THE NEW CAMBRIDGE COMPAN
JOHNSON

Students, scholars, and general readers alike will find *The New Cambridge Companion to Samuel Johnson* deeply informed and appealingly written. Each newly commissioned chapter explores aspects of Johnson's writing and thought, including his ethical grasp of life, his views of language, the roots of his ideas in Renaissance humanism, and his skeptical-humane style. Among the themes engaged are history, disability, gender, politics, race, slavery, Johnson's representation in art, and the significance of the Yale Edition. Works discussed include Johnson's poetry and fiction, his moral essays and political tracts, his Shakespeare edition and Dictionary, and his critical, biographical, and travel writing. A narrated Further Reading provides an informative guide to the study of Johnson, and a substantial Introduction highlights how his literary practice, philosophical values, and life experience provide a challenge to readers new and established. Through fresh, integrated insights, this authoritative guide reveals the surprising contemporaneity of Johnson's thought.

GREG CLINGHAM is emeritus Professor of English at Bucknell University, Pennsylvania, and a Life member of Clare Hall, Cambridge. He is the author or editor of fourteen books and numerous essays on Johnson, Dryden, Boswell, Lady Anne Barnard, Sir George Macartney, memory, historiography, orientalism, translation, archives, and the history of the book. He has been awarded fellowships by the National Endowment for the Humanities; American Society for Eighteenth-Century Studies; the Houghton Library, Harvard; the Beinecke Library, Yale; St Edmund's College, Cambridge; the Bogliasco Foundation; and the University of St Andrews. Between 1996 and 2018, Dr. Clingham was director of Bucknell University Press. Presently, he is editor of the series *18th-Century Moments* with Clemson University Press. Dr Clingham's contribution to eighteenth-century studies is recognized in *A Clubbable Man: Essays on Eighteenth-Century Literature and Culture in Honor of Greg Clingham* (2022).

THE NEW CAMBRIDGE
COMPANION TO SAMUEL
JOHNSON

EDITED BY

GREG CLINGHAM

Bucknell University

CAMBRIDGE
UNIVERSITY PRESS

CAMBRIDGE
UNIVERSITY PRESS

University Printing House, Cambridge CB2 8BS, United Kingdom

One Liberty Plaza, 20th Floor, New York, NY 10006, USA

477 Williamstown Road, Port Melbourne, VIC 3207, Australia

314–321, 3rd Floor, Plot 3, Splendor Forum, Jasola District Centre, New Delhi – 110025, India

103 Penang Road, #05–06/07, Visioncrest Commercial, Singapore 238467

Cambridge University Press is part of the University of Cambridge.

It furthers the University's mission by disseminating knowledge in the pursuit of education, learning, and research at the highest international levels of excellence.

www.cambridge.org
Information on this title: www.cambridge.org/9781108832823
DOI: 10.1017/9781108966108

© Cambridge University Press 2023

First published 2023

A catalogue record for this publication is available from the British Library.

ISBN 978-1-108-83282-3 Hardback
ISBN 978-1-108-96578-1 Paperback

Cambridge University Press has no responsibility for the persistence or accuracy of URLs for external or third-party internet websites referred to in this publication and does not guarantee that any content on such websites is, or will remain, accurate or appropriate.

Contents

Figures

Contributors

MARTINE W. BROWNLEY is Goodrich C. White Professor of English at Emory University. Her research has focused on eighteenth-century historiography and on contemporary women novelists.

SAMARA ANNE CAHILL is a grants editor at Texas A&M University. She is the author of *Intelligent Souls? Feminist Orientalism in Eighteenth-Century English Literature* (2019); the coeditor of *Citizens of the World: Adapting in the Eighteenth Century* (2015); the editor of *Studies in Religion and the Enlightenment;* and the book review editor of *1650–1850: Ideas, Aesthetics, and Inquiries in the Early Modern Era.*

GREG CLINGHAM is emeritus Professor of English and former Director of the University Press at Bucknell University. Among his numerous publications are the *Cambridge Companion to Samuel Johnson* (1987), *Johnson, Writing, and Memory* (2002), and the coedited *Oriental Networks: Culture, Commerce and Communication in the Long Eighteenth Century* (2021). www.greg-clingham.com

LEO DAMROSCH, an emeritus professor at Harvard, has published numerous books on eighteenth-century literature and culture, including *Samuel Johnson and the Tragic Sense* (1972), *The Uses of Johnson's Criticism* (1976), *Jean-Jacques Rousseau: Restless Genius* (2005), *Jonathan Swift: His Life and His World* (2013), and *The Club: Johnson, Boswell, and the Friends Who Shaped an Age* (2019).

ROBERT DEMARIA, JR. is the Henry Noble MacCracken Professor of English at Vassar College. He is the general editor of the Yale Edition and the editor of the *Johnsonian News Letter.* He is the author of *Samuel Johnson: A Critical Biography* (1993) as well as other books on Johnson. With Robert D. Brown, he is editing the Longman's Annotated English Poets edition of Johnson's verse.

CLEMENT HAWES is Professor of English and History at the University of Michigan. Long interested in historical periodization during the Enlightenment, his interests reach back to the English Civil War and such religious radicals as "Digger" Gerrard Winstanley and "Ranter" Abizer Coppe. In addition to Samuel Johnson, he has written on Jonathan Swift, Christopher Smart, and Laurence Sterne.

NICHOLAS HUDSON is Professor of English at the University of British Columbia. Among his books are *Samuel Johnson and Eighteenth-Century Thought* (1988), *Samuel Johnson and the Making of Modern England* (2001), and *A Political Life of Samuel Johnson* (2013). He is editor of *A Cultural History of Race during the Reformation and Enlightenment, 1550–1750* (2021).

FREYA JOHNSTON is Associate Professor and Tutorial Fellow in English at St Anne's College, Oxford. She is the author of *Samuel Johnson and the Art of Sinking, 1709–1791* (2005) and the monograph *Jane Austen, Early and Late* (2021), as well as coeditor of *Samuel Johnson: The Arc of the Pendulum* (2013).

PAUL KELLEHER is Associate Professor of English at Emory University and the Director of Emory's Disability Studies Initiative. He is the author of *Making Love: Sentiment and Sexuality in Eighteenth-Century British Literature* (2015), as well as articles on eighteenth-century representations of sexuality, disability, and animal husbandry. He is completing a book on the rhetoric of "deformity" in Enlightenment-era literature and philosophy.

ANTHONY W. LEE has published books and more than forty-five essays on Johnson and eighteenth-century literature and culture. He has taught at several universities, including the University of Arkansas, Arkansas Tech University, Kentucky Wesleyan College, the University of the District of Columbia, and the University of Maryland University College, where he served as the Director of the English and Humanities Program.

TOM MASON was Senior Lecturer in English at Bristol University, where he ran a special option course on Samuel Johnson. He has written on Johnson's criticism and on Dryden's and Cowley's poems and translations. He is coeditor of *Abraham Cowley: Selected Poems* (1994) and of *The Story of Poetry* (1992), and co-author with David Hopkins of *Chaucer in the Eighteenth Century* (2022).

HEATHER MCPHERSON is emerita Professor of Art History at the University of Alabama at Birmingham. She is the author of *Art and Celebrity in the Age of Reynolds and Siddons* (2017) and *The Modern Portrait in Nineteenth-Century France* (2001). Her research focuses on portraiture, caricature and cultural politics, and the intersection of the visual and performing arts.

LYNDA MUGGLESTONE is Professor of the History of English at Oxford University. She has published widely on the social and cultural history of English, with reference to Johnson, lexical history, and the history of spoken English. Recent publications include *Dictionaries: A Very Short Introduction* (2011), *The Oxford History of English* (2012), and *Samuel Johnson and the Journey into Words* (2015).

FRED PARKER is Associate Professor of English at Cambridge University and author of *Johnson's Shakespeare* (1989) and *Scepticism and Literature* (2003), in which Johnson has a significant place. His most recent book, *On Declaring Love: Eighteenth-Century Literature and Jane Austen* (2020), explores the paradox of finding public language for intimate emotion and how this impacts upon the integrity of the self.

JOHN RICHETTI IS A. M. ROSENTHAL Professor emeritus of English at the University of Pennsylvania. His most recent book is *A History of Eighteenth-Century British Literature* (2017). He continues to record classic English and American verse for the website Pennsound: www.writing.upenn.edu/pennsound/

PHILIP SMALLWOOD is emeritus Professor of English at Birmingham City University and Honorary Senior Associate Teacher in English at Bristol University, where he teaches eighteenth-century literature. He has written and lectured widely on Pope, Johnson, and the history of literary criticism. His *Johnson's Critical Presence* appeared in 2004 and his *Critical Occasions* in 2011.

ANNE M. THELL is Associate Professor of English Literature at National University of Singapore. Her books include *Minds in Motion: Imagining Empiricism in Eighteenth-Century British Travel Literature* (2017) and a critical edition of Margaret Cavendish's *Grounds of Natural Philosophy* (2020). She is now working on depictions of mental illness in the so-called "Age of Reason."

MIN WILD is a lecturer in English at the University of Plymouth. Her research mainly focuses on the poet and satirist Christopher Smart, to whom Johnson was very kind. She is interested in rhetoric and the ways it persuades. Her publications include *Christopher Smart and Satire* (2008) and *Re-reading Christopher Smart in the Twenty-First Century* (2013).

Short Titles and Note on the Text and Cover Art

Unless otherwise specified, citations from Johnson's *Dictionary of the English Language* are from the first edition (1755), online at https://john sonsdictionaryonline.com.

The following short titles are used parenthetically.

The Yale Edition of the Works of Samuel Johnson, ed. Robert DeMaria, Jr., et al. (New Haven: Yale University Press, 1958–2018).

Adventurer	*The Idler* and *The Adventurer*, ed. W. J. Bate, J. M. Bullitt, and L. F. Powell (1963).
BW	*Biographical Writings: Soldiers, Scholars, and Friends*, ed. O M Brack, Jr. and Robert DeMaria, Jr. (2016).
Demand	*Johnson on Demand: Reviews, Prefaces, and Ghost-Writings*, ed. O M Brack, Jr., and Robert DeMaria, Jr. (2018).
DPA	*Diaries, Prayers, and Annals*, ed. Edward Lippincott McAdam, Jr. with Donald and Mary Hyde (1958).
EL	*Johnson on the English Language*, ed. Gwin J. Kolb and Robert DeMaria, Jr. (2005).
Idler	*The Idler* and *The Adventurer*, ed. Walter Jackson Bate, John Marshall Bullitt, and Lawrence Fitzroy Powell (1963).
Journey	*A Journey to the Western Islands of Scotland*, ed. Mary Lascelles (1971).
Lives, 1–3	*The Lives of the Poets*, ed. John H. Middendorf et al. 3 vols. (2010).
Poems	*Poems*, ed. Edward Lippincott McAdam, Jr., with George Milne (1964).

PW	*Political Writings*, ed. Donald J. Greene (1977).
Rambler, 1–3	*The Rambler*, ed. Walter Jackson Bate and Albrecht B. Strauss, 3 vols. (1969).
Rasselas	*Rasselas and Other Tales*, ed. Gwin J. Kolb (1990).
Sermons	*Sermons*, ed. Jean Hagstrum and James Gray (1978).
Shakespeare, 1–2	*Johnson on Shakespeare*, ed. Arthur Sherbo, with introduction by Bertrand H. Bronson, 2 vols. (1968).
Voyage	*A Voyage to Abyssinia*, ed. Joel J. Gold (1985).
Boswell's Scotland	*Boswell's Journal of a Tour to the Hebrides with Samuel Johnson 1773*, ed. Frederick Albert Pottle and Charles Hodges Bennett (New York: McGraw-Hill, 1961).
JM, 1–2	*Johnsonian Miscellanies*, ed. George Birkbeck Hill, 2 vols. (Oxford: Clarendon Press, 1897).
Letters, 1–5	*The Letters of Samuel Johnson*. The Hyde Edition, ed. Bruce Redford, 5 vols. (Princeton: Princeton University Press, 1992–4).
Life, 1–6	James Boswell, *The Life of Samuel Johnson, LL.D., with a Journal of a Tour to the Hebrides*, ed. George Birkbeck Hill, rev. Lawrence Fitzroy Powell, 6 vols. (Oxford: Clarendon Press, 1934–64).
Companion	*The Cambridge Companion to Samuel Johnson*, ed. Greg Clingham (Cambridge: Cambridge University Press, 1997).
AJ	*The Age of Johnson: A Scholarly Annual*
ELH	*English Literary History*
JNL	*The Johnsonian News Letter*

Cover Art: Samuel Johnson by Lady Anne Lindsay Barnard, 1773 and c. 1822

The drawing of Johnson on the cover of this book was made by Lady Anne Lindsay at a social event in November 1773 at Prestonfield, Edinburgh, the home of Sir Alexander Dick, her uncle, while Johnson and Boswell were on their Highland travels. Lady Anne Lindsay (1750–1825) was the eldest child of James Lindsay, the 5th Earl of Balcarres, and, as Lady Anne Barnard, became a distinguished writer, diarist, and watercolorist.

The drawing, which Lady Anne Barnard touched up in the 1810s, was incorporated into a manuscript copy of an unpublished memoir, which she had bound in 1822, presently in the Papers of the Earls of Crawford and Balcarres in the National Library of Scotland (Acc 9769, Personal Papers, 27/4/13, volume 2, fo. 220). The drawing remained unknown until I published it in *The Burlington Magazine*, 161 (March 2019): 220–22. I am grateful to the 29th Earl of Crawford and Balcarres and the Balcarres Heritage Trust for permission to reproduce Lady Anne's drawing of Johnson on the *New Cambridge Companion to Samuel Johnson*.

— Greg Clingham

Introduction: Contemporary Johnson

Greg Clingham

Once a writer – such as Shakespeare, Wordsworth, Austen, or Johnson – has entered the public consciousness, they become, in a sense, invisible. Having become part of the culture and the language, seeing them clearly requires deliberate acts of critical and historical understanding. Johnson felt this about John Dryden. Considering the tradition of English literature in the *Lives of the Poets* (1779–81), he summed up Dryden's transformative contribution: "A writer who obtains his full purpose loses himself in his own lustre . . .. Learning once made popular is no longer learning; it has the appearance of something which we have bestowed upon ourselves, as the dew appears to rise from the field that it refreshes" (*Lives*, 2: 119). That the mark of a writer's distinction is that they become lost in the fullness of their achievement is a paradox that pertains to Johnson as well as Dryden. Indeed, the Samuel Johnson encountered in this book, new and interesting as we hope he is, would not be possible without the contribution of hundreds of scholars, some acknowledged, many invisible though not necessarily forgotten. The interest that Johnson's writings and life continue to stimulate have everything to do with his classic status but also with the possibilities of change, challenge, surprise, and pleasure they offer. The *New Cambridge Companion to Samuel Johnson* is predicated on Johnson's continuing intellectual aliveness and pertinence to our imaginative interests and moral needs. Much has changed in university curricula, critical fashions, and cultural taste since the publication of the first Cambridge Companion to Johnson in 1997, yet Johnson continues to be responsive to new methodologies and relevant to current literary and cultural interests. But how best to see – to adapt Johnson's metaphor about Dryden – that the dew falls from the sky when it appears to arise from the field that it refreshes?

This Introduction aims to sketch out a few essentials of the writer, who is then presented more fully and from different and complementary perspectives in the chapters that follow. If this book is a companion to the reading of Johnson, can Johnson be *our* companion? What are his critical and moral values? How does he write? Can we trust what he says, even if we don't fully agree with every judgment? Are his works helpful in making our way through the minefield of present-day culture? Brief discussions of these issues follow below, and the Introduction then concludes with a brief turn to the chapters that follow.

Johnson Our Companion

In his *Dictionary of the English Language* (1755), Johnson defined the noun "companion" as "One with whom a man frequently converses, or with whom he shares his hours of relaxation. It differs from friend, as acquaintance from confidence." He provides three quotations to illustrate this idea of companionship. The first highlights Macbeth's tormented spiritual isolation after he has murdered Duncan: "How now, my lord, why do you keep alone? / Of sorriest fancies your companions make?" (*Macbeth*, III. ii, 9–10). The second, from the Book of Ecclesiasticus, invokes the idea of reliability and trust: "Some friend is a companion at the table, and will not continue in the day of thy affliction" (VI. 10). And a third, from the seventeenth-century poet Matthew Prior, associates the idea of companionship with emotional support in the act of mourning: "With anxious doubts, with raging passions torn, / No sweet companion near, with whom to mourn" (*Solomon on the Vanity of the World*, Book 3, ll. 91–92). Each quotation designates an idea of companionship in its *absence*: companionship, and its correlative, conversation, provides what these starkly imagined human situations (spiritual loneliness, affliction, anxiety, and mourning) do *not*. Each of these exemplifications, I suggest, points to aspects of Johnson's writings that have always made them powerful and consolatory.

Since December 2019, the world has suffered a pandemic that has placed inconceivable stress on the social, economic, health, and political infrastructures of nations great and small, and on the lives of almost all individuals, millions of whom have suffered sickness, death, grief, and isolation. How should we think about such suffering and loss, exacerbated by the incompetence, folly, or mendacity of governments, political parties, institutions, and individuals, without being overwhelmed by the magnitude of it all? Johnson is a writer who provides tools for understanding, if not entirely addressing, such almost impossible questions. He does so by virtue of his grasp of the relationship between ordinary experience and universal ideas, and by his distinctive tracking of how the world and the mind map onto each other – or fail to. During the pandemic we have waited and watched, suspended between a "normal" past, now irretrievably gone, and a darkly uncertain future, in the meantime trying to occupy ourselves meaningfully. This "meantime," which feels unique to us, is a subject (perhaps *the* subject) of virtually all of Johnson's writings. The question for Johnson as a writer and thinker is, what shall a person do with the time (and with the talents, as in the parable of the talents in Matthew 25: 14–30) allotted to them so they can live a worthy life and to *know* they have done so?

Rambler 41, for example, considers the "present moment" from different, seemingly opposing but complementary perspectives. Starting from the idea of human restlessness ("few of the hours of life are filled up with objects adequate to the mind of man"; *Rambler*, 1: 221), Johnson seems to accept that people routinely look to the past or the future to "relieve the vacuities of our being" (*Rambler*, 1: 221). Because people are rarely *in* the present moment or have little idea what the present *is*, Johnson accepts the necessity of looking to the past and to the future. Because the future is unknown (and unknowable), it is attractive to speculative or fanciful types, but being "pliant and ductile, and . . . easily moulded by a strong fancy into any form," it is not very reliable or satisfying (1: 224). The past, by contrast, is less pliable, its images more "stubborn and intractable" (1: 224); it offers more stable grounds on which to think, feel, and act, for the obvious reason that everything in the past has already happened.

In writing of past and future as diametrically opposite entities, Johnson's key term is "memory," its traces being the remnants of personal experience. Animals have memory, but it is not as prominent in them as in humans because animals have evolved to meet evolutionary needs; they do not need memory as we do (1: 222). Human faculties, by contrast, are conspicuously at odds with each other, but this is not all bad. The cognitive dissonance Johnson sees between the human mind and its "proper objects" is a sign both of the "superior and celestial nature of the soul" (indicating aspiration toward goals) and also of memory as "the purveyor of reason" (1: 222). Because memory is "the power which places those images before the mind upon which the judgment is to be exercised," it "place[s] us in the class of moral agents" (1: 223). The act of remembrance and the contents of the past are thus fraught. If people are seldom in the present, and "the only joys which we can call our own" are the images we have "reposited . . . 'in the sacred treasure of the past'" (1: 224), then every word and deed acquires *future* significance. Just for a moment in *Rambler* 41, the anxiety associated with the present threatens to take a didactic turn, to morph into a mini sermon on the need to live a good life so we can cultivate sustaining images for recollection in a hypothetical future. "Life," Johnson warns, "made memorable by crimes, and diversified through its several periods by wickedness," can only be remembered with "horror and remorse" (*Rambler*, 1: 225).

However, Johnson does something more radical: he questions the nature of time itself and, in a thought suggestive of a postmodern poetics of memory, dissolves past and future into the present: "almost all we can be said to enjoy is past or future; the present is in perpetual motion, leaves us as soon as it arrives, ceases to be present before its presence is well perceived, and is only known to have existed by the effects which it leaves behind" (1: 223–24). Suddenly, it is the *present* (not the past) that is the object of memory, and in a quotation from Dryden's translation of Horace's 29th Ode of the Third Book, Johnson suggests that both present and future are, in fact, produced by memory:

> Be fair or foul or rain or shine,
> The joys I have possess'd in spite of fate are mine,
> Not heav'n itself upon the past has pow'r,
> But what has been has been, and I have had my hour.
>
> (*Rambler*, 1: 225, ll. 69–72)

The power of this passage in the context of Johnson's essay lies in the paradoxical transformation of its explicit statements: the past is irretrievably gone ("what has been has been") and beyond the power even of the gods ("Not heav'n itself upon the past has pow'r"); yet the past is also vitally present in the poetry, especially in the joyousness and the energetic measure of Dryden's translation. In Dryden's translation (an assessment writ large in Johnson's *Life of Dryden*) and in *Rambler* 41, an apparently passive relation to time is transformed through memory into a triumph over the acknowledged limits of life and the anxieties of the present. Johnson's *manner* of embodying this present in *Rambler* 41 has the effect of being joyous "in the meantime." Bleak as the moment might be, "The joys I have possess'd in spite of fate are mine."

Among the fourteen definitions of "time" in Johnson's *Dictionary*, the most literal and the most metaphoric both include the concept of *measure*. In the first definition, we have time as "the measure of duration" and, in the fourteenth, time as "musical measure," the first linking human experience to physics, the second to music. *Rambler* 41 is an example of how Johnson *measures* the discrete particulars of experienced time, and, a little like T. S. Eliot in *Four Quartets*, he creates harmony (temporal and musical measure) by *how* he writes in the "meantime." The implications of this characteristic Johnsonian position can sustain much unpacking.[1] Preliminarily, one might note that Johnson is self-evidently a moral, critical thinker whose vision of life draws on the Christian idea of people as fallen beings, separated from some essential reality. Sometimes he expresses this idea in theological terms in prayers and in sermons he wrote for his friend Rev. John Taylor. Mostly, however, human imperfection is the stuff of ordinary experience for Johnson – what we live with *in the meantime* – and it permeates his large, diverse *oeuvre* – essays (*Rambler*, *Idler*, and *Adventurer*), political tracts, legal commentary, scholarship (e.g., edition of the plays of Shakespeare), *Dictionary*, biography and criticism (*Lives of the Poets*), poems, fiction (*Rasselas*), letters, travel writings, and hundreds of reviews, prefaces, journalism articles, and ghost writings. All Johnson's writings are grounded in principles that he calls "general nature," a loose congregation of experiential and aesthetic terms that escape easy definition[2] but which are fundamental.

General Nature

As a literary critic who was impatient of the cult of sensibility (the cultivation of feeling for its own sake), Johnson was nonetheless a man of large passions and deep feeling. As his many biographers testify, he had many friendships (with men, women, and children) with whom he readily shared life's pleasures and pains. In his letters to Queeney Thrale, Henry and Hester Thrale's little daughter, we see him gayly participating in her childish joys and humors.[3] We also see his open-hearted grief, in his letters to her parents, on the death of her two-year-old brother, Ralph (*Letters*, 2: 239–40, 248). When it comes to literature, however, Johnson's expressions of sympathy are often profoundly complex – as we see in his account of the death of Cordelia in Shakespeare's *King Lear*. In his edition of Shakespeare's plays (1765), Johnson records how powerful he found *King Lear*: "There is perhaps no play which keeps the attention so strongly fixed; which so much agitates our passions and interests our curiosity . . . . So powerful is the current of the poet's imagination, that the mind, which once ventures within it, is hurried irresistibly along" (*Shakespeare*, 2: 702–3).

---

[1] See Greg Clingham, *Johnson, Writing, and Memory* (Cambridge: Cambridge University Press, 2002).
[2] For general nature, see G. F. Parker, *Johnson's Shakespeare* (Oxford: Clarendon Press, 1989).
[3] See Greg Clingham, "Playing Rough: Johnson and Children," in Anthony W. Lee (ed.), *Revaluation: New Essays on Samuel Johnson* (Newark, DE: University of Delaware Press, 2018), pp. 145–82.

Few would disagree. But Johnson balked at what he saw as the unnecessary, even unnatural death of Cordelia: "I was many years ago so shocked by Cordelia's death, that I know not whether I ever endured to read again the last scenes of the play till I undertook to revise them as an editor" (*Shakespeare*, 2: 704). What shocks Johnson is that Shakespeare went out of his way to kill Cordelia by changing his textual sources (in those from which he takes his plot, Cordelia survives) and allowing her father momentarily to believe she lived – only to crush his hopes. These were features that led Nahum Tate to rewrite *King Lear* in 1681 so Cordelia could survive, marry Edgar, and reunite with Lear. Johnson does not say that he prefers Tate's version to Shakespeare's, but he understands its popularity: "Cordelia, from the time of Tate, has always retired with victory and felicity" (*Shakespeare*, 2: 704). Yet, where Tate saw irregularities that he might correct, Johnson saw a vision that he *resists*; he does so by grounding himself in values and experiences that he calls general nature. As Frank Kermode remarks, Johnson saw in Shakespeare's choice "not primitive ignorance but a disregard of publicly endorsed and acceptable answers which terrified him because it did *not* arise out of incompetence or carelessness."[4] Johnson read the play, Kermode continues, "deeply, though not easily" and "fearing that the world might be thus," and in resisting it, "Johnson is responding to tragedy more deeply than we, who profess to be more easily persuaded."[5] That Shakespeare "suffered the virtue of Cordelia to perish in a just cause, contrary to the natural ideas of justice, to the hope of the reader, and, what is yet more strange, to the faith of chronicles" may make for a good play, Johnson says, "because it is a just representation of the common events of human life: but since all reasonable beings naturally love justice, I cannot easily be persuaded, that the observation of justice makes a play worse" (*Shakespeare*, 2: 704).

Johnson is not the only eminent critic who has thought Shakespeare's moral coherence wanting. Unlike Tolstoy, however, who in a notorious essay found Shakespeare's plays to be exaggerated, arbitrary, unnatural, immoral, and implausible,[6] Johnson is appalled by *King Lear* in proportion to values (general nature) that he formulates *from his very reading* of *King Lear* and of Shakespeare's other plays.

[4] Frank Kermode, "Survival of the Classic," in *Renaissance Essays: Shakespeare, Spenser, Donne* (London: Collins, 1971), p. 171.
[5] Kermode, "Survival of the Classic," p. 171.
[6] Leo Tolstoy, *A Critical Essay on Shakespeare*, trans. V. Tchertkoff and Isabella Fyvie Mayo (New York and London: Funk & Wagnalls Company, 1906).

Nothing can please many, and please long, but just representations of general nature . . .. Shakespeare is above all writers, at least above all modern writers, the poet of nature; the poet that holds up to his readers a faithful mirror of manners and of life . . .. Shakespeare's plays are not in the rigorous and critical sense either tragedies or comedies, but compositions of a distinct kind; exhibiting the real state of sublunary nature, which partakes of good and evil, joy and sorrow, mingled with endless variety of proportion and innumerable modes of combination; expressing the course of the world, in which the loss of one is the gain of another; in which, at the same time, the reveller is hasting to his wine, and the mourner burying his friend; in which the malignity of one is sometimes defeated by the frolick of another; and many mischiefs and many benefits are done and hindered without design. (*Shakespeare*, 1: 61–62, 66)

These passages from the *Preface to Shakespeare* celebrate the *multiplicity* of human life in Shakespeare's dramas, which Johnson finds to be painfully violated in *King Lear* by the relentlessness with which it crushes human innocence. While resisting the play's vision, he enjoys other aspects of Shakespeare's drama – "the real state of sublunary nature" – which he values more, and (significantly) which he finds to be *more* indicative of Shakespeare. One way to understand what Johnson means by this is to notice *how* he writes. As we enter into the current of Johnson's imagination in the quotation above, the rhetorical shape and movement of the long sentence generate a sense of an expanding, increasingly abundant, varied, and changing world where we have the sense that both good and bad, and happiness and sadness, exist *at the same time* and where, despite life's uncertainties, we feel deeply at home. The fittingness (Johnson calls it *justness*) of such sentences is a manifestation of what Johnson means by "general nature." This is definitely *not* the experience of the mind that "is hurried irresistibly along" by *King Lear*.

Christopher Ricks observes that as a critic Johnson is committed to principles rather than theory; Johnson's "refusal to elaborate and concatenate the needed concept beyond a certain point . . . was not a refusal to think, but a decision to think thereafter about the application of the principles."[7] "Principles" are applied experientially, and thoughtfully directed. If the aim of literature is just representations of general nature, the language in which we discuss literature should also be "general," accessible to what in the *Life of Gray*, apropos of "An Elegy in a Country Church Yard," Johnson calls the "common reader" (*Lives*, 3: 1470–71). He responds

---

[7] Christopher Ricks, "Literary Principles as Against Theory," in *Essays in Appreciation* (Oxford: Clarendon Press, 1996), pp. 322–23.

to *King Lear* in open, honest, fearful, bold, and classless language – *common* language, though wrought, deliberative, attentive. Furthermore, like Wordsworth, Johnson saw no absolute division between poet and critic; some of his most scholarly discourses, such as the Preface to his *Dictionary*, are also among his most poetic. When expressing his admiration for Dryden's critical prefaces, Johnson's formulation perfectly describes his own practice. They are "not a dull collection of theorems, nor a rude detection of faults," but "the criticism of a poet," "a gay and vigorous dissertation, where delight is mingled with instruction, and where the author proves his right to judgement, by his power of performance" (Lives, 1: 437–38).

"Power of performance" and "delight" are often found in intimate images and moments, as in Johnson's account of the last days of Alexander Pope. As Johnson tells the story in the *Life of Pope*, Pope held tenaciously onto friendships, even as they were falling away from him, as being all that stood between him and the bleakness of death. Of Pope's relationship with Martha Blount, to whom he was once romantically inclined, Johnson writes:

> She is said to have neglected him, with shameful unkindness, in the latter time of his decay; yet, of the little which he had to leave, she had a very great part. . . . if he had suffered his heart to be alienated from her, he could have found nothing that might fill her place; he could have only shrunk within himself. (Lives, 3: 1157–58)

In the context of this biography (a literary form Johnson said he "loved most"; *Life*, 1: 425), Pope's vulnerability and loneliness stand in stark contrast to his poetic stature, which is great. Johnson also delicately alludes to, but does not mention, Pope's diminutive physical stature, his body bent by scoliosis (and relentlessly mocked by his enemies). Johnson – himself nearly blind and scarred from birth – is doing what he can to soften the blow and to treat the "shrunken" heart (and body) respectfully.

Johnson's Skeptical Thinking

Such thoughtfulness is rooted not only in general nature but also in a skeptical sense of human limits and how the human mind works. The discrepancy between the "mind" and the "objects" of our "attention," explored in *Rambler* 41 (and many other texts), is for Johnson the fundamental site of human consciousness. His style is consequently like a moving calculus of these overlapping mechanisms and dimensions, considering the changing ideas, impulses, and perceptions in relation to each other.[8] Not only is the mind at odds with the world, but the world – nature, language, culture, science, and the social realties within which we live – is itself constantly changing. As Johnson says in *Rambler* 63, "to take a view at once distinctive and comprehensive of human life, with all its intricacies of combination, and varieties of connexion, is beyond the power of mortal intelligence" (*Rambler*, 3: 336); and, in *Adventurer* 107, "Life is not the object of science: we see a little, very little; and what is beyond we can only conjecture" (*Adventurer*, 445). This changing reality is why we often disagree with others, and sometimes with ourselves: "we see a little, and form an opinion; we see more, and change it" (444). Crucially, however, we behave as we do "not because we are irrational, but because we are finite beings" (441).

This difference, between human irrationality and finitude, makes all the difference for Johnson. To see war, slavery, poverty, and social injustice as arising *entirely* from human irrationality makes for a very bleak outlook. It leads to the savagery of Swift's satire (characterized by Johnson as "depravity of intellect"; *Lives*, 2: 1020) or to the blinding rationality of the French *philosophes*, criticized by Johnson as being "vain" (these "sceptical innovators, are vain men, and will gratify themselves at any expence"; *Life*, 1: 444). Johnson's analysis of the unhappiness arising from human limitation is less pure than Swift's or Voltaire's view because more forgiving. *Rasselas*, for example, is (*inter alia*) a fiction about the disappointment arising from a well-intentioned but naïve (because too rational) attempt to find happiness. As the characters in this tale *fail* in one attempt after another to "make the choice of life," they become less obsessive and more content with the imperfections of their lot. Eventually, they are pleased to return to the place from which they began, having learned nothing very definite, except that life as it is, is worth living. Johnson treats the will to control implied by the characters' rational purpose with skeptical indulgence: the astronomer (chapters 40–44, 46) who is convinced that he controls the weather by the thoughts in his head is coaxed out of his insipient insanity by conversation. Crucially, however, Johnson's tale frames the whole question of personal responsibility and what is and is not reasonable to expect of ourselves. We should not expect the impossible; as Imlac says to the troubled astronomer, "you are only one atom of the mass of humanity, and have neither such

---

[8] See Adam Phillips, "Johnson's Freud," in Freya Johnston and Lynda Mugglestone (eds.), *Samuel Johnson: The Arc of the Pendulum* (Oxford: Oxford University Press, 2012), pp. 62–71.

virtue nor vice, as that you should be singled out for supernatural favours or afflictions" (*Rasselas*, 163). Limitations may constrain, but they also free us.

Still, Johnson is vigilant about obsessiveness, magical thinking, and exceptionalism. Perhaps because he was himself prone to melancholia and indolence, his prose operates like an early warning system against self-indulgence. Reviewing Soame Jenyns's *A Free Inquiry into the Nature and Origin of Evil* (1757), a work in the vein of Pope's *Essay on Man* that invokes a distant, ultrarational deity and justifies the existence of evil by arguing that individual suffering is offset by a corresponding benefit to the universe, Johnson severely criticized Jenyns's fatuous logic. What angers Johnson is not human suffering (poverty, powerlessness, and death are everywhere in eighteenth-century England) but the indifference of the strong toward the weak. Jenyns's elaborate metaphysical scheme promulgates complacency about other people's deprivation: "The shame is to impose words for ideas upon ourselves or others. To imagine that we are going forward when we are only turning round. To think, that there is any difference between him that gives no reason, and him that gives a reason, which by his own confession cannot be conceived."[9] "Human experience," Johnson insists, "is constantly contradicting theory," and is the "great test of truth" (*Life*, 1: 454). Hence his critique of all theoretical systems – philosophical, social, or political.

Johnson was thus a lifelong advocate for a liberal education for girls, whose socially orchestrated ignorance contributed to the abuses of the "marriage market" (*Rambler*s, 18, 39, 113, 167, 191). His fictional portrayal of Misella, in *Rambler*s 170 and 171, an adolescent abused by an older male relative and then abandoned to the streets, is especially poignant by virtue of his attempt to see events through her eyes, even while acknowledging that he cannot. These liberal principles informed his views, even his respect for monarchy and the hierarchies of Church and aristocracy. They underpin his ethical view of animals and the abhorrence of vivisection (e.g., *Idler*, 10, 17), and they fuel his critique of the injustice and inefficacy of capital punishment (e.g., *Rambler*, 114). Among the great political issues of the day on which he commented (the electoral system, parliamentary representation, taxation, the rule of law), Johnson was especially critical of slavery and the European imperial project. He applied his legal knowledge in writing a brief in defense of Joseph Knight, a Jamaican slave, when, in a Scottish court (1774), he sued his former owner, John Wedderburn. He also put

---

[9] Soame Jenyns' *Free Inquiry*, cited from Samuel Johnson, *A Commentary on Mr. Pope's Principles of Morality, Or Essay on Man*, ed. O M Brack, Jr. (New Haven, CT: Yale University Press, 2004), p. 418.

principles into practice, "adopting" (1752) another former Jamaican slave, Francis Barber (1740–1801), giving him a job, a home, education, and (against the advice of the lawyer Sir John Hawkins, his friend and executor), making Frank the residual legatee of his estate.[10]

These are all forms of attention to social injustices. They indicate that Johnson saw the good life as existing not only in the cultivation of self but in the common good, a view aligning him with his friend Edmund Burke, rather than with utilitarians like Jeremy Bentham and John Stuart Mill.[11] It follows that he was not much impressed by the heroic, whether in its military or literary form. Like Tolstoy in *War and Peace*, Johnson largely deplores the idealization of the military ethos and its destructive impact on people and nations. With few exceptions, his reflections on war and its "heroes" are ironic and critical. For example, in the *Observations on the State of Affairs* (1756), he characterizes the Seven Years War between France and England (over who would own Canada) as "only the quarrel of two robbers for the spoils of a passenger" (*PW*, 188). In his ironic portrayal of King Charles XII of Sweden (1682–1718) in the *Vanity of Human Wishes* (1749), Charles is a romantic individual dedicated to war who achieves memorable victories but (like Napoleon a century later) overreaches in Russia, where he is defeated (1709), thus beginning the decline of the Swedish Empire and the rise of Tsarist Russia. Charles's end is as ignominious as Napoleon's:

> His fall was destin'd to a barren strand,
> A petty fortress, and a dubious hand;
> He left the name, at which the world grew pale,
> To point a moral, or adorn a tale.
>
> (*Poems*, 102, ll. 219–22)

When Johnson does use the term "hero" unironically in a military context, it is to celebrate the "common" soldier ("The Bravery of the English Common Soldiers," *PW*, 278–84).

Johnson's discomfort with heroism is complicated by his recognition of his own claims to greatness. On completing his *Dictionary*, a prodigious intellectual achievement, he identifies himself with Odysseus blinding Polyphemus, the one-eyed, man-eating giant in the *Odyssey* (*Letters*, 1: 92). Contemporaries consistently portrayed Johnson as a classical hero,

---

[10] See Michael Bundock, *The Fortunes of Francis Barber: The True Story of the Jamaican Slave Who Became Samuel Johnson's Heir* (New Haven, CT: Yale University Press, 2015).
[11] See Michael J. Sandel, *The Tyranny of Merit: What's Become of the Common Good* (New York: Farrar, Straus & Giroux, 2021).

such as Hercules strangling the serpent, an engraving incorporated by James Harrison into the frontispiece to his one-volume folio edition of Johnson's *Dictionary* (1786). This trend was understandable given Johnson's extraordinary literary and conversational capacities, the scrutiny accorded his every word and deed by contemporary biographers (not only Boswell, Hawkins, Piozzi, and Murphy, but the many lesser-known writers), and his widespread representation by artists and sculptors of the period – Reynolds, Opie, Barry, Trotter, Cruikshank, and Gillray, among others. But the heroic was never a rational or ethical choice. His love of Shakespeare's plays emphasizes commonality, not specialness: "Shakespeare has no heroes; his scenes are occupied only by men, who act and speak as the reader thinks that he should himself have spoken or acted on the same occasion" (*Shakespeare*, 1: 64). Though Shakespeare's tragic heroes create admiration and wonder, they are not the personages Johnson loves, such as Falstaff. Falstaff has "the most pleasing of all qualities, perpetual gaiety, . . . an unfailing power of exciting laughter" (*Shakespeare*, 1: 523). Johnson loves Falstaff despite (because of?) his faults and weaknesses.

The New Cambridge Companion

Like Dryden, Johnson is "'always another and the same,' he does not exhibit a second time the same elegances in the same form, nor appears to have any art other than that of expressing with clearness what he thinks with vigour" (*Lives*, 1: 443). This multidimensional, flexible, artful, and artless writer who engages with such a wide range of moral, literary, social, and historical material cannot be encompassed within the covers of one book. This new Companion is necessarily selective and has had to be very deliberate about including certain aspects of Johnson's *oeuvre* while excluding others. To recollect Johnson's metaphor about Dryden's freshness, this book is trying to see the dew falling as it refreshes the field. Johnson's *oeuvre* can certainly be divided into genres, for there are moral essays and poems, and there are political treatises and biographies, and there are scholarly editions and works of criticism, and to some extent, genre is honored in the chapters of this book. But Johnson's writings (and conversations) are animated by profound and seamless energies that relate poetry to prose, politics to ethics, fiction to history, biography to criticism, and self to community, all held together by a distinctive, powerful, clear intelligence. Thus, thematically and structurally, the chapters that follow are designed to overlap with each other, trying to suggest how Johnson's synthetic and humanizing imagination operates centripetally to unify, even when topics and points of view under discussion look (or sometimes are) discrepant.

One aspect of Johnson's seamlessness is the remarkable modernity of many of his judgments and of much of his writing, most obviously his advocacy of what we would call social justice (pertaining, for example, to gender, women, and disabilities), his critique of slavery and colonialism, and his understanding of how language and form make meaning. But another aspect is his commitment to truth, rational argument, and the strict rule of law without which – he is clear – individual freedom as well as civil society are impossible. In our post-truth, social-media world, these positions are radical and deserve serious consideration. Running throughout this book is the broad current of Johnson's interest in language and the critical and creative intelligence with which he uses language to speak – and sometimes to make – truth, whether scientific, legal, historical, moral, or fictional. In that vein, we seek to provide the reader with a tool with which to think about current affairs. But we also hope to entice the reader to think historically about Johnson in relation to his moment – not only to political issues, important as they may be, but to the pleasures of reading literature and of thinking critically about particular works, not only by the many writers with whom he engages, but by Johnson himself. For Johnson's classical learning and his relation-ship to Christian apologetics, his roots in Renaissance humanism and in English and Scottish law and history, and his deep knowledge of the French and English critical traditions are all inseparable from the liveli-ness of the writing we encounter on the page.

These chapters are rooted in Johnsonian scholarship, are attentive to specific works and to historical and critical contexts, are well informed as to current theoretical developments, and are written accessibly, appealing to the common reader in us all. We hope they amount to more than the sum of their parts, and that the Johnson we have conjured conveys the excitement and intelligence of which Boswell speaks so memorably in the *Life of Johnson*:

> His superiority over other learned men consisted chiefly in what may be called the art of thinking, the art of using his mind; a certain continual power of seizing the useful substance of all he knew, and exhibiting it in a clear and forcible manner; so that the knowledge, which we often see to be no better than lumber in men of dull understanding, was, in him, true, evident, and actual wisdom. (*Life*, 4: 427–28)

CHAPTER I

Johnson, Ethics, and Living

Min Wild

What does it mean to say something or someone is "Johnsonian?" As an adjective it is most often applied to prose, where it can denote anything from meticulous accuracy in expression to empty, pompous declamation. John Sitter's challenge that "[w]e need to revise Johnson in order to be Johnsonian"[1] leads this chapter to ask what that necessity might signify in ethical terms. It was not only in his own generous actions that Johnson presented an ethical model, but also in and through his writing. Every time Johnson's quill hit paper it carried an ethical charge, and much of his writing demonstrated, in style and content, in flexibility, and most of all in its will to precision, ways in which one can think and live ethically or morally. His balanced, knowing, and prescient style in itself showed how language can carry and convey the ethical: its burdens, pleasures, rewards, and punishments. In Johnson's thought, ethics is distinct from, though necessary to, religious piety. In his *Dictionary of the English Language* (1755), he illustrates the definition of "Ethicks" with a quotation from Francis Bacon's *Considerations Touching a War with Spain* (1624) by noting its subservience to divinity: "true *ethicks* are but as a handmaid to divinity and religion."

In his Preface to *The Preceptor* (1748), an educational work for the publisher Robert Dodsley, Johnson defines "Ethicks" as both a "doctrine" and "system of morality," but it is a "doctrine" communicated in his secular writings as a kind of ethics by "allurement" (*Demand*, 168–93). Johnson said that to impart knowledge, including ethics, the "roving curiosity" of the reader – perhaps the dizzy young – must be captured by "scattering in its way such allurements as may withhold it from a useless and unbounded dissipation" (*Demand*, 172). Others, such as Joseph Addison in his moral and religious essays, recommended by Johnson

---

[1] John Sitter, "Academic Responsibility and the Climate of Posterity," *Interdisciplinary Studies in Literature and Environment*, 21:1 (2014): 164–73.

(*Demand*, 188), had tried to sweeten an everyday popular ethics for the reading public, but it took Johnson to bring truly rigorous, combative, vivid, and accurate ways of talking about morality to the new forums of the secular: the tea table, the coffeehouse, and the schoolroom.

We have the word of Bishop Thomas Percy that Johnson declared his Preface to *The Preceptor* was the "best thing he ever wrote" (*Life*, 1: 192). Unusually, he revised it for a second edition (*Demand*, 169). This partiality may be explained by the color and life of Johnson's brief introductions to many different kinds of topics listed in the Preface, most notably in the section on "Ethics," "[t]his great science," which "ought to begin with the first glimpse of reason, and only end with life itself" (*Demand*, 187). Involved intimately in his description of ethics are the two main forces of culture that shaped Johnson's thought: the classically derived valorization of logic and ratiocination, and the pure force and emotion of Christian faith. These are not simply divisible, and Johnson insists on their consanguinity. I will trace his relationship with three of his favored ethical writers – Isaac Watts, William Law, and Cicero – who offer differing insights into how the tangled relationship of logic and feeling, "reason" and "life," may govern our understanding of our own behavior.

Ethics, for Johnson in this Preface, is the study of human beings, of ourselves, both men and women: "the knowledge of his own station in the ranks of being, and his various relations to the innumerable multitudes which surround him," and with whom "his Maker has ordained him to be united for the reception and communication of happiness" (*Demand*, 187). Johnson will have selected his words with care, and he evidently remembered them with pleasure. The power of clear thought is central to his ethics: "he that thinks reasonably must think morally," he says in his Preface to Shakespeare (*Shakespeare*, 1: 71). In recommending the study of themselves to schoolboys, the arrow flight of Johnson's initial definition of ethics lands in an unexpected place, perhaps; not on stern duty or austerity, but on happiness. This is felicity in union with other humans and all living creatures: those "innumerable multitudes." Each living entity is made by God, who has "ordained" humans to "unite" with all other beings. Johnson's choice of words is precise: The primary task of this union is not to exploit or destroy, but simply to receive and to communicate happiness.

Reference to sterner duties follows in the *Preceptor*, but still within the context of this community of beings, "to consider these [the 'innumerable multitudes'] aright is of the greatest importance," because "from these [studies] arise duties which he cannot neglect." Johnson's revision for the second edition substituted this injunction for the previous, milder "duty from which he cannot deviate without much danger" (*Demand*, 187nf). Ethics is the paramount subject, in its role as gateway to divinity. All other "acquisitions" of knowledge are merely "temporary benefits," as set against those of the "practice of morality and piety." Johnson the writer would not be himself were he not to complete the sentence with balance and musicality: The fragile temporal dimension of these "benefits" is alleviated by the clinching end to the sentence, looking forward to the "increase" of "happiness through endless duration" (*Demand*, 187).

Samuel Johnson was not a prig. His own frailty and despondency were part of a mobile and vigorous expression in thought and language. In a sermon he asked, "What can any man see, either within himself or without himself, that does not afford him some reason to remark his own ignorance, imbecillity and meanness?" (*Sermons*, 94). In his Preface to *The Preceptor*, morality's "excellence" is self-reflective, "proving the deformity, the reproach, and the misery of all deviations from it[self]." The next powerfully compacted sentence includes a strikingly visual contrast, for, while the laws of morality may please the cool thinker, "the reasoner in the shade" – where "the appetites are secluded from their object" – stepping beyond this sequestration entails a more severe test. These laws "will be of little force against the ardour of desire, or the vehemence of rage, amidst the pleasures and tumults of the world" (*Demand*, 188). How to behave ethically when so many forces urge the contrary?

To combat "the power of temptations," and all that mars human relationships with the "innumerable multitudes" that share our world, Johnson then summons "hope" – of "reward" – and "fear by the expectation of punishment": largesse and terror, those well-tested devices of control. These powers are called on to balance the "panegyrics" of morality, but also the "authority" of religion, inextricable from each other on the path to "virtue." The "obligations of morality" and the "sanctions of Christianity" give "strength and lustre to each other," and here Johnson further refines the weights on the rhetorical scales: thus, "religion will appear to be the voice of reason, and morality the will of *God*" (*Demand*, 188).

For the study of logic, Johnson recommended in this Preface a book by Isaac Watts, whom he considered a good reasoner, although, as he says in a review of Elizabeth Harrison's *Miscellanies* (1756), "he stood not in the first class of genius" (*Demand*, 356). Watts's *Logick* (1674) was essentially theological; like Johnson, he saw reason as ultimately directed by – and toward – the will of God. Michael Suarez notes that for Johnson, "the best exercise of reason leads us to the higher truths of religion."[2] With breath-taking certainty, Watts makes "right reason" and God's laws synonymous: "the very Essence of Virtue or Holiness consists in the Conformity of our Actions to the Rule of Right Reason, or the *Law of God*."[3] In his *Life of Watts*, Johnson notes how closely Watts's actions and teachings followed his devotion: "Few men have left behind such purity of character, or such monuments of laborious piety" (*Lives*, 3: 1306).

Watts's attitude to the cultivation of right judgment and the careful discrimination of truth is that of a rather cross "modern." Just because we "admire [a writer] for his Virtues," we should not follow him blindly: "It is this Prejudice that has . . . inclined [many great scholars] to defend Homer or Horace, Livy or Cicero, in their Mistakes" (*Logick*, 199–200). Reason is the "common Gift of God to all Men" (1),[4] giving its "daily Service to Wisdom and Virtue," and logic, "in rescuing our reasoning powers from their unhappy Slavery and Darkness," "offers an humble Assistance to divine Revelation" (vi, v). Although Watts was a nonconformist, a member of the Protestant religion in England at the time who dissented from the liturgy and ecclesiastical structure of the established Anglican Church – thus making him, to Johnson, an imperfect model thinker for others – Johnson nevertheless admired him and other dissenters for their charity, "which might well make their failings forgotten" (*Demand*, 357). Or, as Johnson says in the *Life of Watts*, "Happy will be that reader whose mind is disposed . . . to imitate him in all but his non-conformity" (*Lives*, 3: 1307). Theologically speaking, however, Johnson's moral universe was focused elsewhere.

Religion, guiding eighteenth-century thought and action in ways it is now difficult to fully appreciate, was the cornerstone of Johnson's being. His Anglican practice tended to be "high church": indeed, he singled out the Nonjuror William Law as central to his life as a Christian. Law's *Serious Call to a Devout and Holy Life* (1686), with its strenuous commitment to a devout Christian life, galvanized him:

> When at Oxford, I took up Law's "Serious Call to a Holy Life," expecting to find it a dull book, (as such books generally are,) and perhaps to laugh at it. But I found Law quite an overmatch for me; and this was the first occasion

---

[2] Michael F. Suarez, SJ, "Johnson's Christian Thought," *Companion*, p. 192 (pp. 192–208).
[3] Isaac Watts, *Logick: Or, the Right Use of Reason in the Inquiry after Truth* (London: Richard Hett and James Brackstone, 1740 [1674]), p. 27.
[4] Women are not addressed; see *Logick*, pp. 231–32.

of my thinking in earnest of religion, after I became capable of rational enquiry. (*Life*, 1: 68)[5]

Law, said Johnson, wrote "the best piece of Parenetick Divinity," but added that he was nonetheless, and unlike Watts, "no reasoner" (*Life*, 4: 287 n3).[6]

William Law seriously calls us to focus our lives intensively upon God; the logic of faith should sustain an everyday Christian life: "If we are to follow Christ, it must be in our common way of spending every day."[7] It is "our strict duty to live by *reason*, to devote *all* the actions of our lives to God" (*Serious Call*, 3). Action, a Christian's "manner of using the world" (9), is paramount, but reason should guide all choices. Reason, as with Watts, is also godliness, and its highest function is demonstrating how to please God in following the tenets of the Gospels. Law's uncompromisingly stringent requirements ask Christians to "renounce the world" in order to "live as pilgrims in spiritual watching"; "deny ourselves"; "profess the blessedness of mourning"; to "seek the blessedness of poverty of spirit"; "forsake the vanity of pride and riches"; "take no thought for tomorrow"; "live in the profoundest state of humility"; "rejoice in worldly sufferings"; "reject the lusts and the pride of life"; "bear injuries, forgive and bless our enemies"; "love mankind as God loves them"; and finally, the most demanding of all, "to give up our whole hearts and affections to God" (*Serious Call*, 8–9).

Johnson struggled to follow these prescriptions among the "pleasures and tumults of the world," as he acknowledged in the Preface to *The Preceptor* – as who would not? Boswell remarked that Johnson's youthful "amorous inclinations" were "strong and impetuous" (*Life*, 4: 395–96). Where Johnson best followed Law's strictures, however, was in the churchman's call to *caritas*. While Johnson in no way "love[d] mankind as God love[d] them" (*Serious Call*, 9), his charity was painstaking, habitual, and astonishingly wide-ranging: "He loved the poor as I never yet saw any one else do, with an earnest desire to make them happy," said his close friend Hester Thrale Piozzi (*JM*, 1: 204–5). The Rev. William Maxwell remembered that "he frequently gave all the silver in his pocket to the poor, who watched him, between his house and the tavern where he dined" (*Life*, 2:

---

[5] Suarez notes, Johnson learned "self-examination" from Law, *primus inter pares* (*Companion*, p. 201).
[6] The *Oxford English Dictionary* (online) defines the now obsolete "parenetic" as "A text or speech composed in order to give exhortation or advice" and as "advisory or hortatory." Oddly, "parenetick" is not in Johnson's *Dictionary*.
[7] William Law, *A Serious Call to a Devout and Holy Life* (London: William Innys, 1729), p. 10.

119). More than that: in responding to the destitute and the outcast, he made significant personal commitments:

> Coming home late one night, [Johnson] found a poor woman lying in the street, so much exhausted that she could not walk; he took her upon his back, and carried her to his house, where he discovered that she was one of those wretched females who had fallen into the lowest state of vice, poverty, and disease. Instead of harshly upbraiding her, he had her taken care of with all tenderness for a long time, at a considerable expence, till she was restored to health, and endeavoured to put her into a virtuous way of living. (*Life*, 4: 321–22)

The personal discomfort and difficulty occasioned by his charity carried over into his household, which Frances Burney and Hester Thrale viewed as eccentric. It included the blind Mrs. Anna Williams, Mrs. Elizabeth Desmoulins – the daughter of Johnson's godfather, Samuel Swynfen, whom he rescued from near-destitution – as well as Robert Levet, a disheveled medical doctor who in his turn helped the poor for payment in kind, and on whose death, Johnson wrote the moving elegy, "On the Death of Dr. Robert Levet" (*Poems*, 313–15). Burney's account in her diary helps us see the incidental comedy of these ill-assorted housemates, but sometimes their quarreling drove Johnson away: "Mrs. Thrale has often acquainted me that [Dr Johnson's] house is quite filled and over-run with all sorts of strange creatures, whom he admits for mere charity, and because no one else will admit them, – for his charity is unbounded, – or, rather, bounded only by his circumstances."[8] Burney's attitude toward Johnson's eccentric kindness would be that of well-to-do London society. "The Town," though, was not Johnson's preceptor: "When you make a feast, call the poor, the lame, the maimed, the blind," says Christ, not "the rich and wealthy" (*Luke* 14: 12–14).

The exercise of boundless generosity – a compensatory will to charity – was one way Johnson could meet Law's prescriptions, and I offer here two more. Johnson's was a kind of pragmatic ethics: how best to negotiate one's inadequacy? He turned to a kind of healing vigor, for human beings should act, should seek to make things happen: we are, he says in Sermon 10, "in full possession of the *present* moment; let the *present* moment be improved" (*Sermons*, 113). What would "driv[e] on the system of life" and what would blur or negate it? (*Life*, 4: 112). Where Christianity did not absolutely prescribe behavior – as it did with his charity to the poor and his

---

[8] Frances Burney, *Diaries and Letters of Madame D'Arblay*, ed. Charlotte Barrett, 4 vols. (London: Swan Sonnenschein & Co., 1893), 1: 62–63.

house guests – Johnson always preferred activity, movement, and life to stagnation and vacuity, and his own system of rational ethics would (haltingly and painfully at times) guide his own actions. His advice to others, as in *Adventurer* III, was to act: "To strive with difficulties, and to conquer them, is the highest human felicity; the next is, to strive, and deserve to conquer: but he whose life has passed without a contest, and who can boast neither success nor merit, can survey himself only as a useless filler of existence" (*Adventurer*, 455). His own terrible self-castigation for falling short in this is well documented in his diaries, annals, and prayers, as in an entry for Easter Day 1777, at sixty-eight years of age: "When I survey my past life, I discover nothing but a barren waste of time" (*DPA*, 264).

Johnson's pragmatic ethics were mostly resigned to issues on which he was bound to fail. Their third characteristic element is a sustained observation of how people actually are, producing a set of realistic expectations. How can we live, given how often we stumble? Accumulated learning will help: "Human experience, which is constantly contradicting theory, is the great test of truth. A system, built upon the discoveries of a great many minds, is always of more strength, than what is produced by the mere workings of any one mind" (*Life*, 1: 454). Thus, truth is only to be gained by reading; it is not simply an individual's experience across one lifetime, but the accumulated knowledge of ages. To Boswell's uncle, Johnson was this "robust genius, born to battle with whole libraries" (*Life*, 3: 7). He lived Watts's recommendation that "A Treasure of *Observations* and *Experiences* collected by wise Men, is of admirable Service in the judging of what is good" (*Logick*, 244). Yet, to Johnson this was not enough, because, as he says when praising Shakespeare: "There is a vigilance of observation and accuracy of distinction which books and precepts cannot confer" (*Shakespeare*, 1: 88). "Truth must arise from a conjunction of theory and experience, where each continues to test and refine the other."

Johnson's ethical thinking is shaped not only by his prodigious reading and reflection alone, but the way he balances these with an acute observation of how humanity – himself, his friends, his enemies – behaves. Johnson looks. He looks unceasingly, sees what people do and say, and thinks always with vivid perceptions based in daily living – as Adam Gopnik puts it, he "endeavour[s] to see things as they are, and then enquire whether we ought to complain."[9] Such lifelong attention meant a realistic expectation of what was ethically possible. People are not consistent, especially with themselves. They do, for instance, officiously recommend

[9] Adam Gopnik, "Johnson's Boswell," *The New Yorker* (November 27, 2000): 158.

codes of behavior to others, and then ignore their own advice. Johnson implicates himself, as he puts it in *Adventurer* 107: "We have less reason to be surprised or offended when we find others differ from us in opinion, because we very often differ from ourselves" (*Adventurer*, 442).

This constant looking translates into the written observations we see in Johnson's many essays (*The Rambler*, *The Idler*, and *The Adventurer*), which are like laboratories that set imagined people in motion, who act like models exemplifying the ethical dilemmas that ordinary people encounter. Like "these familiar histories," as the realistic novel was then called, Johnson's essays more alluringly "convey the knowledge of vice and virtue" than "the solemnities of professed morality" (*Rambler*, 4; 1: 21). But it is not just in Johnson's writing style where we see what moral philosophers call the "method of reflective equilibrium" but also in his rehearsal of fictional cases where, as Thomas Nagel argues, "coherence in . . . moral views is achieved through mutual adjustment between particular moral judgements, general principles, and theoretical constructions."[10] In the portrait of Misella in *Ramblers* 170 and 171, Johnson powerfully voices a young woman who was forced onto the streets by an older relative who abused her when barely more than a child, and then, when she was pregnant, attempted to "lull her conscience with the opiates of irreligion." Misella's internal rejection of his "impious gabble" and her return to the "general principles" (Nagel's term) of her "natural reason and early education" (*Rambler*, 3: 141) gives a striking and tragic example of Johnson's mode of shaping the ethical in the periodical.

What else created Johnson the pragmatic ethicist? If, as Watts required, "with diligence [you] . . . read the best Books," you will gain the power to think for yourself: "your Soul, like some noble Building, shall be richly furnished with original Paintings" (*Logick*, 72–73). "The best books": for an educated person in the eighteenth century this meant the classics. In the Preface to *The Preceptor*, Johnson recommended five titles in which one could study morality as the "will of *God*." The first – and the only classical text – is "Tully's *Offices*" (*Demand*, 188). Cicero's *De Officiis* (*On Duties*, 44 BCE) enjoys a towering status in the story of British education. In Cicero's own "serious call" to a virtuous life, boys in British classrooms from the seventeenth to the early twentieth century were given their conduct manual. The turn here to "Tully" was founded in Johnson's own education, and it underscores and also complements Law's insistence on activity.

---

[10] Thomas Nagel, "John Rawls," in Ted Honderich (ed.), *Oxford Companion to Philosophy* (Oxford: Oxford University Press, 1995), p. 746.

If a Christian life according to the Gospels was to be run according to the dictates of reason (Law's "strict duty"), then so too was the life of a good Roman, a *vir virtutis*. In his own "parenetick" writings Johnson tended to cite Cicero, rather than Horace or Virgil, other eighteenth-century favorites; the editors of the Yale edition of the *Idler*, for example, notice that Cicero is quoted "twice as often as Virgil" therein (*Idler*, xxvii).

Arranged with the careful formality of a master of rhetoric, *On Duties* takes its readers through what is to be expected from a gentleman of Rome via four cardinal requirements: his devotion to truth, in the form of wisdom, prudence, and "the intelligent development of the true"; his obligations to society in terms of justice and charity, of service, and debt; his attention to the increase of his own personal power through courage and strength; and lastly the development of his own rational judgment in the realm of personal behavior, with attention to temperance and control, along with decorum, his judgment of what is fitting in any given circumstance.[11] No intelligent young person could wade through or translate *De Officiis* without measuring the applicability of Cicero's injunctions to their own lives, and the brighter ones would also be wondering how much the Ciceronian code tallied with the ethical prescriptions they heard in their weekly Sunday sermon. Cicero, like Law, makes impossible demands: "moral goodness, in the true and proper sense of the term, is the exclusive possession of the wise and can never be separated from virtue; but those who have not perfect wisdom cannot possibly have perfect moral goodness, but only a semblance of it" (3:3:12). What is this wisdom, the lack of which precludes having "perfect moral goodness"? Whatever it is, it is only attainable through reason. At the very start of *De Officiis*, Cicero states that the "most marked difference" between men and animals is that the former are "endowed with reason" (1:4:11). Watts also begins here, in the second sentence of *Logick*: "Reason is one of the chief Eminencies by which we are raised above our Fellow-Creatures the Brutes" (1). Consider, though, as quoted earlier from the Preface to *The Preceptor*, that to Johnson these "brutes" are part of the "innumerable multitudes" of other beings with which God wants us to "unite" (*Demand*, 187).

Johnson noted that Law "was no reasoner," but Cicero was. Where then do Cicero and Law most disagree? Most tellingly in their treatment of generosity, *caritas*. Cicero, unlike Law, is interested in something that his Loeb editor has translated as "expediency," a sort of kindness hedged with

---

[11] Cicero, *De Officiis*, trans. Walter Miller (Cambridge, MA: Harvard University Press, 1913), Bk. 1, section 5, para. 15.

warnings and exceptions. Charity, Cicero says, should be based on value judgments about the worth of the recipient (3:6:30). William Law, conversely, cites the passage from Luke (above), and calls for the wealthy to give without stint to "the *widow* and the *orphan*, the *sick* and the *prisoner*" (*Serious Call*, 21). Johnson was with Law and Luke on this, as Hester Thrale Piozzi so vividly recorded in her *Anecdotes*:

> What signifies, says some one, giving halfpence to common beggars? they only lay it out in gin or tobacco. "And why should they be denied such sweeteners of their existence (says Johnson)? it is surely very savage to refuse them every possible avenue to pleasure, reckoned too coarse for our own acceptance. Life is a pill which none of us can bear to swallow without gilding; yet for the poor we delight in stripping it still barer, and are not ashamed to show even visible displeasure if ever the bitter taste is taken from their mouths." (*JM*, 1: 204–5)

It is "very savage," says Johnson, to use value-based judgments to justify refusing common charity to the poor. Here "savage" signifies brutal cruelty among supposedly civilized people. When Cicero concludes that "it is never expedient to do wrong, because wrong is always immoral; and it is always expedient to be good, because goodness is always moral" (*De Officiis*, 3:15:64), it sounds as if he stands with Law, and Luke too. For the Roman, though, charity is in fact a matter of logical calculation, not moral law: "in acts of kindness we should weigh with discrimination the worthiness of the object of our benevolence." Factors to juggle include "his moral character, his attitude toward us, the intimacy of his relation to us, and our common social ties, as well as the services he has hitherto rendered in our interest" (1:14:45). Johnson evidently departs radically from this measured calculus.

Cicero asks: "suppos[ing] a wise man were starving to death, might he not take the bread of some perfectly useless member of society?" (3:6:29). Yes, he replies, if your life is worth more than theirs. If taking something from a "perfectly worthless fellow" would keep you alive "to render signal service to the state and to human society," this "would not be a matter for censure" (3:6:30). This is where logic gets you. There are many similar examples in Johnson's writings, such as when a philosopher's belief in reason in *Rasselas* fails him at the death of his daughter (*Rasselas*, 75–76). Cicero's expediency is not the same as Johnson's pragmatism, because Johnson's is not, like the Roman's, strictly rational and quasi-utilitarian, but follows the simple and absolute prescription of the Christian Gospels: you help those in need because they are in need.

Johnson's ethics, then, were founded not only in the classics but also in Christianity. Yet, they were also pragmatic in that he knew about relativism – how time, place, and culture affect what is considered to be good, of value. To be Johnsonian, some think, is to be "universalist,"[12] to erase or elide how time, place, and circumstance create important differences in human behavior and experience, as when Johnson states in *Adventurer* 95 that the "influence [of the passions] is uniform, and their effects nearly the same in every human breast" (*Adventurer*, 427). *Adventurer* 95, though, also refines those statements, and includes a startlingly current idea about the spectrum as a tool for thought. Citing the rainbow, Newton's "distinct and primogenial colours," Johnson modifies his sweeping claim about the universal nature of human feeling, for through "infinite diversifications of tints" of circumstance, these primal passions will always be subject to "external causes . . . and modified by prevailing opinions and accidental caprices" (*Adventurer*, 428–29). Roman *mores*, like ours, rest on value judgments about humans that have no rational basis. Johnson does not calculate that he should take the bread of, in Cicero's phrase, some "perfectly useless member of society" (3:6:29).

Let us return to John Sitter's suggestion that "we need to revise Johnson in order to be Johnsonian." Johnson's ethics suggest that we should stop talking and thinking, once and for all, about Johnson as hidebound or dogmatic. *Adventurer* 107 confirms this view, returning us to his "pragmatic ethics," and his emphasis on action, on change – on "driving on the system of life." People can and should change their attitudes – "a man's mind" has "suffered many revolutions" in the course of his life (*Adventurer*, 442). Why is this so? Because acquiring a comprehensive understanding of any complex phenomenon is nigh impossible for the individual human mind. Complex issues need to be seen from more than one angle, as part of a spectrum, and as shaped by particular circumstances.

Isaac Watts asked his readers to be patient and to withhold judgment "when such Propositions offer themselves to us as are supported by *Education, Authority, Custom, Inclinations, Interest* or other powerful Prejudices" (*Logick*, 241). Wise men may disagree among themselves, says Johnson, for "no man can be happy by the prescription of another" (*Adventurer*, 444). And even the virtuous may put their own self-interest before pity, as in Johnson's remark in 1763 to Boswell, his uncle Dr. John Boswell, and William Dempster: "When I am on my way to dine with

---

[12] See, for example, Nicholas Hudson, "The Nature of Johnson's Conservatism," *ELH*, 64:4 (1997): 931 (925–43).

a friend, and finding it late, have bid the coachman make haste, if I happen to attend when he whips his horses, I may feel unpleasantly that the animals are put to pain, but I do not wish him to desist" (*Life*, 1: 437). If Watts's "custom" and the emotion of anxiety combine to make Johnson only "happen to attend" to the pain of a fellow creature, reason will nonetheless show him he is wrong, and will make him uneasily aware of this ethical falling away. To the same company, Johnson said: "pity is acquired and improved by the cultivation of reason" (1: 437). "Being Johnsonian," then, might mean having the flexibility, wit, experience, and knowledge to appreciate "the different faces shewn by the same objects, as they are viewed on opposite sides, and of the different inclinations which they must constantly raise in him that contemplates them" (*Adventurer*, 442), and thus to seek the broadest and most comprehensive view. To be Johnsonian is also to know that reason itself calls us to put aside expediency when feeling for others and other species asks more of us than arriving on time for dinner.

Johnson's education in rhetorical technique made it fatally easy for him to argue with passion for completely opposing ideas, to the confounding of scholars ever after. Boswell and others noted "the spirit of contradiction" in Johnson's talk (*Life*, 3: 66): he "would sometimes in conversation maintain opinions which he was sensible were wrong," reveling in the power of the spoken word to persuade (*Life*, 3: 23). Quentin Skinner has shown how central to a humanist education were the exercises where schoolboys argued a topic, in turn, on both sides – "*in utramque partem*" [taking both parts].[13] William Hamilton noted Johnson's pleasure "in maintaining the wrong side of an argument." But "if you could contrive to have his fair opinion on a subject, and without any bias from personal prejudice, or from a wish to be victorious in argument, *it was wisdom itself, not only convincing, but overpowering*" (*Life*, 4: 111). To "be Johnsonian" is thus to be full of knowledge, full of practiced rhetorical power, but also to be flexible and alert, and to actively argue in the most convincing way for being the best we can be.

In discussing Johnson's essay "On the Character and Duty of an Academick" (*Demand*, 610–12), John Sitter suggests that we still need Johnson's way of living and thinking. For ethical thinking demands that civilization is more than collective self-interested expediency: we need to "understand ethics as more than a human-to-human affair, extending our

---

[13] Quentin Skinner, *Reason and Rhetoric in the Philosophy of Hobbes* (Cambridge: Cambridge University Press), pp. 9–10, 27.

moral concern to the nonhuman world as well."[14] Two main forces of culture shape Johnson's pragmatic ethics and his balanced, alluring writing, and to lose either impoverishes our ability to extend our ethical framework. One is the Ciceronian insistence on using expedient reason to act for the good of the state, and, I suggest here, for our own home, the world. We can alter Cicero: "one native planet embraces all our loves" (1:17:57).[15] The other is a Christian, broadly moral, and humane insistence on going beyond reason to care for all beings: to include in our "processes of reflective equilibrium" those "innumerable multitudes" surrounding us, including that fellow whose bread we will not take, even if we are "Samuel Johnson."

---

[14] Sitter, "Academic Responsibility," 169.
[15] I have adapted Cicero's words, "one native country embraces all our loves" (1:17:57).

CHAPTER 2

Johnson and the Essay

Philip Smallwood

"The chief art of learning, as Locke has observed, is to attempt but little at a time. The widest excursions of the mind are made by short flights frequently repeated" (*Rambler*, 137; 2: 361). This citation by Samuel Johnson of John Locke might serve as a personal rationale for Johnson's periodical essays where, in the same place, he goes on to say that "the proper ambition of the heroes in literature" should be "to find [their] way through the fluctuations of uncertainty, and the conflicts of contradiction" (*Rambler*, 2: 362) – terms I suggest that also offer a reasonably precise summary of Johnson's ventures as an essayist. Essays on every subject are a staple of the eighteenth-century literary canon; they are a key intellectual and stylistic development within the Johnsonian *oeuvre*; they are an avenue by which his writing would try to do good. Johnson gained from the great tradition of the essay, which came to maturity in the eighteenth century, and in his major periodicals – *The Rambler, The Adventurer,* and *The Idler* – he measured his present performance against the past, variously sharing, or deserting, his predecessors' structures, styles, and intentions. Johnson's papers channel his poetic and linguistic creativity. Though no one writes quite like him, his papers mark an influential evolution in English prose of the age.

Yet because the essay can be many things, the periodicals we commonly call Johnson's essays share traits with forms also known by other names: the history, the review, the sermon, the life, the introductory preface, or the critical observation. Johnson contributed throughout his early career to journalistic publications of many kinds, and certain pieces have "essay" in their title. One of Johnson's earlier works of prose, *An Essay on Epitaphs*, was published in the *Gentleman's Magazine* in 1740 (*BW*, 496–508). However, Johnson's relation to the essay as practitioner and critic does not suggest the attributes of any determinate list of texts: to speak of an "essay" is typically to say less about textual features than the virtuoso spirit to which variant formal features are bound. The term signals not an inherent property of a given work but a quality of performance.

The modality of the essay has traces everywhere in Johnson's writing: commentators unimpressed by his novelistic skills in *Rasselas* (1759) have sometimes complained that the chapters are really moral dissertations modeled on *The Rambler* (1750–52). Elsewhere, the forensic logic of Johnson's political writings invites us to number them among his most powerful essays; so likewise we appreciate the rhetorical arc and judicious sweep of the prefaces to Shakespeare (1765) and to the *Dictionary* (1755), the latter with its emotional, almost tragic, conclusion. Even as textual annotation, Johnson's Shakespeare edition can comprise a small but perfectly formulated essay on the "mixed character" of the elderly Polonius from Shakespeare's *Hamlet* (*Shakespeare*, 2: 974). Lengthier "General Observations," such as the endnote to *King Lear*, move similarly from editorial apparatus to summative essays-in-miniature, while, from his later career, we likewise accept unquestioned his *Lives of the Poets* as essays, whether long or short, on the complex relations of writing to life. Turning to the periodical essays themselves, we see they embrace mock correspondence, allegories in prose, stories, comic *jeux d'esprit*, solemn deliberation, and much else critical and creative.

The Sallying Forth of the Mind

Johnson's attempts to define the essay in his *Dictionary* of 1755 reflect the elusiveness of its generic attributes. He here glossed "ESSAY, n.s." as "loose sally of the mind" and "an irregular indigested piece; not a regular and orderly composition" (sense 2); but the *essay* is also an "attempt; [an] endeavour," and he adds the near synonyms "trial" and "experiment" (sense 3). As these senses imply, Johnson's idea of the essay could incorporate a nuance of the French language equivalent, the *essai*, and its denotation of a literary endeavor pioneered in the sixteenth century by Michel de Montaigne (1533–92), whose *Essais* (1570–92) did not in their time signify an established genre; Johnson, who noted in his *Dictionary* a stress on either syllable of the English noun, and thus the lingering resonance in English usage of the French, suggests how, after the very different manner of Montaigne, his own written thoughts may in their own fashion express "'trials,' 'attempts,' [and] 'soundings.'"[1] "The transition was not difficult

---

[1] As applied to the *Essais* by Terence Cave, *How to Read Montaigne* (London: Granta Books, 2007), p. 21.

from Montaigne and his imitators," wrote William Hazlitt in 1819, "to our Periodical Essayists."[2] Johnson had at his call the English predecessors who helped frame his major achievements. But despite the absence of any expressed debt, Johnson's explorations of the conduct of life, the pursuit of happiness, the fear of death, the pleasure of books and conversation, politics, friendship, uncertainty, consolation, and the connection between the details of experience and grand secular and religious concerns make it natural to place Montaigne and Johnson together. English influences include the moral-philosophical *Essayes* of Francis Bacon (1561–1626) and, with a lighter touch, those of the seventeenth-century poet Abraham Cowley (1618–67), whose *Several Discourses by Way of Essays In Verse and Prose* (1656) Johnson praised in his "Life" of the poet.

The periodical paper is a special case of the essay. Narratives and critical examinations may take up two or more papers or revisit at a later point their stories or themes, but the individual periodical by Johnson is generally a self-contained experience; its meaning, however, depends at the same time on the structural character and embracing aesthetic of the series it sustains. This form of the periodical emerges as an important genre in the eighteenth century, and its understandings arise as "short flights" sensitive to the contours of weekly, daily, or occasional reflection on the part of their author. We experience periodical long-form only with the passage of time – by accretion. Through acquaintance with each new paper in turn, we get to know the essayist. We accommodate his mode of thinking progressively and with growing confidence in his judgment; different readers can enjoy an exchange of opinions as the same paper does the rounds. Johnson's authorial timeliness appears strikingly to the fore in the reliable promptness and fortitude of his periodical practice. To this end, Addison's papers from *The Spectator* offered a template on which Johnson could advance his different ambitions. As early as *Rambler* 23 (Tuesday June 5th, 1750), Johnson registers "the great force of preconceived opinions" generated by Addison's example: "My readers having, from the performance of my predecessors, established an idea of unconnected essays, to which they believed all future authors under a necessity of conforming, were impatient of the least deviation from their system, and numerous remonstrances were accordingly made by each, as he found his favourite subject omitted or delayed" (*Rambler*, 1: 128). Johnson struggled to be light in his first solo attempt at periodical composition. He was inspired by aspects of

---

[2] William Hazlitt, *Lectures on the English Comic Writers* (London: Taylor and Hessey, 1819), p. 185.

Addison's practice with which he could not compete, but he also introduced a philosophical depth and complexity to the periodical essay missing from Addison – a writer more completely immersed in the fashionable topicalities of the society from which he writes.

As a critic of writing, Johnson adjudicated essays written in poetry. The poetical excursions by John Sheffield, Earl of Mulgrave, on the subject of poetry (1682), by the Earl of Roscommon on translated verse (1684), and George Granville, Lord Lansdowne, on poetry's unnatural flights (1701) are given their due in the *Lives*, as is Pope's series of satirical poems known as his *Moral Essays*. These suppose an ethical purpose for the essay in poetry. Standing superior to all such works, however, Johnson could praise Pope's *An Essay on Criticism* (1711) as simultaneously an essay and an excellent poem, remarkable for "selection of matter, novelty of arrangement, justness of precept, splendour of illustration, and propriety of digression" (*Lives*, 3: 1200). Yet the freedom of poetical expression could set a damaging precedent. In *Rambler* 158, Johnson views with suspicion the formal liberties encouraged by the notorious irregularities of lyric, a genre receiving his mixed approval in the *Lives*. "[S]et free from all the laws by which other compositions are confined," Johnson complains, essayists are "allow[ed] to neglect the niceties of transition, to start into remote digressions, and to wander without restraint from one scene of imagery to another." For inciting these errors, Johnson homes in on a particular author:

> A writer of later times has, by the vivacity of his essays, reconciled mankind to the same licentiousness in short dissertations; and he therefore who wants skill to form a plan, or diligence to pursue it, needs only entitle his performance an essay, to acquire the right of heaping together the collections of half his life, without order, coherence, or propriety. (*Rambler*, 3: 77)

Could this licentious writer be Montaigne? Johnson feels under no obligation to say. But it is apparent that chaotic writings claimed as essays, whether they are long or short, offer no good basis for imitation. In what follows we see that even as he draws this damning caricature, Johnson is taking to heart a more morally responsible, intellectually coherent, sense of what the essay might be. His practice in the periodicals confirms this.

"Pure Wine" – A Project Moral and Devotional

Many essays from the periodicals have their lighter side. Appearing weekly from 1758 to 1760 in the pages of the *Universal Chronicle*, Johnson's papers published as *The Idler* picture the jauntier proto-Dickensian world of the politicos Tom Tempest and Jack Sneaker (number 10), of the marriageable Miss Dolly Juniper (number 12), "the great philosopher Jack Whirler" (number 19), the "eminent oilman" Timothy Mushroom (number 28), and the "lethargick virgin" Lady Biddy Porpoise (number 53). There are more topical allusions than appear in the *Ramblers* (to wars, politics, etc.) alongside "readers' letters," while number 9 offers good-humored advice on how to be idle. But not all the *Idlers* are light, and some share the moral project of *The Rambler*. Number 41 appeared a few days after Johnson's mother had died and is a meditation on human loss and the consolations of religion: "Philosophy may infuse stubbornness," Johnson concludes, "but religion only can give patience" (*Idler*, 131). Others stand out for their humanity. *Idler* 4 argues for charitable giving and the "unabated" pleasure "of having contributed to an hospital for the sick" (14). The argument then pivots to the unreliability of charity in the interests of public health. Johnson's advice anticipates the communitarian good sense of Nye Bevan: "Whatever is left in the hands of chance must be subject to vicissitude; and when any establishment is found to be useful, it ought to be the next care to make it permanent" (15).

As in *The Rambler*, Johnson's ethical, social, and legal intelligence in *The Idler* are intertwined. Number 22 condemns the evil of debtors' prisons. Johnson exposes the absurdity of locking up people who then have no means of paying you back. If defaulting on debt is wrong, the creditor must share part of the blame: "He that trusts one whom he designs to sue, is criminal by an act of trust" (71). Generally shorter than the *Ramblers*, the *Idlers* are the source of such critical essays as the two quietly hilarious, though not wholly unkind, satires on Dick Minim the critic in numbers 60 and 61 and the thoughtful definition of Easy Poetry in number 77. Number 60 mocks the affectation of close reading by reference to a passage from Butler's *Hudibras*. Number 77 illustrates specimens of stylistic "ease" from Addison's play *Cato* (1712) and from Cowley, and it confutes any suggestion that Johnson's poetic taste was peculiarly ruled by decorous elevations of style. Between the years 1753 and 1754, Johnson supplied 29 out of 140 essays to *The Adventurer*, a periodical undertaken in collaboration with Johnson's friend John Hawkesworth (1715–73), and a joint endeavor notable for distinguished papers on Shakespeare's *King Lear* and *The Tempest* by the critic Joseph Warton (1722–1800). *The Adventurer* is a comradely enterprise; *The Rambler* a work of lonely repetitive toil and individual tenacity.

Hazlitt called the essays of *The Rambler* "scholastic theses."[3] Johnson, however, defined the purpose of his great project of 1750 with a beautiful and moving prayer to his Maker: "Almighty God, the giver of all good things, without whose help all Labour is ineffectual, and without whose grace all wisdom is folly, grant I beseech Thee, that in this my undertaking thy Holy Spirit may not be withheld from me, but that I may promote thy glory, and the Salvation both of myself and others" (*DPA*, 43). When writing essays is accountable to God, it follows that Johnson should be judged on the redemptively moral explorations and searching self-examinations that connect his essays with his trials of conscience, his markings of time, and his devotional life.

The experience of Johnson's periodical essays is one of serendipitous surprise. His voice is an anchoring presence – grave, laconic, questioning, emphatic, trenchant, sometimes playful, and often satirical. As he adapts the English periodical to his own intellectual temperament, Johnson combines an Addisonian schema with a return to a range of Montaigne's miscellaneous themes. Johnson's wife died on March 17, 1752, and only a few days before, on March 14, while yet innocent of this devastating event, Johnson had published his valedictory *Rambler* (number 208). This was the last of the punishing twice-weekly commitment he had made almost exactly two years earlier and that was commenced, according to Thomas Tyers, "by way of relief" from his *Dictionary* labors.[4] Unlike *The Idler* or *The Adventurer*, *The Rambler* was a serial publication entirely on Johnson's terms, and at first appeared anonymously, though its author would have been easy to guess. The project was a matter of particular pride to Johnson: "My other works are wine and water," he observed, "but my *Rambler* is pure wine" (*Life*, 1: 210 n1).

He "desired no assistance," writes Arthur Murphy, "relying entirely on his own fund."[5] But not quite everything is Johnson's. Three of the *Rambler* essays were contributed by friends, of which two, numbers 44 and 100, were composed by Elizabeth Carter, the translator of the Stoic philosopher Epictetus, and number 30, a riddle on "Sunday," by Catherine Talbot. Number 97 was written by Samuel Richardson the novelist. Sixty-three out of the 208 were formulated in "letter-to-the-editor" guise, again borrowing the practice of Mr. Spectator and reaching out to actual readers even as Johnson dreams up the named or anonymous correspondents

---

[3] Hazlitt, *Lectures*, p. 195.
[4] Thomas Tyers, "A Biographical Sketch of Dr. Samuel Johnson" (1785), in *JM*, 2: 350.
[5] Arthur Murphy, "An Essay on the Life and Genius of Samuel Johnson, LL.D." (1792), in *JM*, 1: 391.

whose letters he prints. Such devices are sometimes the occasion for self-
ridicule. The absurdly naive Bellaria in number 191 complains in this vein
to Mr. Rambler that she is forced by learned aunts to expose herself to the
indigestible philosophical vocabulary of his papers. Johnson later wrote of
Addison (approvingly enough) that he "detects follies rather than crimes"
(*Lives*, 2: 647), and, as a comedian of manners on his own account,
Johnson humorously lays bare individuals' vanity and folly more often
than real evil. In *Rambler* 61, Mr. Frolick comes down from London twice
a year. His entire purpose is to condescend to the residents of the countryside whence he started life and to boast:

> His dress, his language, his ideas, were all new, and he did not much
> endeavour to conceal his contempt of every thing that differed from the
> opinions or practice, of the modish world. He shewed us the deformity of
> our skirts and sleeves, informed us where hats of the proper size were to be
> sold, and recommended to us the reformation of a thousand absurdities in
> our cloaths, our cookery, and our conversation. (*Rambler*, 1: 326)

Gathered with the social-satirical sketches of *The Rambler*, this is one of
Johnson's "pictures of life" – a category coined in summing up his
achievement in *Rambler* 208, the others being "excursions of fancy,"
"disquisitions of criticism," and "essays professedly serious" (*Rambler*, 3:
319–20). In common with *The Idler*, the *Rambler*s host a gallery of types –
critics, readers, writers, fathers, daughters, husbands, guardians, servants,
men on the make, and people who come down from London. Boswell
remembers Johnson relating to him, "with much satisfaction, that several
of the characters in *The Rambler* were drawn so naturally, that when it first
circulated in numbers, a club in one of the towns in Essex imagined
themselves to be severally exhibited in it, and were much incensed against
a person who, they suspected, had made them objects of publick notice"
(*Life*, 1: 215–16). The audience for *The Rambler* in Essex was perhaps less
discriminating than Johnson had predicted, but their disapproval afforded
a pleasing validation.

   The Rambler does not ignore the darker side of human nature. Johnson
had bridled at censure in *Rambler* 23 "for not imitating the politeness of his
predecessors, having hitherto neglected to take the ladies under his protection, and give them rules for the opposition of colours, and the proper
dimensions of ruffles and pinners" (*Rambler*, 1: 129). In response, Johnson
discharges his obligation in tales of female crisis, illustrations of the fate of
women as victims of male condescension, narratives of misplaced ambition, exploitation, or innocent misfortune, as in the story of Misella from

*Rambler*s 170 and 171. In company with *The Spectator*, *The Rambler* sometimes seems to anticipate the satirical strokes of Jane Austen (who knew the papers), but Johnson is more outspoken. In number 35, on arranged betrothals, one of a series devoted to marriage, he writes that "I could not but look with pity on young persons condemned to be set at auction" (1: 193). In *Rambler* 45 there are listed aside this abuse the shabby maneuverings and mindless haste by which some marital ties are cemented:

> When I see the avaricious and crafty taking companions to their tables, and their beds, without any enquiry, but after farms and money; or the giddy and thoughtless uniting of themselves for life to those whom they have only seen by the light of tapers at a ball; when parents make articles for their children, without enquiring after their consent; when some marry for heirs to disappoint their brothers, and others throw themselves into the arms of those they do not love, because they have found themselves rejected where they were more solicitous to please; when some marry because their servants cheat them, some because they squander their own money, some because their houses are pestered with company, some because they will live like other people, and some only because they are sick of themselves, I am not much inclined to wonder that marriage is sometimes unhappy, as that it appears so little loaded with calamity; and cannot but conclude that society has something in itself eminently agreeable to human nature, when I find its pleasures so great that even the ill choice of a companion can hardly over-balance them. (*Rambler*, 1: 246)

Building paratactically from one semi-colon to the next, Johnson's clauses register Mr. Rambler's mounting perplexity at the venal, frivolous, or pitiful preludes to the most solemn of alliances. But the sentence concludes in the inescapable recognition of human sociability and the good that survives. The surprise that commitments contracted from the lowest of ulterior motives, or explained by defects of character, are not more destructive depicts society as greater than the sum of individual conduct.

Among the "essays professedly serious," several *Rambler*s reflect Johnson's appreciation of the legal brief. Boswell, a lawyer, commended "the astonishing force and vivacity of mind," the "bark and steel" of *The Rambler*, and that "no mind can be thought very deficient that has, by constant study and meditation, assimilated to itself all that may be found there" (*Life*, 1: 213–14). At the same time, the spiritual motives of other essays enabled Thomas Bellamy (1745–1800) to characterize Johnson's ghosting of sermons for delivery by others as "the religious essays of the *Rambler*."[6] Elsewhere,

---

[6] Thomas Bellamy, *The General Magazine and Impartial Review*, 2 (June 1788): 311.

Johnson can bring real-world economic insights to the notice of Christian moralists and politicians alike. His correspondent in *Rambler* 57, one Sophron, suggests how poverty and wealth are relative: "he that has less than any other is comparatively poor" (*Rambler*, 1: 307). Johnson highlights the irony of our acquisitive follies in *Rambler* 58:

> Wealth is nothing in itself, it is not useful but when it departs from us, its value found only in that which it can purchase . . . . With respect to the mind, it has rarely been observed, that wealth contributes much to quicken the discernment, enlarge the capacity, or elevate the imagination; but may, by hiring flattery, or laying diligence asleep, confirm error and harden stupidity. (*Rambler*, 1: 313)

The essayistic mode of *The Rambler* advanced Johnson's moral-philosophical opportunities and, consequentially, strengthened the historical role of the essay in English philosophical thought. Among compositions of a philosophical cast is number 28 on self-knowledge, while number 29 on destructive anxiety about a future state reveals Johnson's grasp of moral psychology in its troubled relation to time. In number 32, Johnson challenges the ancient Stoics who claimed to eliminate pain from their catalogue of evils. If pain "be not an evil," reasons Johnson, "there seems no instruction requisite how it may be borne," so that philosophers "may be thought to have given up their first position" when they try to instruct their followers by arguments against it (1: 175). This brusque rebuttal at the time of *The Rambler* contrasts with the vulnerability of stoical convictions sympathetically portrayed nine years later in one of the most distressing chapters of *Rasselas*, where we learn that the philosopher of Nature has lost his only daughter. In the unbearable grief of family bereavement, philosophy cannot, ultimately, sustain him (*Rasselas*, 70–76).

Literary criticism is a practice where hot tempers often prevail. Johnson's "disquisitions of criticism" substantiate the essay as bringing analytic method to critical thoughts repeated or modified or reversed in later life. Among his topics are biography (number 60), the impossibility of defining comedy according to its attributes (number 125), the rules of tragic drama (number 156), and Shakespeare's "force of poetry" (number 168). Johnson's critical pieces match analysis with evaluation. Two essays on the laws of pastoral poetry (numbers 36 and 37) are prescient of Johnson's ridicule of Milton's *Lycidas* and the pastorals of other practitioners in the *Lives*. Johnson can be withering. He concludes number 37 with a swingeing dismissal of pastoral imitators who "have written with an utter disregard both of life and nature, and filled their productions with mythological allusions, with incredible fictions, and with sentiments which neither passion nor reason could have dictated, since the change which religion has made in the whole system of the world" (*Rambler*, 1: 205).

Johnson's discussions of literary issues express a high degree of self-awareness. Recalling the "young enthusiast" of *The Vanity of Human Wishes* (ll. 135–64), Johnson evokes the humiliations of a beginning author (a condition recalled from experience) and satirizes correspondents desperate to enjoy "the bliss of publication" (*Rambler*, 56; 1: 303). He examines the art of fiction in *Rambler* 4, but Johnson also reveals his own short-story skills in periodical fabulation, or "excursions of fancy" (including five oriental tales). Individual stories, including the testimonies and imprecations of "correspondents," can extend over two or more papers, providing a sequel to the narrative begun in the first.

The Experience of Style

Johnson writes of Dryden's critical prefaces: "Nothing is cold or languid; the whole is airy, animated, and vigorous; what is little, is gay; what is great, is splendid" (*Lives*, 1: 443). He goes on to apply his compositional standards negatively to the essays of Blackmore, whose "prose [by contrast with Dryden's] is not the prose of a poet; for it is languid, sluggish, and lifeless: his diction is neither daring nor exact, his flow neither rapid nor easy, and his periods neither smooth nor strong" (*Lives*, 2: 766). The character of the essayist, this contrast suggests, is partly occasioned by their performance of style; Johnson reads the literary personality of other essayists in how they write. A distinction of Johnson's *Rambler* essays is the stylistic experience they too afford, and, as the self-satire of *Rambler* 191 suggests, he was in turn alive to the effects of his singularity upon readers. Johnson's expression animates the complex moral analysis, social comedy, spirit of philosophical curiosity, protest, or resignation we have encountered in the essays.

Johnson's vocabulary calls attention to itself, albeit that in some early *Ramblers* a learnedly polysyllabic diction can seem cumbrous. For example, he writes in *Rambler* 24 of the "terraqueous globe"; in *Rambler* 49 of the "adscititious passions." In number 65, a river is said to water a region "with innumerable circumvolutions" (1: 131, 265, 346). As Milton elevates the style of his heroic poem, so for the essay Johnson finds a defamiliarizing register in words of Latin origin where Anglo-Saxon derivatives would otherwise do. His phraseology at the same time plays an arresting contributory role – as in the triple ascent: "the prejudice of faction, the stratagem of intrigue, or the servility of adulation" (*Rambler*, 106; 2: 201). Johnson's sentences are often constructs, elaborately subordinated, a practice that generated mockery of him as "Dr. Pomposo" by the contemporary poet Charles Churchill. The syntactic intricacies of his prose have always drawn criticism. But Johnson's longest sentences never lose their way, and a wonderful metaphoric life often marks his expressions. So, for example, Johnson's female correspondent complains of the preposterous Frolick that one must conclude "his faculties are benumbed by rural stupidity, as the magnetick needle loses its animation in the polar climes" (*Rambler*, 1: 329). "His mind was so full of imagery," writes Boswell, "that he might have been perpetually a poet" (*Boswell's Scotland*, 7) and perhaps, as such "heterogeneous ideas" suggest, a metaphysical one.[7]

Johnson gives weight and force to abstract nouns: Hope, Vanity, Criticism, etc. are charged with the moral drama and agency reminiscent of Johnson the poet. Abstractions likewise become *things* at the level of the phrase, where Johnson beautifully and memorably combines an abstract noun with a concrete one: hence in *Rambler* 103, the "cobwebs of petty inquisitiveness," or in *Rambler* 104, "the mist of pride," "the precipice of falsehood," and "the shackles of dependence" (*Rambler*, 2: 187, 193, 194). Nor is Latinate vocabulary necessarily an *unconscious* habit: blunt monosyllables can alert by deliberate contrast with more exalted diction. Writing of the student's enthusiasm for study in *Rambler* 108, Johnson observes that the scholarly mind returns from "occupations less pleasing" with greater alacrity than "when it is glutted with ideal pleasures, and surfeited with intemperance of application" (2: 213). Johnson highlights the embodied quality of an act – here "to glut" – as against the propensity to "surfeit" the mind. In the Eastern tale of Nouradin, Latinism marks the speech of Almamoulin, whose exotic grandeur is the moral question at issue: "a frigorifick topor encroaches upon my veins," he complains ornately (*Rambler*, 120; 2: 277).

In an image adopted from Hazlitt by Freya Johnston and Lynda Mugglestone, Johnson's sentences are said to describe "the arc of the pendulum."[8] Sometimes a sentence sways judicially between equal halves: "They that encourage folly in the boy, have no right to punish it in the man" (*Rambler*, 109; 2: 220), where twenty syllables split into sets of ten.

---

[7] Johnson's definition of metaphysical wit in the *Life of Cowley* has such ideas "yoked by violence together" (*Lives*, 1: 26).

[8] Freya Johnston and Lynda Mugglestone, *Samuel Johnson: The Arc of the Pendulum* (Oxford: Oxford University Press, 2012).

Elsewhere, many sentences succeed as sustained flights: the extended sentence I have quoted on cynical or shallow-minded routes to matrimony has 190 words. A contrasting stylistic feature less frequently observed is the power of the Johnsonian sentence to confront readers with unassailable truth for which we are not prepared. "Sorrow is a kind of rust on the soul" (*Rambler*, 47; 1: 258); "Without hope there can be no caution" (*Rambler*, 119; 2: 270). Such directness recalls conversational interventions by Johnson that Boswell reports. Sometimes a witty about-face clinches the point, as when Johnson repudiates capital punishment for robbery: "To equal robbery with murder is to reduce murder to robbery" (*Rambler*, 114; 2: 244). Johnson's balanced style need be no less pithy, brisk, or barbed. In *Rambler* 158, the rules of critics are "the arbitrary edicts of legislators, authorised only by themselves" (3: 76). Echoing Johnson's spoken remarks, the printed voice of Johnsonian prose sounds exceptionally sharp.

"Their premises precede their conclusions," writes Hazlitt of the *Rambler*s.[9] However, Johnson took corresponding care with "the niceties of transitions" he believed ignored by later essayists: "To proceed from one truth to another, and to connect distant propositions by regular consequences," he announces in *Rambler* 158, "is the great prerogative of man" (*Rambler*, 3: 78). Thus, "It is allowed," reads the opening of *Rambler* 145, "that vocations and employments of least dignity are of the most apparent use" (3: 8). But in the next paragraph bar one this becomes only "one of the innumerable theories" destroyed when reduced to practice. Those who labor for a living "must be content . . . to form the base of the pyramid of subordination" (3: 8–9) – and so on until the substance of the essay is addressed: esteem for the lowly labor of authors. John Ruskin noted how "the turns and returns of reiterated *Rambler* and iterated *Idler* fastened themselves in my ears and mind."[10] The recursive patterns enact the essays' skeptical and exploratory spirit: Johnson's finding his way through Locke's "fluctuations of uncertainty."

Periodical Form and Moral Inquiry

Several *Rambler*s (for example numbers 54, 56, and 58) have a "therefore" or "Let us therefore" signaling their conclusion. The Johnsonian periodical paper at the "professedly serious" end of its range is invariably

---

[9] Hazlitt, *Lectures*, p. 179.
[10] John Ruskin, *Praeteritia*, *The Complete Works of John Ruskin*, ed. E. T. Cook and Alexander Wedderburn, 39 vols. (London: Allen, 1903–12), 35: 225–26.

a tightly organized work of deduction. Yet thinking analytically is not a precondition of the moral action Johnson commends: "No man needs stay to be virtuous," he declares in *Idler* 37, "till the moralists have determined the essence of virtue" (*Idler*, 117). Johnson had made the background to this verdict explicit in *Rambler* 63: "To take a view at once distinct and comprehensive of human life, with all its intricacies of combination, and varieties of connexion, is beyond the power of mortal intelligences" (*Rambler*, 1: 336). It is in response to such limitation that periodicals are "works . . . not sent into the world at once, but by small parts in gradual succession" (*Rambler*, 23; 1: 126). Or, to recall once again the teaching of Locke, "short flights" that together compose the "widest excursions of the mind" (*Rambler*, 137; 2: 361). There is a fresh start with each successive periodical essay: Mr. Rambler conveys the authorial emotion of the moment – purposeful, curious, sometimes bright and fanciful, and sometimes earnest and melancholic; yet Johnson's structure means that conclusions reached in any one number are exposed to the critical context of issues examined in other papers. Essays constituting the genre of the periodical each channel values and qualities not fully expressed generically. No topic is completely exhausted.

Compared with the *Spectators*, some *Ramblers* are somber; in this they both reflect a phase in his emotional life and mark Johnson's seriousness of purpose. But laughter keeps on breaking in. Quoting Dryden's explanation for translating the first book of the *Iliad*, Johnson's final *Dictionary* gloss of "ESSAY, n.s." is the "First taste of any thing" (sense 4) – a meaning recalling the accomplished writer of prefaces and introductions that Johnson was. The pages of Johnson's periodical essays are a storehouse of moral unresolvables and unaccountable contradictions, and he is devoted throughout to testing the ethical and critical platitudes of his day. In this pursuit, his practice brings a discipline of thought to the essay as "loose sally of the mind," and by his short and often intensely focused contributions, Johnson redeems the essay's inclination to wander "without restraint from one scene of imagery to another." At the same time, personal ownership of his project means that Johnson's individual compositions for *The Rambler* are not "unconnected" (*Rambler*, 23; 3: 138). In the original pamphlets costing tuppence a time and appearing unfailingly every Tuesday and Saturday over a period of two years, Johnson's deliberations unfold as interim reports, but they also show how moral, spiritual, political, and economic questions, literary ideas and judgments, comedies of manners, cries from the heart, and philosophical speculations are related. The "gradual succession" of papers coheres to suggest that good can be done under conditions often hostile to virtue and knowledge. Montaigne, whose self-founding as an essayist is recalled by Johnson's lonely and original struggle for truth in *The Rambler*, would be the first to understand his endeavor.

CHAPTER 3

Johnson and Renaissance Humanism

Anthony W. Lee

What is humanism? Correctly speaking, plural responses are required to answer that question. We have the broadly subjective and relativistic humanism of the pre-Socratic philosopher Protagoras: "Man is the measure of all things," as well as more recent iterations: the anti-modernist conservatism of the early-twentieth-century New Humanists (Irving Babbitt and Paul Elmer More); the atheistic humanist existentialism of John-Paul Sartre; and, more recently, Donna Haraway's cyborg humanism. The present chapter uses the term to refer to the European-wide cultural flowering of the Renaissance. The genealogy of this movement extends at least as far back as Cicero's *studium humanitatis* (which itself harkens back to the model Greek education, *paedeia*), denoting a liberal arts education,[1] and an afterlife reaching later authors such as John Dryden and Samuel Johnson.

European Renaissance humanism – a literary, intellectual, and cultural "movement" roughly spanning the fourteenth through the seventeenth centuries, from Petrarch to Milton, from Italy to Britain – has two major distinguishing characteristics: (1) reverence for learning and books of the past, especially classical (Greek and Roman) literature; and (2) a focused effort to bring the wisdom of earlier authors to bear on contemporary life. My concern is primarily with the backward-looking Johnson, whose focus may be seen in a representative text such as *Adventurer* 58 (1753), where he writes of "the authors of antiquity":

> [T]hose whose works have been the delight of ages, and transmitted as the great inheritance of mankind from one generation to another: surely, no man can, without the utmost arrogance, imagine, that he brings any superiority of understanding to the perusal of those books which have been preserved in the devastation of cities, and snatched up from the

I wish to thank Robert G. Walker and Robert DeMaria, Jr., for reading drafts of this essay and offering helpful commentary.
[1] See Nicholas Mann, "The Origins of Humanism," in Jill Kraye (ed.), *The Cambridge Companion to Renaissance Humanism* (Cambridge: Cambridge University Press, 1996), pp. 1–19, p. 1.

wreck of nations; which those who fled before barbarians have been careful
to carry off in the hurry of migration, and of which barbarians have repented
the destruction. (*Adventurer*, p. 372)

Johnson's interest in the authors of antiquity is one with his interest in
civilization itself. His intellectual affiliations with sixteenth-century
teachers and scholars underpin his desire, as recorded by Boswell in 1784,
to write a specialized history, the

> History of the Revival of Learning in Europe, containing an account of
> whatever contributed to the restoration of literature; such as controversies,
> printing, the destruction of the Greek empire,[2] the encouragement of great
> men, with the lives of the most eminent patrons and most eminent early
> professors of all kinds of learning in different countries. (*Life*, 4: 382 n1)

Johnson never pursued this project, but clues about what such a history
might have included may be gathered from other points in his *oeuvre*. In
the Preface to the *Dictionary of the English Language* (1755), he writes of the
illustrative quotations appended to the definitions: "I have studiously
endeavoured to collect examples and authorities from the writers before
the restoration, whose works I regard as *the wells of English undefiled*, as the
pure sources of genuine diction" (*EL*, 95). Later in the same text he specifies
some of the authors he has in mind: "I shall not think my employment
useless or ignoble . . . if my labours . . . add celebrity to *Bacon*, to *Hooker*, to
Milton, and to *Boyle*" (110). In his *Life of Ascham* (1757; *BW*, pp. 427–72), he
favorably contrasts the great learning of that period with that of his own:

> New studies of literature, and new tenets of religion, found employment for
> all who were desirous of truth, or ambitious of fame. Learning was at that
> time prosecuted with that eagerness and perseverance which in this age of
> indifference and dissipation it is not easy to conceive. (*BW*, p. 429)

Johnson was learnedly receptive to and engaged with numerous English
and Continental humanist thinkers and writers, far more than can be listed
here. To get a sense of this, one only needs to thumb through the sale
catalogue of his library or to consider his proposals for the *Harleian
Catalogue* (*Demand*, 74–106) and the "Plan" (1747) for his *Dictionary*
(*EL*, 25–59).[3] His *Dictionary* is itself in the lineage of such scholar-heroes

---

[2] It was long thought that the fall of Constantinople in 1453 was a decisive catalyst for Renaissance
humanism. However, it was a much more gradual process; see Douglas Bush, *The Renaissance and
English Humanism* (Toronto: University of Toronto Press, 1968), p. 14.

[3] See Donald Greene, *Samuel Johnson's Library: An Annotated Guide*. English Literary Studies, No. 1
(Victoria, BC: University of Victoria, 1975). The Harleian Catalogue (1743–45) was commissioned by
bookseller Thomas Osborne to advertise his sale of the enormous library of Tory minister Robert

as Joseph Scaliger (1540–1609), compiler of an Arabic dictionary, Robert Estienne's (d. 1559) *Thesaurus Latinae Linguae* (1531), and his son, Henri Estienne's (d. 1598) *Thesaurus Graecae Linguae* (1572).[4] Johnson's edition of Shakespeare (1765) – to say nothing of his edition of Sir Thomas Browne's (1605–82) *Christian Morals* (1756) – had as their precursors such great editions as Isaac Casaubon's (1559–1614) Athenaeus of Naucratis's *Deipnosophistae* (1657) – a work of literary, historical, and antiquarian references set in Rome as a series of banquets that Johnson alludes to in *Rambler* 48 – and Erasmus's Greek New Testament (1516), as well as Erasmus's editions of the early Church Fathers, such as St. Jerome.

When Johnson was twenty-one years of age (1734), he issued proposals for an edition of the works of Angelus Politian (1454–94), a neo-Latin poet and Italian humanist. As the title to his (now lost) proposals indicates,[5] Johnson intended to append to this edition a life of the writer and a history of Latin poetry from Petrarch to Politian. Likewise, Johnson began a translation of Father Paolo Sarpi's (1552–1623) *Council of Trent* (1738–9), but only the Proposals have survived, as has his short biography of Sarpi (*BW*, 1–18). Known today by only a few specialists, Sarpi's history made an important contribution to the literature of the Counter-Reformation and has been highly valued by historians Hugh Trevor-Roper and Anthony Grafton. There is more in this vein. Near the end of his life, Johnson contemplated a biography of the French Renaissance historian Jacques Auguste de Thou (1553–1617). He also wanted to create a critical edition of Edward Fairfax's translation of Torquato Tasso's *Jerusalem Delivered* (1600), Machiavelli's *History of Florence* (1532), Girolamo Benzoni's *History of the New World* (1565), and of the works of the English poet Abraham Cowley (1618–67), whose "Life" he did eventually write in the *Lives of the Poets* (1779–81). Essentially, Johnson knew many of the Renaissance humanists as well as the back of his hand. In what follows – skimming but the surface of Johnson's engagement with the Renaissance and the neo-Latin humanists – I shall consider his relationship with three in particular: Sir Thomas More, Sir Francis Bacon, and Michel de Montaigne.

Harley, Earl of Oxford, and his son Edward. The manuscripts in the collection became the core of the British Museum (later Library).

[4] See Paul Korshin, "Johnson and the Renaissance Dictionary," *Journal in the History of Ideas*, 35:2 (1974): 300–12.

[5] *Angeli Politiani Poemata Latina, quibus, Notas cum historia Latinae poeseos, a Petrarchae aevo ad Politiani tempora deducta, et vita Politiani fusius quam antehac enarrata, addidit* Sam Johnson. See *Life*, 1: 90.

More and Johnson

In 1775 Johnson, accompanied by Mr. and Mrs. Thrale and their eldest daughter Queeney, and cicerone Giuseppe Baretti, spent two months touring France, the only time he ventured outside Britain (*Life*, 2: 389–401). However, there are occasional xenophobic hints toward the French in Johnson's writing,[6] for example, in *London* (1738):

> Nor hope the British lineaments to trace,
> The rustic grandeur, or the surly grace,
> But lost in thoughtless ease, and empty show,
> Behold the warrior dwindled to a beau;
> Sense, freedom, piety, refin'd away,
> Of France the mimick, and of Spain the prey.
> . . .
> No gainful trade their industry can 'scape,
> They sing, they dance, clean shoes, or cure a clap:
> All sciences a fasting Monsieur knows,
> And bid him go to hell, to hell he goes.
>
> (*Poems*, 53, 54, ll. 101–6, 112–16)

Here, Johnson unites his apparent disdain for France with ridicule of the English "beau" who apes French manners, to his degradation. We might compare this passage from *London* to the following epigram by Sir Thomas More (1478–1535):

> A friend and chum I have, called Lalus, who
> Was born in Britain and in Britain bred, ...
> Lalus holds British ways and fashions cheap,
> Doting upon the French.

He struts about

> In cloaks in fashion French. His girdle, purse,
> And sword are French. His hat is French.
> His nether limbs are cased in French costume.
> His shoes are French. In short, from top to toe
> He stands the Frenchman.[7]

---

[6] For Johnson's French Journal, see Anthony W. Lee, "Travel," in Jack Lynch (ed.), *The Oxford Handbook of Samuel Johnson* (Oxford: Oxford University Press, 2022), pp. 244–59.

[7] J. H. Marsden, *Philomorus: Notes on the Latin Poems of Sir Thomas More* (London: Longmans, Green, Reader, and Dyer, 1878), p. 223. Like Johnson's, More's satire of the French is complicated: after a reproach about it from his best friend, Erasmus, More seems to have regretted it.

London, of course, is not an "original" poem, but an imitation of Juvenal's 3rd satire.

Whether or not we can trace the *London* passage to More's epigram, their thematic congruence suggests an affinity between More and Johnson, and it illustrates a larger point. In the diary that he kept in 1774 when traveling in Wales with Hester Thrale and Queeney, Johnson approvingly transcribed a Greek epigram that suggests how highly he thought of More: "From the Muses, More carried off the first crown, / Erasmus the second, and [Jacob] Micyllus has the third" (*Poems,* 389).[8] Johnson owned at least two editions of More's works, and even as an undergraduate he had a copy of More's *Utopia* (1515).[9] In the "History of the English Language," part of the introductory matter to his *Dictionary,* Johnson quotes more specimens of Thomas More's poetry and prose than any other author's (*EL,* 210–48). He was interested in the biography of More by his son-in-law, William Roper (written 1553–78, published 1626), and apparently thought of writing one himself (*EL,* 211 and *Letters,* 1: 112–13).[10] In addition to their disparagement of the French, Johnson shares More's disdain for would-be or irreligious doctors (as seen, for example, in the *Life of Garth* and *Rambler* 9, respectively) and for urban wits making fools of themselves in the country (see *Rambler,* 62, 101).[11] While it is likely that both Johnson and More are drawing upon common topoi, that they share objects of satire suggests a commonality of interests. Indeed, More was the type of intellectual that Johnson tended to value most. He did not cloister his learning in the study but used it to pursue the *activae vitae* (active life), as seen in his rise to the highest political office in England, Lord Chancellor, the first non-churchman to do so. Johnson's strong interest in the law also forms a connective strand between him and More.

Furthermore, both More and Johnson wrote fictions that have defied easy categorization: *Utopia* (1516), More's most celebrated work,[12] and *Rasselas* (1759), Johnson's major work of fiction. Both describe travels beyond the boundaries of Europe. Apart from being a travel narrative, *Rasselas* is a *contes philosophiques,* an experimental novel, a romance, an

---

[8] Jacob Micyllus (1503–58) was a German humanist and Neo-Latin poet.
[9] Greene, *Samuel Johnson's Library,* p. 85; Aleyn Lyell Reade, *Johnsonian Gleanings,* 11 vols. (New York: Octagon Books, 1968), 5: 214. For Johnson's undergraduate library, see Reade, *Johnsonian Gleanings,* 5: 213–29.
[10] See Anthony W. Lee, "Hearne, Roper, More, and *Rambler* 71," *Notes and Queries,* 67:3 (2020): 422–26.
[11] For English translations of More's epigrams, see Thomas Pecke (b. 1637), *Parnassi puerperium* (London: J. Cottrel, for Tho. Bassett [etc.], 1659).
[12] Other humanist works by More include his *Letters on Humanism,* especially the "Letter to Dorp" (1515) and "Letter to a Monk" (1519–20).

oriental or Eastern tale, a satire upon human nature, and an allegory of life. *Utopia*, in turn, is a satire upon society and culture, both European and English, an innovative literary experiment, a penetrating social critique, and, like Erasmus's *Praise of Folly* (1511), written almost contemporaneously, an elaborate comic cock-and-bull story. Both works resist a single, comfortable genre. Further, they both feature a place suggestive of an Edenic golden age, although More presents his as an ideal paradise, while the Happy Valley in *Rasselas* is more a dismal dystopian prison from which all inhabitants yearn to escape. Both works feature a seemingly wise mentor, Raphael Hythloday and Imlac – however, the name of the former means something like "Mr. Nonsense," a false idol, while the latter's leadership leads to an inconclusive and uneasy acceptance of the status quo. Both works are humanistic in their appropriation of the details of a learned tradition deployed in a new medium accessible to a contemporary audience.

Compare, for example, More and Johnson's championing of more humane ways to deal with crimes such as theft. In *Utopia*, More writes of the abolition of private property and money:

> [O]nce the use of money was abolished, and together with it all greed for it, what a mass of troubles was cut away, what a crop of crimes was pulled up by the roots! Is there anyone who does not know that fraud, theft, plunder, strife, turmoil, contention, rebellion, murder, treason, poisoning, crimes which are constantly punished but never held in check, would die away if money were eliminated?[13]

Johnson, in his turn, does not propose so radical a solution; he advocates a more modest yet more realistic approach to crime and unjust laws in *Rambler* 114:

> For, who can congratulate himself upon a life passed without some act more mischievous to the peace or prosperity of others, than the theft of a piece of money?
>   This scheme of invigorating the laws by relaxation, and extirpating wickedness by lenity, is so remote from common practice, that I might reasonably fear to expose it to the publick, could it be supported only by my own observations: I shall, therefore, by ascribing it to its author, Sir Thomas More, endeavour to procure it that attention, which I wish always paid to prudence, to justice, and to mercy. (*Rambler*, 2: 242–43, 246–47)

---

[13] Sir Thomas More, *The Essential Works of Thomas More*, ed. Gerard B. Wegemer and Stephen W. Smith (New Haven, CT: Yale University Press, 2020), p. 210.

While their solutions are different, both men share a fierce humanistic anger against unjust laws and the harm they inflict upon the poor and powerless. And it is a decisive point that Johnson calls upon More as the authority supporting his own attempts at reform. As Robert DeMaria, Jr. notes, "Johnson's real country was humanist Europe."[14]

Bacon and Johnson

Johnson is one of the great essayists in English literature. Though he admired the essays of his eighteenth-century precursors, Addison, Steele, and Swift – authors he read in his youth – the roots of Johnson's essayistic style lie in two Renaissance humanists, both of whom shaped his thought significantly: Sir Francis Bacon and Michel Eyquem de Montaigne.

Johnson admired and respected Bacon, planned to edit his English works, and also wanted to write his life (*JM*, 2: 302). He was particularly impressed by Bacon's breadth of knowledge and its application to human life. In the Preface to the *Dictionary*, Johnson wrote: "If . . . the terms of natural knowledge [were extracted] from Bacon . . . few ideas would be lost to mankind, for want of English words in which they might be expressed" (*EL*, 96). Sir Joshua Reynolds reported Johnson as saying of Bacon's *Essays* (1597): "[T]heir excellence and value consisted in being the observations of a strong mind operating on life; and in consequence you find there what you seldom find in other books" (*Life*, 3: 194 n). A "strong mind operating on life" signifies a certain kind of wisdom admired and exemplified by Johnson, which he articulates in *Adventurer* 85:

> It is observed by Bacon, that "reading maketh a full man, conversation a ready man, and writing an exact man." As Bacon attained to degrees of knowledge scarcely ever reached by any other man, the directions which he gives for study, have certainly a just claim to our regard; for who can teach an art with so great authority, as he who has practised it with undisputed success? (*Adventurer*, 411–12).

Having begun with Bacon's aphorism from the essay "Of Studies," Johnson proceeds to expound on and exemplify the importance of reading, conversation, and writing for a humanist education, and in the process translates what he finds inspiring in Bacon into his own particular terms. Not only does Johnson advocate for Baconian principles but also exemplifies in *his very style of writing and thinking* the necessity of their unity.

[14] Robert DeMaria, Jr., *The Life of Samuel Johnson: A Critical Biography* (Oxford: Blackwell, 1993), p. xiv.

Adventurer 85 is not only about learning but also about turning learning into practice, for "who can teach an art with so great authority, as he that has practised it with undisputed success?" Most of our learning comes from writers of the past, such as Bacon. Indeed, gathering a little learning from writers from the past is about as much as most people are capable of, for "To understand the works of celebrated authors, to comprehend their systems, and retain their reasonings, is a task more than equal to common intellects." Yet, Johnson concedes, this is no mean feat, for "he is by no means to be accounted useless or idle, who has stored his mind with acquired knowledge, and can detail it occasionally to others who have less leisure or weaker abilities" (*Adventurer*, 413).

However, to become useful learning needs to be turned into knowledge, into practice, but, as Johnson elaborates, this is extremely difficult because the limits of the human mind, along with social pressures, constantly throw up obstacles. One obstacle is ego or smallness of mind, signified by what Johnson calls reclusive learning. Like the deluded astronomer in *Rasselas*, the reclusive learner does not have the "facility of inculcating his specula-tions" (414), as Bacon does. They are thus likely to erect half-baked, fantastic ideas into absolute and universals truths, and to go into the world touting foolish or dangerous falsehoods because this "gratifies the pride of airy petulance" (415). What counters this slide into prideful folly, for Johnson, is conversation and writing, both, significantly, social modes of existence that operate in different yet complementary ways to enable active knowledge.

Conversation exposes obstinately held individual ideas and fantasies to the light of day in the form of contending, different views, thus enabling one to qualify, test, and expand one's ideas and to make one's thinking sounder and more reasonable. In *Adventurer* 85, and in most of Johnson's writing, truth is not an object that is possessed outside of the *process* necessary to realize it. Truth-finding is mirrored and inculcated in Johnson's language and argument, which, as he says in *Adventurer* 85, necessitate "many artifices ... to procure admission for the most evident proposition into understandings frighted by their novelty" (415). Artifice is required to insinuate even the simplest truths into minds that are habit-ually closed. Johnson's prose in these passages *mirrors* the flexibility and suppleness of thought that is one expression of his humanism, thus inculcating the truth to experience that he aims to convey as a Baconian value: "nothing but long habit and frequent experiments can confer the power of changing a position into various forms, presenting it in different points of view, connecting it with known and granted truths, fortifying it with intelligible argument, and illustrating it by apt similitudes" (415). If conversation opens the mind, writing (as we witness in Johnson's own writing) refines it in acts of self-knowledge, without which the humanistic understanding of nature, science, and experience remains unrealized: "To fix the thoughts by writing, and subject them to frequent examinations and reviews, is the best method of enabling the mind to detect its own sophisms, and to keep it on guard against the fallacies which it practices on others" (416).

Not only has Johnson "comprehended their systems," as he says of the Renaissance humanists, he finds his own way to actively inculcate and diffuse Bacon's wisdom. In the *Harleian Catalogue* (1743–5), Johnson characterized Bacon as "a truly great man, distinguished by unusual intellectual gifts: naturally strong perception, a faithful memory, penetrating judgment, and eloquence."[15] It is rare for him to devote an entire essay to a single author. He does so only for Virgil (*Adventurer*, 92), Shakespeare (*Rambler*, 168), and Milton (*Rambler*, 86, 88, 90, 94, 139, and 140). In *Adventurer* 85, he added Bacon – like Milton, an English "classic."

Montaigne and Johnson

Johnson's association of knowledge of self with Bacon suggests why a skeptic like Montaigne might have appealed to him. Though careful not to promote the writings of those whom many in the eighteenth century perceived as "atheists," such as Hobbes, Hume, and Voltaire, Johnson is often interested in the work of reputedly skeptical writers.[16] Indeed, Montaigne was not a skeptic of ontology (the study of being, substance, and ultimately God), but rather of epistemology (the study of how we know what we know). He subjects to introspective doubt the capacity of his own mind – and that of others – to arrive at truth. For example, in "On the Education of Children," Montaigne quotes from Dante's *Inferno* (Bk. II, line 93), "*Che non men che saper dubbiar m'aggrado*" ("For doubting pleases me as much as knowing),"[17] a phrase that suggests his own method. Like a later French author, Descartes, Montaigne uses doubt to strip away comfortable illusions to arrive at truth.

[15] Quoted in DeMaria, *The Life of Samuel Johnson*, p. 101).
[16] See Anthony W. Lee, "Johnson, Machiavelli, and *Rambler* 156," *JNL*, 69:2 (2019): 53–56, and Fred Parker, *Scepticism and Literature: An Essay on Pope, Hume, Sterne, and Johnson* (Oxford: Oxford University Press, 2003), chapters 1 and 6.
[17] Michel de Montaigne, *The Complete Essays*, trans. M. A. Screech (London: Penguin, 1991), p. 170.

Johnson's moral essays consistently explore the thrust of Montaigne's "An Apology for Raymond Sebond" (1580–8),[18] which examines the limitations and misuses of reason as it props up vain delusions to support individual pride, self-importance, and self-delusion, a common theme in the writings of many of the Continental humanists, including Erasmus, More, Rabelais, and Cervantes. The moral imperative of Johnson's *Vanity of Human Wishes* (1749) strikes a similar note, which also echoes Montaigne's position that we should submit to God and let go of petty intellectual quibbles:

> Implore his Aid, in his Decisions rest,
> Secure whate'er he gives, he gives the best.
> Yet with the Sense of sacred Presence prest,
> When strong Devotion fills thy glowing Brest,
> Pour forth thy Fervours for a healthful Mind,
> Obedient Passions, and a Will resign'd.
>
> (*Poems*, 108, ll. 355–60)[19]

This philosophical doubting is quite different from the skepticism that Johnson ferociously combated throughout his life, as expressed, for example, by David Hume. The sanctity and authority of religion was of the highest importance to Johnson. This is perhaps because he himself entertained – or was assailed by – skeptical thoughts that accompanied doubts of his own sanity. The skepticism that Johnson saw as repugnant to the truth of Christianity may be seen in his portrait of Pertinax in *Rambler* 95 and of Misargyrus in *Adventurer* 34. That both fictional characters share aspects of Johnson's own intellectual profile suggests the uneasiness he must have felt as a religiously conservative person seeking to quell internal dissension, but, conversely, it also indicates how intellectually adventurous he was in embracing Montaigne.[20]

In less obvious but equally important ways, Montaigne also modeled self-scrutiny for Johnson, applying his skeptical essayistic style to the analysis not only of his culture but his own mind and thought. The parallel with Johnson's moral and religious thought is significant. Under the mask

---

[18] Raymond of Sabunde (c. 1385–1436) was a Spanish theologian who sought to prove the existence of God through pure reason, eschewing faith. We know that Johnson read this essay; see Anthony W. Lee, "Johnson's 'French Authors': Rambler 5 and 87," *ANQ: A Quarterly Journal of Short Articles, Notes, and Reviews*, 34:2 (2021): 121–28; see *Ramblers* 13 and 98 for additional references to Montaigne.

[19] See also Johnson's *Life of Boerhaave, BW*, 53.

[20] See Greg Clingham, *Johnson, Writing, and Memory* (Cambridge: Cambridge University Press, 2002), pp. 77–88.

of such fictional personae as a "rambler," an "idler," and an "adventurer," Johnson engages in deep introspection and self-scrutiny in his essay collections bearing those titles. In her *Anecdotes* (1786), his friend Hester Thrale Piozzi exclaimed of this intellectual tendency, "Will *any* body's mind bear this eternal microscope that you place upon your own so?" (*JM*, 1: 207). Donald J. Greene has attributed this habit to religious motives, and he may well be partially right.[21] However, others – including myself – agree with W. Jackson Bate when he writes:

> As in no other classical moralist, we have a profound anticipation of what was to be the wide-scale nineteenth- and twentieth-century discovery about the mind that went on from the major Romantics down through the clinical exploration of the unconscious that follows Freud. . . . Johnson . . . really anticipates psychoanalysis.[22]

Johnson explores the depths of the human mind with an acuity rivaled, in early modern literature, only by Montaigne. His humanistic achievement as an essayist was to unite empirical inquiry and the external, discovered in Bacon's writings, with the exploration of the dimensions of inner human worlds, exemplified by Montaigne's essays.

Both Johnson and Montaigne were booklovers, yet both recognized that the proper function of books is to prepare human beings for an active life. As Montaigne writes in "On Educating Children":

> I share Plutarch's conviction that Aristotle never spent much of the time of his great pupil Alexander on the art of syllogisms nor on the principles of geometry: he taught him, rather, sound precepts concerning valour, prowess, greatness of soul and temperance, as well as that self-assurance which fears nothing.[23]

The right balance between books and action, as discussed in *Adventurer* 85, is a recurring theme of Johnson's writings: the importance, as he calls it, of immersing oneself in the "living world." What he says of Alexander Pope in the *Life of Pope* is highly autobiographical: "When he [Pope] entered into the living world, it seems to have happened to him as to many others, that he was less attentive to dead masters; he studied in the academy of Paracelsus, and made the universe his favourite volume" (*Lives*, 3: 1182).

---

[21] Donald J. Greene, *Samuel Johnson* (New York: Twayne, 1970), pp. 118–19.
[22] Walter Jackson Bate, *Samuel Johnson* (London: Chatto & Windus, 1978), pp. 300, 307.
[23] Montaigne, *Complete Essays*, p. 183.

Coda

The humanists of the fifteenth and sixteenth centuries formed a powerful cadre of intellectuals seeking to remake Europe intellectually, to reform human nature on a progressive footing. Though conservative in some respects – both More and Erasmus remained Catholic in the face of the Protestant Reformation – they valued not only the texts of ancient Greece and Rome but also the early Church Fathers, such as Jerome and Augustine. Hence their designation (and others, like Johnson) as the Northern or Christian Humanists. But their attempts to reclaim humanity from folly and vanity ended in profound disappointment. Sir Thomas More's attempts to compromise, to fuse traditional pedagogy with "new learning" and with the realities he faced as a lawyer, politician, and Christian apologist, ended in his decapitation at the hands of a public executioner. This provoked a Europe-wide scandal among humanists residing in France, Germany, Italy, and Spain. His greatest and closest friend, Erasmus, was devasted by this loss: it was not merely the death of a best friend; it was the annihilation of a progressive idealism and its consequent vision of reforming a deeply flawed historical past. However fresh the ideas and ideals might have been, they were quickly crushed by what the Italian philosopher Antonio Gramsci has called the Repressive State Apparatus – the political and economic instruments of power deployed, through violence, actual or threatened, to preserve the status quo. The religious wars of the sixteenth century on the Continent and the Civil Wars of seventeenth-century England witness the futility of Renaissance humanism to impact European society in any significant or lasting way.

There are many similarities between Johnson and the humanist writers of the Renaissance. Like them, Johnson was a distinguished Latinist who could write, appreciate, and severely critique neo-Latin poetry. Like Justus Scaliger, he compiled a major dictionary. Like Erasmus, he produced a critical edition of canonical texts (Shakespeare's plays). Like Thomas More, he wrote biting satires exposing the corruption and folly of contemporary England. Like many of the early Renaissance humanists (such as More and Machiavelli), he devoted his immense learning to the political life of his country, especially in the four political tracts he wrote later in life.[24] Like Erasmus, he attained a Europe-wide reputation, receiving

---

[24] "The False Alarm" (1770), "Thoughts on the Late Transactions Respecting Falkland's Islands" (1771), "The Patriot" (1774), and "Taxation No Tyranny" (1775).

commendations from the learned societies of Italy and France for the single-handed accomplishment that is his *Dictionary*. Like Grotius, Johnson was fascinated by the law and its implementation to improve the human condition and contributed to it importantly in his collaboration with Robert Chambers on *A Course of Lectures on the English Law* (1767–73).[25] Like Lilly, Colet, Smith, and Cheke – all teachers associated with the introduction of Renaissance humanism into England (especially at Oxford University) in the early sixteenth century – he adapted the "new learning" derived from the resurrected Classics to advocate for a humanist pedagogical curriculum.

However, Johnson lived within a very different cultural landscape from his Renaissance humanist precursors. His society witnessed the rise of egalitarian sentiments, the pressures exerted by an increasingly powerful merchant class upon traditional feudal hierarchies, the rise of science, and the development of a British Empire that would place Britain at the forefront of global expansion: something that Johnson vigorously opposed throughout his lifetime.[26]

This new world required specific measures to meet its demands and problems. What Harold Mason wrote of Erasmus and More might in this context be applied to Johnson:

> If we wish for a touchstone by which to try any work claiming to be animated by the Humanist spirit, we can find it here. . . . In every age the task of the humanist is different, but the same. For it is an aspect of all civilisation to struggle for renewal by attacking inert ideas. It has also been the practice of all renewers of value to seek for an ally in the past.[27]

What Johnson inherited from Erasmus, More, Bacon, Montaigne, and others he used as a platform from which to engage and improve his own culture and society. As we have seen, in introducing the English works of Roger Ascham, he remarked, "Learning was at that time prosecuted with that eagerness and perseverance which in this age of indifference and dissipation it is not easy to conceive" (*BW*, 429). His major poems, the *Rambler*, *Rasselas*, and the *Lives of the Poets*, among other works, seek to

---

[25] See Greg Clingham, "Law," in Jack Lynch (ed.), *The Oxford Handbook of Samuel Johnson* (Oxford: Oxford University Press, 2022), pp. 333–49, and J. T. Scanlan, "Johnson's Legal Thought," in Greg Clingham and Philip Smallwood (eds.), *Samuel Johnson After 300 Years* (Cambridge: Cambridge University Press, 2009), pp. 112–30.

[26] See Thomas Curley, "Samuel Johnson and *Taxation No Tyranny*," in Anthony W. Lee (ed.), *New Essays on Samuel Johnson: Revaluation* (Newark: University of Delaware Press, 2018), pp. 87–108.

[27] Harold Andrew Mason, *Humanism and Poetry in the Early Tudor Period* (London: Routledge and Kegan Paul, 1959), pp. 261–62.

dismantle those forces of "indifference and dissipation" and to generate a new humanist tradition. Not least, he "made it new" (Ezra Pound, derived from Chinese classic texts) by fusing, with charismatic authority, religious conservatism with political progress and by applying an intellectual legacy to solving contemporary problems in education, politics, literature, and culture. If he was at times backward-looking, this did not undermine his embrace of the contemporary, the modern. To recognize and appreciate the productive tension of such dichotomies today is, perhaps, to crack open the shell of language that often dissuades young readers from pursuing and understanding Johnson. To do so invites us to embrace Johnson the humanist in order to confront and seek to resolve the pressing and complex issues of our own world today. If we do so, we are then humanists as well and bear the torch lit centuries ago, passed on to us by Johnson.

CHAPTER 4

Johnson and Language

Lynda Mugglestone

Johnson's approach to, and treatment of, language has long been a site of fertile debate. His *Dictionary of the English Language*, first published in 1755 (a fourth revised edition appeared in 1773), can be seen as marking a newly modern lexicography, characterized by his attentive collection and scrutiny of evidence alongside a detailed engagement with contextual nuance as a way of deriving meaning and sense.[1] Conversely, Johnson is often remembered for his contribution to prescriptive (and proscriptive) linguistics – a domain in which the dictionary-maker's remit is interventionist and normative, drawing on models established by the *Vocabulario* of the Accademia della Crusca in 1612 and the *Dictionnaire de l'Académie Française* (first edition, 1640). That Johnson "fixed" English spelling is another commonplace assumption in this respect.

Johnson's partisan prejudices present other well-established narratives in which, for example, French or Scottish resistance is seen as imbricated in the *Dictionary* as text, offering subjective testimony where modern reference works prefer a stance of unwavering impartiality. Johnson's definition of *oats* ("A grain, which in England is generally given to horses, but in Scotland supports the people") remains a well-rehearsed set-piece. Nevertheless, antecedents in earlier lexicography are plain ("it is forage for Horses in all places; and in some, provision for Men," wrote Richard Hogarth in his *Gazophylacium Anglicanum* [1689]). Plain, too, is its assimilation into eighteenth-century lexicography more widely. "In most parts of England, and in others, as also in Scotland, the chief support of the people," wrote Nicol Scott in his *New Universal Etymological English Dictionary* (1755). The geographical specificities embedded in the definition of *kohlrabi* in the *Oxford English Dictionary* ("cultivated as food for

---

[1] Patrick Hanks, "Johnson and Modern Lexicography," *International Journal of Lexicography*, 18:2 (2005): 243–66.

cattle in England, and as a vegetable in India and Germany") have, in comparison, attracted far less attention.

"Every other authour may aspire to praise; the lexicographer can only hope to escape reproach, and even this negative recompence has been yet granted to very few," Johnson presciently observed in the Preface to his *Dictionary* (*EL*, 73). This chapter will explore language and lexicography in Johnson's hands from a range of perspectives while examining the basis, and rationale, of the assumptions discussed above. Formally hired in 1746 for a fee of £1,575 by Robert Dodsley (and other members of the booksellers consortium with which the dictionary project originated), it is, for example, undeniable that Johnson's work was, from the beginning, embedded in the impulse to codify an authoritative (and national) model of English. Over 650 dictionaries involving English were, in reality, already in existence. Johnson's popular status as "the father of the dictionary" is tenuous at best. Nevertheless, an English dictionary with a normative remit like those produced by academies abroad was, Dodsley stressed, "a Work which of all others we most want"[2] – and would undoubtedly "be well received by the publick" (*Life*, 1: 182). Advertising in 1749 drew further attention to ambitions of this kind: "It is hoped, that our language will be more fixed, and better established when the publick is favoured with a new dictionary, undertaken with that view," the *Gentleman's Magazine* announced.[3]

Johnson's *Plan of a Dictionary of the English Language* (printed in 1747 and dedicated to Lord Chesterfield) expressed similar attitudes. Earlier lexicography was subject to critical review. "The title which I prefix to my work has long conveyed a very miscellaneous idea," Johnson stated: "they that take a dictionary into their hands have been accustomed to expect from it, a solution of almost every difficulty" (*EL*, 30). Instead, a detailed focus on documenting words rather than things, alongside core elements of prescriptive rhetoric, took precedence. "My idea of an English dictionary," Johnson notes toward the end of the *Plan*, is one "by which the pronunciation of our language may be fixed, and its attainment facilitated; by which its purity may be preserved, its use ascertained, and its duration lengthened" (*EL*, 57). That the *Plan* was itself an advertisement, reissued as publication of the *Dictionary* approached, is a further strand in the prescriptive positioning of Johnson's text.

[2] [Robert Dodsley], "Review of *The Plan* of a DICTIONARY of the EL," *The Museum: Or, the Literary and Historical Register*, 3 (1747): 385–90.
[3] [Dodsley], "Review."

Johnson's original "idea of a dictionary" had, however, been somewhat different. Modern scholars of Johnson are fortunate in the number of working documents for Johnson's *Dictionary* that remain extant. One of these is a manuscript "Fair Copy" – an antecedent version of the *Plan*, written by an amanuensis and replete with annotations in various hands. It offers not only an illuminating account of Johnson's early thinking on what a record of English might be but an explicit consideration of the challenges that linguistic control presents. As Johnson admits, stasis – and the kind of linguistic certainty advocated by popular prescriptivism – is a tantalizing prospect. "Desires" of this kind readily conceive a state in which the "fundamental atoms of our speech might obtain the firmness and immutability of constituent particles" such that words might "remain essentially the same" (*EL*, 461–62).

Even so, certain reservations are already clear. Such "Desires," as Johnson notes, are also "Phantoms" – the products of "Imagination," alluring but ultimately insubstantial. In the "Fair Copy," their opposition to what he terms the "shackles of Lexicography" is made overt (*EL*, 461). Johnson, in this early draft, contemplates two irreconcilable trajectories while delineating what is, in essence, a fundamental crux in practical lexicography. If the "Phantoms of Desire" are pursued, this is, critically, at the expense of the "shackles of Lexicography" that bind the dictionary-maker to his craft, and the discipline that this requires.

Exploratory thinking of this kind, long before the final text of the *Dictionary* took shape, presents an interesting challenge to familiar narratives by which Johnson, seen as originally prescriptive in aims and thinking, acquires descriptive wisdom from his experience of practical lexicography such that, by 1755, fixity as aspiration is overtly shed. Instead, across his work on the *Dictionary*, we can detect marked continuities in his thinking about language and the problematic nature of linguistic control. In his "Preface" to the completed *Dictionary*, for example, Johnson's metaphors reprise those of the "Fair Copy." As the "slave of science," the dictionary-maker is shackled once more, committed to the pursuit of knowledge about words and meaning in which fancy plays no part (*EL*, 73). Meanwhile, the "Phantoms of Desire" take the form of the "elixir that promises to prolong life to a thousand years" (*EL*, 105) – a prospect that meets marked skepticism on Johnson's part. Its linguistic counterparts fare no better:

> with equal justice may the lexicographer be derided, who being able to produce no example of a nation that has preserved their words and phrases

from mutability, shall imagine that his dictionary can embalm his language, and secure it from corruption and decay, that it is in his power to change sublunary nature, and clear the world at once from folly, vanity, and affectation. (*EL*, 105)

Johnson's "Phantoms of Desire" might now exist in a canceled passage in the "Fair Copy," but their salience across his work is clear.

The *Plan* can seem outwardly prescriptive. As Reddick notes, in the transitions between "Fair Copy" and published text, the normative agenda is clearly sharpened.[4] Contributions by Chesterfield himself, as well as other critical readers, were incorporated in ways that steered Johnson toward the ambitions with which the project began. An originally expressed tolerance for the current state of spelling ("settled with such propriety that it may be generally received") disappears, for example, in response to Chesterfield's criticism and the need for greater regulation (*EL*, 385). Other annotations (in an unknown hand) urge the need to "brand with some mark of reprobation" variations in sound or form (*EL*, 436). Even so, the echoes of the "Fair Copy" are not entirely displaced. "Who upon this survey can forbear to wish, that these fundamental atoms of our speech might obtain the firmness and immutability of the primogenial and constituent particles of matter," Johnson declares. But, as he adds, wishes, however widespread, cannot always be granted:

> This is a privilege which words are scarcely to expect; for, like their author, when they are not gaining strength, they are generally losing it. Though art may sometimes prolong their duration, it will rarely give them perpetuity, and their changes will be almost always informing us, that language is the work of man, of a being from whom permanence and stability cannot be derived. (*EL*, 44)

Johnson both advances and undercuts the fixity that popular language attitudes desired.

The real matter of the *Dictionary* lies, of course, within the entries themselves and the evidence they contain. Here, too, surviving archival materials are illuminating. While the French Academy had adopted the authoritarian "on dit" ("one says") in specifying recommended norms, Johnson embarked on what he described as a series of "excursions into books" (*EL*, 84). Armed with black-lead pencil, he marked out words and meanings in use, underlining potential headwords and carefully

---

[4] Allen Reddick, *The Making of Johnson's Dictionary, 1746–1773* (Cambridge: Cambridge University Press, 1996), p. 18.

demarcating the textual boundaries of citations that might be used in documenting particular words or senses. The fourteen marked-up texts that survive are testimony to the industry required by practical dictionary-making in Johnson's hands. While his reading is piecemeal – some pages are densely annotated, others pristine – his chosen methodology reflects a determination to engage in primary research rather than relying on work done by his lexicographical predecessors. Earlier dictionaries were consulted but, Johnson points out, their "deficiency" in collecting evidence was "immediately apparent" (*EL*, 84). Their inclusion of words for which he could find no supporting use raised critical apprehensions. The label "*Dict.*," subjoined to words such as *omniferous* ("all-bearing") or *pedaneous* ("going on foot") served to remind readers of the limits of lexicographical authority. "Of these I am not always certain that they are seen in any book but the works of lexicographers," he wrote (*EL*, 87). Words might exist in the dictionary – but this did not guarantee their existence in the realities of use.

"To attain *clear* and *distinct* Ideas of what we read or hear, we must search the *Sense of Words* ... We must consider in what Sense the same Author uses any particular Word or Phrase," Isaac Watts advised in his *Logick: or, The Right Use of Reason in the Enquiry after Truth*. The eighth edition, published in 1745 and preserved in the British Library, is one of Johnson's surviving marked-up texts.[5] As Johnson's in-text annotations confirm, Watts's words were taken to the letter, yielding citations, for example, for *delusive* ("one great part of the *Design of Logick* is to guard us against the delusive Influences of our meaner Powers, to cure the Mistakes of immature Judgment"), or *judgement* ("Judgement is that Operation of the Mind, whereby we join two or more Ideas together by some Affirmation or negation"), or *speaker* ("In Conversation or Reading be diligent to find out the true sense or distinct Idea, which the Speaker or Writer affixes to his Words"), as well as evidence for phrasal structures such as *strip off* or *take off*, or the pragmatic familiarities of *pencil*. *Dictionary*, too, in the finished text of 1755, is documented courtesy of Watts, as part of Johnson's lexical and semantic anatomization of his work. "An army, or a parliament, is a collection of men; a *dictionary*, or nomenclature, is a collection of words," an illustrative citation affirmed. Johnson's model of an authoritative dictionary, as his annotations indicate, was a literally collective process, founded on the creation of an extensive citation file and

---

[5] Isaac Watts, *Logick: or, The Right Use of Reason in the Enquiry after Truth* (London: T. Longman, 1745).

the scrutiny of words in use. Some 114,000 citations appear in the print text of 1755. As the surviving marked-up texts confirm, Johnson in fact gathered far more.

Johnson, in the *Plan*, stressed his commitment to the eighteen canonical writers originally suggested as source-texts by Alexander Pope (*EL*, 55). Nevertheless, as his reading of the dissenting preacher Isaac Watts's works suggests, the realities of dictionary-making involved documentary practices that ranged far outside this selective grouping. Johnson's "excursions into books" were, he confirms, both "fortuitous and unguided," while the "feasts of literature" originally envisaged were displaced by the pragmatic necessities of locating evidence (*EL*, 84, 100). "Words," he reminded his readers in 1755, "must be sought where they are used; and in what pages, eminent for purity, can terms of manufacture or agriculture be found?" (*EL*, 94). The *Dictionary* as text is indeed replete with citations from canonical writers such as Shakespeare, Dryden, and Pope, but, within individual entries, Milton can find himself located next to William Hale, a writer by no means commended for the excellence of his prose (but attentively read by Johnson), while Walter Raleigh (firmly excluded by Pope) is used some 700 times in 1755 as under *diet, gluttonous, facility*, and *harpy*, among others. Other writers on Pope's list who gained merely qualified approval as "authorities for familiar dialogue" – such as Vanbrugh, Congreve, and Ben Jonson – secured extensive representation. So, however, did writers such as the physician John Arbuthnot, and John Mortimer, a well-established writer on agriculture and husbandry, or the Royalist surgeon Richard Wiseman, or the cleric William Holder, whose work on language was used, for example, under *language, labiodental*, alongside his *Discourse Concerning Time* (see, e.g., *decade, fathom*, or *noctidial* ["Comprising a night and a day"]). Evident, too, is Johnson's attentive observation of modern novelists such as Defoe, Richardson, or Swift (in particular *Gulliver's Travels*), alongside women writers such as Jane Collier, Anne Morton, Charlotte Lennox, or Margaret Cavendish in domains of evidence certainly never contemplated by Pope. At least traditionally, women, as in Robert Cawdrey's *Table Alphabeticall* (1604) or Thomas Blount's *Glossographia* (1656), were deemed the recipients of lexicographical authority rather than writers by whom usage might be exemplified and derived. Johnson's female citations might be relatively few (see, e.g., *just* [sense 10], *perish, marital, prink, starry, unravel, uncle*), but they represent, even so, a significant shift in both practice and visibility.

While the *Dictionary* is, for many critics, hallmarked by its use of "great writers," Johnson's interest in their ordinary use, traced across the private communications of Swift and Pope, John Donne, the writer Richard Steele, the physician John Arbuthnot, or the cleric Thomas Pierce (among many others), cannot pass unremarked. "A great beauty of letters does often *consist* in little passages of private conversation, and references to particular matters," a letter from the poet and politician William Walsh affirms, for example (used in illustrating sense 3 of *consist* [v.]). Johnson's entry for *letter* is appropriately accompanied by an extract from a missive from Swift in 1728 ("Mrs. P. B. has writ to me, and is one of the best *letter* writers I know; very good sense, civility, and friendship, without any stiffness or constraint"). Other letters by Swift were appropriated in documenting the colloquial *blab* ("I should have certainly gone about shewing my letters, under the charge of secrecy, to every *blab* of my acquaintance"), while the letters of the writer and critic John Dennis (1657–1734) pithily document *gambado*, glossed as "boots worn upon the legs above the shoe" ("The pettifogger ambles to her in his gambadoes once a week"), or *leash* ("Thou art a living comedy; they are a *leash* of dull devils") or, say, *unbacked* in the sense "untamed" ("They flinch like *unback'd* fillies") as well as *bawdy-house*. Pope's own letters – commended by Johnson for their "epistolary excellence" (*Lives*, 3: 1122) – presented a plentiful source of evidence. Relevant citations are marked by their idiomatic vigor: "You'll say the whole world has something to do, *something* to talk of, *something* to wish for, and something to be employed about; but pray put all these somethings together, and what is the sum total but just nothing" (s.v. *something*); "I am satisfied to trifle away my time, rather than let it *stick* by me" (s.v. *stick*). Similar is *scrap*, attested by an extract from a letter to Lady Mary Wortley Montagu during her stay in Constantinople ("I can never have too many of your letters: I am angry at every *scrap* of paper lost"). Letters, writes Cusack, are "substitute speech."[6] Material of this kind, in lexicography and language history, remains highly valuable.

Words, for Johnson, were not merely atomistic units even if their alphabetical organization in a dictionary might foster impressions of this kind. Instead, context and register – how and where words are used – contribute decisively to the polysemies he strove to record. "Being arbitrary," he later wrote in his *Life of Cowley*, words "must owe their power to association, and have the influence, and that only, which custom has given them" (*Lives*, 1: 76). Formal specifications of register – the situational

---

[6] Bridget Cusack, *Everyday English 1500–1700: A Reader* (Edinburgh: Edinburgh University Press, 1998), p. 190.

diversities of use – are, for example, apparent across many entries. An *annulet* is used "in architecture" and *remission* "in physick" when signifying the point "when a distemper abates"; meanwhile, *peccant*, meaning "injurious to health," is "chiefly used in medical writers"; *brace*, meaning "A crooked line inclosing a passage, which ought to be taken together," is used "in printing"; while *degradation* gains specific meanings "in painting" ("A term made use of to express the lessening and rendering confused the appearance of distant objects"). Tone demanded similar consideration. Denotatively, a word such as *stargazer* might be synonymous with *astrologer* or *astronomer*. Connotatively, it was, Johnson noted, freighted with "contempt" in ways that underpinned both usage and meaning. Similar is, say, the metalanguage of age. A *graybeard* might be glossed as "old man," but "contempt" is integral to its use.

At the other end of the scale were, say, the "low" and "ludicrous." What is deemed "ludicrous" might, to modern ears, sound pejorative. "Burlesque; merry; sportive; exciting laughter," Johnson conversely explains. His labels offer a form of pragmatic marking. The ludic pertained to verbal play and humor such that *devil* is "a ludicrous term for mischief" ("A war of profit mitigates the evil; / But to be tax'd, and beaten, is the *devil*," states a supporting citation from the poet and playwright George Granville). *Deadly* likewise gains an incongruous playfulness. "It is sometimes used in a ludicrous sense, only to enforce the signification of a word," Johnson comments, using a quotation from Roger Boyle in illustration ("Mettled schoolboys set to cuff, / Will not confess that they have done enough, / Though *deadly* weary"). "Low" and "cant," in similar ways, referred to slang and the vigorously colloquial, as in *flapdragon* ("to swallow") or *lace* meaning "sugar." As Johnson's comments clarify under *bamboozle* (v.), the word is robustly familiar, inappropriate for formal occasions ("a cant word not used in pure or grave writings"). Cant has, in other respects, its own polysemies, referring, for example, to the in-house slang of various activities as a further aspect of register (*dawk* is a "cant word among workmen"). Johnson's evidence was testimony to a spectrum of styles, vividly exhibiting the diversity with which English could be used.

Associative meanings of this kind widely reflected Johnson's interest in what he defines as "applied" use. He might, for instance, initially explain *absurdity* (n.) as "The quality of being absurd." But, he continues, the nature of such absurdity varies depending on the context such that it signifies "want of judgment" when "applied to men" but "want of propriety" when "applied to things." Across the *Dictionary*, he teases out these prosodies of use. As he observes, *anguish*, in general, means "excessive pain either of mind or body," but "applied to the mind, it means the pain of sorrow, and is seldom used to signify other passions." In similar ways, *haul* (v.) gains a general definition of "To pull; to draw," even if Johnson immediately points out its inadequacy; "applied to things, [it] implies violence" but when applied "to persons," associative meanings instead incline to "aukwardness or rudeness." Six illustrative citations enabled readers to examine these patterns for themselves. As Johnson confirmed, "those quotations which to careless or unskilful perusers appear only to repeat the same sense, will often exhibit, to a more accurate examiner, diversities of signification ... different shades of the same meaning" such that "one will shew the word applied to persons, another to things; one will express an ill, another a good, and a third a neutral sense" (*EL*, 97).

Earlier dictionaries had exhibited relatively little sense-differentiation. Nathan Bailey, in his *Universal Etymological Dictionary* (1721),[7] had, for example, defined *clear* (adj.) in a single line of text as "fair, fine, pure." Johnson's corresponding entry spanned seventeen separate sense divisions, actively drawing on evidence from the citation file he had assembled. He carefully disambiguated the adjectival clustering on which Bailey relied. Johnson's sense 2 hence focuses on *clear* in the sense "Free from clouds; serene, as a *clear* day." The state of being "Without mixture; pure; unmingled" is detailed in sense 3. Other sense divisions turned to *clear* as signifying that which is "perspicuous; not obscure; not hard to be understood" (illustrated by citations from Temple and Locke), or its use in referring to that which is "indisputable; evident" and hence "undeniable" (exampled by Milton's *Paradise Lost*), or, in sense 10, *to clear*, meaning "free from deductions or incumbrances" – a sense illustrated from Johnson's reading of Locke, Swift, and Jeremy Collier. He probes, too, the ways in which, when used with *from*, it signifies "free, guiltless," or, when used in conversation, and with reference to individual people, it means "distinguishing" and "judicious." Spoken as well as written uses can, as here, attract attention.

In this interest in multiple patterns of signification, Johnson's model of ascertainment moved away from the ambitions of rigid fixity and stasis with which the dictionary project began. What is "sometimes" used is a property of many entries. Variation can be conspicuous, whether of co-existing spellings (*jail/gaol, frenetick/phrenetick, risk/risque; screen/skreen*) or

---

[7] Nathan Bailey, *An Universal Etymological English Dictionary* (London: E. Bell, J. Darby, A. Bettesworth, et al., 1721).

specifications of sound. "Our authors write almost indiscriminately *embassador* or *ambassador, embassage* or *ambassage,*" he noted under *embassy*; "This word, with many others of the same termination, are indifferently written with *ance* or *ence, ancy* or *ency,*" his entry for *dependency* observes. An interest in *acceptance* ("the meaning of a word as it is received or understood") or what he termed *acceptation* ("The meaning of a word, as it is commonly received") was part of this. As Johnson explains, it is by "common talk" that "*fowl* is used for the larger, and *bird* for the smaller kind of feathered animals" (s.v. *bird*). Other communalities underpin the difference, say, between *forge* and *smithy* such that, in "common language," "we use *forge* for large work, and *smithy* for small" while, as under *fair* (adj.), gendered prosodies meant that "*fair* seems in the common acceptation to be restrained, when applied to women, to the beauty of the face." If, as under *buffoonery*, we are told that "*Dryden* places the accent, improperly, on the first syllable," the normative judgment derives from the norms of "common speech," just as an *admirer* is, in "common speech," deemed delicately euphemistic for "a lover." What is "common" is usual and widespread. Johnson's *Dictionary* is often seen in relation to the exceptional and difficult, as in words such as *depascent* ("feeding greedily") and *traducible* ("Such as may be derived"), or his decision to define *poultice* (n.) as "a cataplasm; a soft mollifying application" (or *nose* as "The prominence on the face ... the organ of scent and the emunctory of the brain"). However, as his iterated interest in what "we say" affirms ("we say, *girded* for the battle" (s.v. *brace*); "We say, properly, the *shore* of the *sea*, and the *banks* of a *river, brook,* or small water" (s.v. *bank* (n.), sense 1), it is also rooted in the familiar and the shared practices that define a language and its use. Johnson's entries also include *cheesevat* and *poulterer, brick-dust, gingerbread,* and *apple-tart. Stewpan* ("A pan used for stewing") is added in the fourth edition.

That words such as *quietude* ("rest; repose") were "not in common use" is equally important. The tensions of a language that, as the Preface affirms, is always "budding" and "falling away" even as dictionaries "hasten to publication" (*EL,* 110), often claim attention. "Disused" or "antiquated" words and senses – no longer common but preserved in earlier texts – attract careful elucidation. *Gloom* as verb, however eloquent it might have been ("to shine obscurely, as the twilight," Johnson notes), is "not now in use." *Ope* for *open* is likewise "scarcely used but by old authors"; *wrack* is fading into obsolescence ("the later writers of prose commonly [use] *wreck*"). Johnson's interests in temporality, and the dictionary as a form of historical narrative, underpin other aspects of his exploratory thinking.

Other forms of restricted currency attract comment, too. The standard variety – delocalized in use – is at the heart of his text. But localized uses such as *cibol* (described as "a small sort of onion used in sallads" and "common in the Scotch dialect") or *laird* (defined as "The lord of a manor in the Scottish dialect") attract careful observation. Similar is Johnson's account of *mortal* as used "in the middle counties" where, he states, it functions as "a particle of amplification; as, 'mortal tall,' 'mortal little,'" or of *deemster*, explained as "yet in use" in Jersey and the Isle of Man (in preference to standard English *judge*). Differences of this kind confirmed other aspects of the arbitrariness of the sign and the play of convention in space and place.

Literary texts could present more troubling instances of restricted currency. Shakespeare, for example, might be one of Johnson's most cited sources. But citation does not always mean endorsement. Usage can be anomalous. Johnson can hence direct attention to uses that require explication, but which are by no means representative. *Dear* "seems to be sometimes used in Shakespeare for ... sad; hateful; grievous," he notes, separating this from the core meanings anatomized under this entry. "In *Shakespeare* it seems once to signify *abhor*," he stated under *despise* (v.), providing evidence accordingly. Lexical and semantic outliers, they are included when Johnson judges it useful or necessary. As under *model* (n.), senses 5 and 6, they are "unexampled uses" – forms for which evidence, here in Shakespeare, can be found, but which are not, to Johnson's knowledge, "exampled" elsewhere. These might be defined, at least conjecturally ("Something formed or produced"; "something small and diminutive"), but "common acceptation" is different and must take precedence.

Even so, the limits of literary innovation can, at times, prompt a conspicuous lapse in neutrality. "Freshness; coolness. A word foolishly innovated by Dryden," Johnson states under *fraischeur* (n.), defined as "freshness." *Falsify*, used (again by Dryden) in the sense "to pierce, to run through" (on the basis of Italian *falsere*), is similar. Johnson provides Dryden's justification and defense: "Why am I forbidden to borrow from the *Italian*, a polish'd language, the word which is wanting in my Native Tongue?" he had stressed: "I used the word *falsify*, in this place, to mean that the shield of Turnus was not of proof against the spears and javelins of the Trojans, which had pierced it through." Johnson remained unconvinced. "*Dryden*, with all this effort, was not able to naturalise the new signification, which I have never seen copied, except once by some obscure nameless writer, and which indeed deserves not to be received," he declared under this entry. Dryden's use of *perfectionate* (another "word proposed by *Dryden*, but not received"), *renounce* in the French-derived sense of "to declare renunciation," or *rapport* (given as introduced by Sir William Temple but "not copied by others") provide other examples. As Johnson indicates, assimilation – and the communality of use – was key. In ways that also impact on the dictionary enterprise more widely, individuals, as Johnson stresses, cannot change language on their own.

These liminal territories were, however, undoubtedly difficult to negotiate. Like *gout* in the sense "taste," many forms of this kind were fashionable and elite code-switches – and dismissed by Johnson as part of "affected cant [i.e., slang] use." As in Dryden's *fraicheur*, "Frenchness" could be precisely the point. Words of this kind were indeed on the borders of discourse. Spatial metaphors by which forms such as *finesse* are depicted as "creeping into the language" can suggest a form of surreptitious invasion. *Finesse*, another loan from French, is "unnecessary," Johnson declares, even as his present progressive ("is creeping") verifies the fact of change. The critical reception accorded to non-native uses of this kind clearly contributes to other well-established stereotypes in which patriotic lexicography in Johnson's hands not only aimed to reclaim the "palm of philology" from the "nations of the continent" (*EL*, 109) but to protect English from the unwarranted incursion of foreign forms. "Preserving the purity" of English was, as we have seen, an early aspect of Johnson's thinking (*EL*, 379). This might, he admitted, "seem to require nothing more than that our language be considered so far as it is our own" (*EL*, 29). Nevertheless, here, too, reality was more complex. To exclude all "foreign words" would, he pointed out, produce a work "little regarded, except by critics, or those who aspire to criticism" (*EL*, 30).

Instead, in the metaphors of citizenship he adopts, some words are "denizens" and, irrespective of etymology, indistinguishable by "common" use from the original inhabitants of the native tongue. Spanish *chocolate* and *renegade*, *peccadillo* and *matadore* ("A hand of cards so called from its efficacy against the adverse player") are recorded with impartial hospitality, alongside, say, *devise* and *devotee* (from French), *broccoli* and *magnifico* (from Italian), and *ogle* from Dutch. Others, however, remain as "aliens" – "auxiliaries" rather than "subjects" in the state of language (*EL*, 31). Conceptions of this kind underpin what Johnson variously describes as *Latinisms* ("A Latin idiom; a mode of speech peculiar to the Latin") or *Gallicisms* ("A mode of speech peculiar to the French language: such as, he *figured* in controversy; he *held* this conduct; he *held* the same language that another had held before"), just as an *Anglicism* is "A form of speech peculiar to the EL; an English idiom." Comments such as "merely French," as under *delices* ("pleasures"), or "scarce English" under French-derived *trait*, might therefore seem to possess proscriptive force. But, as accompanying evidence suggested, considerations of usage often intervene. "Neither this word, nor *adroit*, seem yet completely naturalized into English," Johnson notes, for example, under *adroitness*, providing evidence from Charles Jervas's translation of *Don Quixote* (posthumously published in 1746). His insertion of "yet," however, deftly reminds of the possibility of change and the ongoing negotiations that must take place between words and use.

Even so, descriptive and prescriptive can, at times, present a complex interface in which subjectivities (of reception, or acceptability, or grammaticality) can be superimposed on the objectivities of evidence so carefully assembled. Loanwords such as *ruse* ("A French word neither elegant nor necessary") were, for Johnson, seen as both redundant and undesirable. Idioms such as *to make bold* or *spick and span* elicit resistance. "This word I should not have expected to have found authorised by a polite writer," he writes of the latter. To make bold is "not grammatical" (if "common"), Johnson declares; "To *be bold* is better," as in "I was bold to speak." *Would* in the sense "wish" likewise "ought not to be imitated" even if "used in good authors." Seen quantitatively, Johnson's own prescriptive comments are relatively limited. The "Phantoms of Desire" might, as we have seen, formally have been elided. But, as here, their legacy can remain, influencing Johnson's sense of the language and the boundaries it ought, preferentially, to observe.

Johnson's role as lexicographer can, as such, remain conflicted in ways that contribute to the conflicts of interpretation with which we began. The 1755 Preface (in reality, the final part of the *Dictionary* to be composed) nevertheless reflects his wider conclusions, both on the inevitability of linguistic change and the innovations it brings, as well as the fallibilities by which the dictionary-maker is constituted as a border-guard, repelling intruders or impeding words that might, for various reasons, be departing. Discourses of power again intervene. So do Johnson's metaphors of slavery and submission, alongside a firm reminder of the distance between what is, in language, achievable and what merely desired:

> With this hope, however, academies have been instituted, to guard the avenues of their languages, to retain fugitives, and repulse intruders; but their vigilance and activity have hitherto been vain; sounds are too volatile and subtile for legal restraints; to enchain syllables, and to lash the wind, are equally the undertakings of pride, unwilling to measure its desires by its strength. (*EL*, 105)

Johnson's critical engagement with his own discipline, and its imperfection, remains an arresting aspect of his work. While his *Dictionary*, in important ways, reflects his dedicated acts of reading, it is characterized, too, by the honesty with which human desire, linguistic pragmatism, and the real demands of lexicography are both confronted and deftly anatomized.

CHAPTER 5

Johnson and British Historiography

Martine W. Brownley

Johnson's reaction to Iona in his *Journey to the Western Islands* is frequently invoked to illustrate his beliefs about the power of history:

> We were now treading that illustrious island, which was once the luminary of the Caledonian regions, whence savage clans and roving barbarians derived the benefits of knowledge, and the blessings of religion. . . . Whatever withdraws us from the power of our senses; whatever makes the past, the distant, or the future predominate over the present, advances us in the dignity of thinking beings. . . . That man is little to be envied, whose patriotism would not gain force upon the plain of Marathon, or whose piety would not grow warmer among the ruins of Iona? (*Journey*, 148)[1]

Johnson always stressed the significance of history for individuals, emphasizing that no one could understand or judge the present without knowledge of the past. In both private and public life – "Whether we provide for action or conversation, whether we wish to be useful or pleasing" – he ranked "an acquaintance with the history of mankind" second only to "the religious and moral knowledge of right and wrong" (*Lives*, 1: 117).

Johnson described the study of history as "one of most natural delights of the human mind" (*Demand*, 180), and it was clearly one of his. He was a serious and deeply engaged student of history throughout his life. He read a variety of histories; William Cooke wrote that "In history he possessed an intimate knowledge of the ancient and modern parts, as well as in the annals and chronologies of most countries."[2] Among the plans for writing projects found after his death were a "History of the State of Venice," a "History of the Revival of Learning in Europe," and a "History of the Constitution," along with translations of Machiavelli's *History of Florence*,

---

[1] R. W. Chapman: "The mark of interrogation was still (and later) often used where we now use the mark of exclamation" (quoted in *Journey*, 148).
[2] William Cooke, "Life of Samuel Johnson, LL.D" (1785), in O M Brack, Jr. and Robert E. Kelley (eds.), *The Early Biographies of Samuel Johnson* (Iowa City: University of Iowa Press, 1974), pp. 91–135, 128.

Plutarch's *Lives*, and Benzoni's *History of the New World* (*Life*, 4: 381–82, n2). Even his emotional response to Iona resulted in part from his historical knowledge. As J. D. Fleeman notes, like many eighteenth-century visitors to Iona, Johnson's reaction to it was mediated through the early ecclesiastical historian Bede (672–735).[3]

In marked contrast to the high regard for history reflected in his personal life and career is the deep skepticism that Johnson repeatedly expressed about history as both the knowledge and the narrative of the past. From this vein of skepticism derive his numerous reductive remarks about history: "There is but a shallow stream of thought in history"; "in historical composition, all the greatest powers of the human mind are quiescent" (*Life*, 2: 195; 1: 424). These two comments occurred during conversations, where Johnson's eagerness to win arguments could sometimes make him reductive. But the same kind of comments recur in his writings, particularly in his dismissive descriptions of historians' roles: "He that writes the history of past times, undertakes only to decorate known facts by new beauties of method or of style, or at most to illustrate them by his own reflections" (*Idler*, 291).

Throughout Johnson's life, his recognition of history's potential as a powerful influence shaping human lives was countered by his doubts about historical knowledge and writing and his reductive expressions of these reservations. Commentators have accounted for his negativity in various ways, but some assessment of how his attitudes relate to the British historiographical conditions of his time can offer additional perspectives. Many of Johnson's misgivings stem directly and indirectly from his reactions to the kind of English history that was being written in the first half of the eighteenth century. Little in his experience with contemporary histories and historians led him to find either of them satisfactory.

Johnson's Requirements for History

Johnson's requirements for history were the two traditional requirements from classical times. A historian must tell the truth, and that truth should be related in a middle style, neither overly plain nor excessively elaborate. Acceptable history had to satisfy both requirements. He lavishly praised Lord Hailes for accuracy, for the "stability of dates," "certainty of facts," and "punctuality of citation" in his *Annals of Scotland* (1776–9). But since

---

[3] John David Fleeman, "Commentary," in Samuel Johnson, *A Journey to the Western Islands of Scotland* (Oxford: Clarendon Press, 1985), p. 239, n4.

Johnson considered truth a necessary but not sufficient requirement for written history, he recognized that the "mere dry particulars" in the *Annals* ultimately relegated it to the status of a dictionary (*Life*, 3: 58, 404). Similarly, he commented that Tacitus "seems to me rather to have made notes for an historical work, than to have written a history" (*Life*, 2: 189).

The middle style appropriate for historical writing has sometimes been misconstrued as artless and unembellished prose. It is actually a mean between extremes. Johnson described Joseph Addison's prose as a "model of the middle stile": "on grave subjects not formal, on light occasions not grovelling; pure without scrupulosity, and exact without apparent elaboration; always equitable, and always easy, without glowing words or pointed sentences" (*Lives*, 2: 678). Although Johnson's own prose was much more formal, he was a perceptive critic of historical styles. He often retreated to the seventeenth century for examples of what he considered effective English historical prose. In *Rambler* 122, he praised Sir Walter Raleigh's "elegance" and overpraised Richard Knolles for "all the excellencies that narration can admit." Even while criticizing Lord Clarendon's "negligence" as a stylist, Johnson admired his "rude inartificial majesty" (*Rambler*, 2: 289–90). In his *Dictionary*, Johnson defined written history as a narrative "delivered with dignity," a quality he believed many contemporary histories lacked. For example, despite delighting in the first part of Gilbert Burnet's *History of His Own Time* (1724–34) as "one of the most entertaining books in the English language," he dismissed its style as "mere chit-chat" (*Life*, 5: 285; 2: 213).

Johnson was more concerned about the elaborate historical prose of some of his contemporaries. He frequently attacked "that painted form which is the taste of this age," such as Sir John Dalrymple's "foppery," William Robertson's "*verbiage*," and Thomas Blackwell's "luxuriant stile" (*Life*, 3: 58; 2: 236–37; *Demand*, 295). Johnson distrusted these styles as symptoms of possible historical inaccuracy. He complained to Hester Thrale that "historians magnify events expected, or calamities endured [by] collecting all the big words they can find" (*JM*, 1: 203). He believed that historians caught up in their own rhetoric risked substituting imagination for fact; in his view, the traditional middle style was more likely to convey historical truth.

For Johnson, many of the problems in British historiography involved questions of authorial control. In *Rambler* 122 on historians, he wrote that "some have doubted, whether an Englishman can stop at that mediocrity of stile, or confine his mind to that even tenour of imagination, which narrative requires" (*Rambler*, 2: 289). (In this context the word "mediocrity," of course, refers to the middle stylistic level appropriate for history; it is not disparaging.[4]) Contemporary English historians were in Johnson's view failing to restrain – "stop"; "confine" – both their thought and their expression.

Production and Forms of History

During the first half of the eighteenth century, the quality of most British historical writing was inversely proportional to its quantity, a bad sign since so much history was being published. An enormously expanded audience for history generated increasing demands. D. R. Woolf writes that by the eighteenth century, for most readers, history was "the single most important branch of literature other than fiction or religion."[5] Even some large tomes proved surprisingly popular. In 1745, Johnson noted that histories of England were "so far the prevailing object of literary curiosity" that there were "three or four several editions, now publishing . . . in folio," with an additional one "yet in embryo" (*Demand*, 125–26). Because folios were expensive, a variety of cheaper and briefer historical forms proliferated to serve the needs of less wealthy readers. Chronologies and geographies – "the necessary preparatives and attendants" for history, according to Johnson (*Demand*, 85) – also thrived in this market.

Eighteenth-century authors wrote, revised, edited, continued, excerpted, indexed, abridged, epitomized, anthologized, reviewed, serialized, and translated histories. Others made extracts and digests from historical texts, and still others wrote sequels or assembled collections from popular predecessors. Above all, they compiled, with many of them doing so in the sense of the word's Latin root *compīlāre*, "to plunder, pillage, rob, steal, snatch together and carry off," as the *Oxford English Dictionary* defines the verb "compile." Johnson had no objections to historical compilations as long as they were competently done. Before a detailed demolition of Blackwell's style in his review of the *Memoirs of the Court of Augustus* (1753–63), Johnson emphasized that the works of qualified writers could be useful even if they added no new information. Different organization or expression could potentially attract diverse readers: "No writer pleases all, and every writer may please some" (*Demand*, 293). His infamous claim that Oliver Goldsmith "stands in the

---

[4] Johnson's *Dictionary* does not include the negative connotations that "mediocrity" usually carries now.
[5] Daniel Robert Woolf, *Reading History in Early Modern England* (Cambridge: Cambridge University Press, 2000), p. 7.

first class" as a historian has often been dismissed as Johnson's love of defending unlikely argumentative positions and his particular glee in criticizing the Scots to Boswell, who in this case was championing his compatriot Robertson. But Johnson's description of Goldsmith's *Roman History* (1772) as "an abridgement" superior to Lucius Florus's *Epitome* and Eutropius's *Summary* clearly indicated that he understood the limitations of the kind of history that Goldsmith was writing. He credited Goldsmith with "the art of compiling," and recognized that within that category, a large one in eighteenth-century Britain, Goldsmith excelled (*Life*, 2: 236–37).

From classical times, the best historians were considered to be participants in great events who later wrote about their experiences. Alternatively, historical writing could be entrusted to scholars. As the number of British historians grew during the early eighteenth century, relatively few of them came from these elite groups. This development, sometimes viewed as a democratic expansion of opportunity by modern critics, displeased Johnson. With "the inclosures of literature . . . thrown open," he lamented in *Reflections on the Present State of Literature* (1756) that "It is not now, as in former times, when men studied long, and past through the severities of discipline, and the probation of public trials, before they presumed to think themselves qualified for instructors of their countrymen" (*Demand*, 256–57). Not all of the compilers of histories were Grub Street hacks, but some of them earned their places in Pope's *Dunciad* that way.

In content and in form, many of the problems facing eighteenth-century historians were inherited from the later seventeenth century. With the sheer volume of historical material continually becoming available, organization remained a problem. Antiquarians offered valuable historical materials but no formal models, and integrating their discoveries into narrative histories was at best awkward. Johnson had some doubts about the document collection, a popular seventeenth-century form that survived into the eighteenth century. Questioning the utility of such "naked papers" in a letter to Edmund Cave about a proposed historical project, he wrote that "without an historical treatise interwoven," the necessary documents would "require some other book to make them understood" (*Life*, 1: 155–56).

Above all, as both the book trade and political journalism flourished after the Licensing Act lapsed (1695), politics blatantly saturated historiography. Historical writing is of course always ideologically charged discourse. But in the early eighteenth century, the politicization of all English historical writing was strikingly overt in its concentration primarily on the short-term political applicability of the past. The emphasis on immediate political relevance that characterized histories is equally clear in the ubiquitous historical parallels that recur in the literature and journalism of the period. In 1724, Bolingbroke wrote to Pope that "our Histories are Gazettes ill digested, & worse writ."[6]

By the early eighteenth century, both Whigs and Tories had evolved their own competing interpretations of the past, resulting in binary schematic histories. Tzvetan Todorov has described two models for narrative construction: the narrative of contiguity, organized around events and marked by relations of causality and succession (logical and temporal order), and the narrative of substitutions, marked by symmetry and repetition, where the organization occurs at the level of ideas rather than events.[7] Most historical writing has elements of both kinds of narrative, with contiguous narration prevailing in traditional histories and the narrative of substitutions prominent in more schematized productions like providential histories. In later seventeenth- and early eighteenth-century histories, substitutive narrative was increasingly augmenting or displacing contiguous narrative.

Even in historical works that maintained chronologically linear structures, the pervasive political emphases demanded a high percentage of substitutive narrative to convey their messages to the present via the past. Whig interpretations of the reign of Charles I and the civil wars generated specific readings of the Restoration, the Exclusion Crisis, the Glorious Revolution, Jacobitism, and the Hanoverian succession. Tories countered with their own schematic versions. Obviously, variations existed among individual historians, but during this period the simplified political binary overwhelmingly predominated.

Since Whig and Tory histories in many cases relied on the same basic historical materials, only the commentary differentiated historians on the two sides. Analyses naturally became more prominent. In addition, swollen commentaries often displaced narrative elements, in the process losing much of the variety and richness of the past purportedly being depicted. Historical writing lost immediacy, when, as Johnson noted of Thucydides, "there is more said than done" (*Lives*, 1: 217). As events gave way to the substitutive narrative created by historians' commentaries, the premium

---

[6] Alexander Pope, *Correspondence of Alexander Pope*, 5 vols. ed. George Sherburn (Oxford: Clarendon Press, 1956), 2: 220.
[7] Tzvetan Todorov, *Genres in Discourse* (Cambridge: Cambridge University Press, 1990), pp. 135–36.

on analysis left history particularly vulnerable to being misused for polemical purposes.

Despite Johnson's approval of competent compilations, when historians moved from compilers to commentators he became concerned. As historians filled their texts with elaborate political analyses, his objections focused on the ways conjecture functioned in their texts. On political histories, he writes in *Thoughts on . . . Falkland's Islands* (1771):

> It seems to be almost the universal error of historians to suppose it politically, as it is physically true, that every effect has a proportionate cause. . . . The caprices of voluntary agents laugh at calculation. . . . Obstinacy and flexibility, malignity and kindness, give place alternately to each other, and the reason of these vicissitudes, however important may be the consequences, often escapes the mind in which the change is made. (*PW*, 365–66)

Johnson emphasized that some of the motives of figures in earlier periods were particularly impervious to historical conjecture. Having considered "interest and policy," historians treating past decisions were still "obliged at last to omit more frequent and more active motives of human conduct, caprice, accident, and private affections" (*BW*, 442).

Surrounded by politicized commentary disfigured by conjecture, Johnson reacted in conversation in 1775 with the philosopher James Harris by insisting on truth as the bedrock of history: "We must consider how very little history there is; I mean real authentick history. That certain Kings reigned, and certain battles were fought, we can depend upon as true; but all the colouring, all the philosophy, of history is conjecture." In discussing antiquarian research with the historian William Robertson in 1778, he spoke similarly: "All that is really *known* of the ancient state of Britain is contained in a few pages. We *can* know no more than what the old writers have told us; yet what large books have we upon it, the whole of which, excepting such parts as are taken from those old writers, is all a dream" (*Life*, 2: 365–66; 3: 333).

These comments were made in conversations, where Johnson occasionally exaggerated for effect. To his remark about "authentick history," Boswell objected that Johnson was "reduc[ing] all history to no better than an almanack, a mere chronological series of remarkable events" (*Life*, 2: 366). Boswell was right, although his description does accurately reflect the practices of some contemporary compilers. On ancient Britain, too, Johnson was overstating, this time about the paucity of information available. By the early eighteenth century, antiquarians had actually assembled much more documentation than he suggests.[8] However, Johnson's overstatements are significant because they show the strength of his objections to the proliferation of historical commentary around him and his belief that historians should keep their focus on factual material. Again, the key for him was authorial control, to ensure the integrity of historical truth.

Johnson's Alternatives

Although much of Johnson's thought generalizes, his negativity about history can best be understood in more specific terms, as a reaction to the kind of historiography that he observed for over half his life. What are often taken as general comments about history are in part reflections of the contemporary historiographical situation. For example, given the predominance of politics and polemic in contemporary histories, in most cases when Johnson refers to "history," the reference is specific, not general: he means "*political* history." His negative assessments of history are often not so much denigrations of history in general as either subject or narrative, but specific reactions to the prevailing politicized histories of his era.

   Again and again, when Johnson disparages history in comparisons with other genres, history is described entirely in political terms. His famous comparisons favoring biography are good examples. When in *Idler* 84 he explains why, despite their "weight of truth," the "examples and events of history" are more often deployed in conversing casually than in guiding individual lives, he takes his examples from political history:

> Few are engaged in such scenes as give them opportunities of growing wiser by the downfal of statesmen or the defeat of generals. The stratagems of war, and the intrigues of courts, are read by far the greater part of mankind with the same indifference as the adventures of fabled heroes, or the revolutions of a fairy region. (*Idler*, 262)

Similarly, in *Rambler* 17 he notes that "miscarriages of the designs of princes are recorded in the histories of the world, but are of little use to the bulk of mankind, who seem very little interested in admonitions against errors which they cannot commit" (*Rambler*, 1: 96). Throughout his remarks on historical writing, one of Johnson's major concerns is that the predominantly political histories available failed to engage or serve the majority of the readers of history during the period.

---

[8] Graham Parry, *The Trophies of Time* (Oxford: Oxford University Press, 2007), pp. 358–61.

To expand history beyond the confines of politics, Johnson championed different historical genres and subgenres to create other more useful perspectives for this audience. Imlac in *Rasselas* is most likely speaking for Johnson when he praises intellectual history:

> There is no part of history so generally useful as that which relates the progress of the human mind, the (gradual) improvement of reason, the successive advances of science, the vicissitudes of learning and ignorance, which are the light and darkness of thinking beings, the extinction and resuscitation of arts, and the revolutions of the intellectual world. (*Rasselas*, 113)

Characteristically, Johnson brings in political history for contrast, to emphasize that even those who lead the state, the traditional audience for such history, could benefit from different historical perspectives: "If accounts of battles and invasions are peculiarly the business of princes, the useful or elegant arts are not to be neglected; those who have kingdoms to govern have understanding to cultivate" (*Rasselas*, 113).

Along with intellectual history, another subgenre Johnson favored was "the history of manners, of common life." He remarked that he especially wished to see that branch of history well done (*Life*, 3: 333), and he agreed with Lord Monboddo's opinion that "The history of manners is the most valuable." For this kind of social and cultural history, he also turned to the genre of biography, telling Monboddo that he esteemed its perspective for "giving us what comes near to ourselves, what we can turn to use" (*Life*, 5: 79).

Biography had traditionally been categorized as a branch of history, although with inferior status and less demanding standards than history itself. Laurence Echard, in his 1718 *History of England*, reflected the generic position of biography, writing that he had "several times deviated and descended from the Dignity of an *Historian*, and voluntarily fallen into the lower Class of *Biographers*." He explained that he did so because of the enlarged audience for history; he sought "to answer the Expectations of a numerous sort of Readers, curious in some Particulars," because he thought it would be "acceptable and useful to the Generality of the Nation." Echard also contrasted "the Rules of History" and "the Liberty of Biography."[9]

In the early eighteenth century, English biography was even less developed as a genre than history. The largescale transformations in methods

---

[9] Laurence Echard, *History of England*, 3 vols. (London: Jacob Tonson, 1718), 2: v, 714.

and materials that marked historical research over the seventeenth century had left biography mostly untouched. Since classical times it had been a static and atemporal form that usually depicted the public lives of moral exemplars rather than the private lives of individual human beings. In the early eighteenth century, although its form remained largely unchanged, some of the same market forces impacting historiography also influenced biography. Like history, biography fell into the hands of many compilers with limited knowledge, who assembled lives from public sources. Instant biographies immediately followed the deaths of well-known figures, and sensationalized criminal lives became popular. Although panegyric had predominated in earlier English biographies, in the heated early eighteenth-century political environment invective also came to the fore. Either way, the subjects remained lifeless and wooden.

Johnson was well aware of British deficiencies in biography. He asserted in *Rambler* 60 that "most accounts of particular persons are barren and useless" (*Rambler*, 1: 322), and in the *Life of Cowley* he lamented "the penury of English biography" (*Lives*, 1: 5). Johnson's high esteem for the genre stemmed from its potential rather than its current state. His famous treatment of it in *Rambler* 60 criticizes biographers as much or more than it praises biography itself, as he shows what the genre should be.

To situate biography in relation to history, in *Rambler* 60 Johnson again emphasized the distance of political history from the experience of most readers: "Histories of the downfal of kingdoms, and revolutions of empires, are read with great tranquility." In contrast, he stressed the importance of "the minute details of daily life" that biography offered (*Rambler*, 1: 319, 321). Johnson's focus was not new. Plutarch had differentiated the biographer from the historian in similar terms, writing that "a slight thing like a phrase or a jest often makes a greater revelation of character" than "illustrious deeds."[10] But Plutarch's practice had been largely ignored by centuries of subsequent biographers, who had instead produced, in Johnson's words, "whole ranks of characters adorned with uniform panegyric" (*Rambler*, 1: 323).

Johnson's treatment of the "minute details of daily life" in *Rambler* 60 highlights an element of biography that history was unable to assimilate, since such particulars "have no place in those relations which never descend below the consultation of senates, the motions of armies, and the schemes of conspirators" (1: 320). In biography, however, these everyday details

---

[10] Plutarch, *Plutarch's Lives: Demosthenes and Cicero. Alexander and Caesar*, trans. Bernadette Perrin. Loeb Classical Library Volume 7 (Cambridge, MA: Harvard University Press, 1919), p. 225.

functioned to ensure its wide applicability, because "A great part of the time" of all people, whatever their differences, "must unavoidably pass in the same manner" (1: 320). Ironically, then, by including details of daily life common to everyone, biography actually covered more of human life than history can, with its focus on "imperial tragedy" (1: 319). These details of character and behavior are to Johnson "invisible circumstances," unseen in historical writing but available in effective biography. It is partly on the basis of their importance that he elevates the status of biography over history – and particularly over the political history characteristic of the early eighteenth century: "There are many invisible circumstances which, whether we read as enquirers after natural or moral knowledge, whether we intend to enlarge our science, or increase our virtue, are more important than publick occurrences" (1: 321).

With biography, Johnson repeatedly stressed its usefulness, but for the memoir, the last genre he favored as an alternate to political history, he emphasized its truthfulness. In a review of the Duchess of Marlborough's *Account* (1742), he asserted that truth is not "any where more likely to be found than in private memoirs." This conclusion is undercut by Johnson's prefatory discussion in which his case against memoirists' reliability is actually more convincing than the claims for their truthfulness. When his arguments apparently dead-end in the "distrust [of] every relation" by memoirists, he suddenly veers to convert that negative into a positive, assuring the reader that "distrust is a necessary qualification of a student in history" (*Demand*, 67–68.).

When Johnson wrote this review in 1742, he was taking a strong stand on a dubious genre. Memoirs in England were a historiographical development of the late 1650s; the first English work with that title was published in 1658. By 1711, Shaftesbury commented on the genre's popularity: "The whole writing of this age is become indeed a sort of memoir-writing."[11] Historical memoirs also functioned as weapons in party warfare. In 1734, for instance, Tory opponents of Walpole published Sir John Reresby's *Memoirs* to counteract the second volume of Burnet's Whig *History of His Own Time*.[12] Although early memoirs were predominantly historical, the form rapidly mutated in autobiographical directions. The *OED* dates the first use of the word "memoirs," meaning accounts of events from an individual perspective, in 1659. By 1676, the word could also refer to

---

[11] Anthony Ashley Cooper, Earl of Shaftesbury, *Characteristics of Men, Manners, Opinions, Times*, ed. John M. Robertson (Indianapolis: Bobbs-Merrill, 1964), p. 132.

[12] John Reresby, *Memoirs of Sir John Reresby*, ed. Andrew Browning (Glasgow: Jackson, 1936), pp. ix–x.

"autobiographical observations."[13] During the period, a number of scandalous secret histories were also published as memoirs. These writers both reflected and hastened the declining historical credibility of the genre as it mutated again, this time toward fiction. By the time Johnson was writing, although historical memoirs still occasionally appeared, most of the English works entitled "memoirs" were fictional, such as John Cleland's *Fanny Hill: Memoirs of a Woman of Pleasure* (1749) or the *Memoirs of Miss Sydney Bidulph*, by Johnson's friend Frances Sheridan (1761).

Johnson claimed that memoirs, like biography, offered "a more exact knowledge than can be expected from general histories" because of the perspectives from characters' "private apartments," where "they indulged their own inclinations" (*Demand*, 69). In both memoirs and biography, Johnson preferred historical evidence from participants or eyewitnesses. He recognized the compelling reasons not to trust either one, and he detailed them fully; as Arthur Murphy noted, "no man better understood the nature of historical evidence" than Johnson (*JM*, 1: 479). Nevertheless, Johnson's commitment to the kind of truthful immediacy only such witnesses could provide – the kind of "volatile and evanescent" details he had described in *Rambler* 60 in connection with biography, which escape both memory and tradition (*Rambler*, 1: 323) – overcame the "distrust" characteristic of Johnson in dealing with history. In his view, memoirs also provided documentary stability to anchor details too often altered or lost over time in later accounts. He emphasized "how soon a succession of copies will lose all resemblance of the original" (*Rambler*, 1: 323).

Coda: Hume, Robertson, and Gibbon

Johnson's description of the ongoing problems in English historiography in terms of authorial control – the need for an "even tenour of imagination" and "mediocrity of style" – succinctly summed up the failures of his contemporaries. Then the situation radically changed. Starting in 1754 when the first volume of David Hume's *History of England* appeared, and continuing for over three decades, Hume, William Robertson, and Edward Gibbon, three of the finest historians Britain ever produced, began publishing their works.[14] The "distrust" that had served Johnson so well as

---

[13] "Memoir, n." *OED*.
[14] Hume, *History of England* (1754–61); Robertson, *History of Scotland* (1759), *History of the Reign of the Emperor Charles V* (1769), *History of America* (1777); Gibbon, *Decline and Fall of the Roman Empire* (1776–88).

a lifelong student of history was misapplied with these historians, and he was unwilling to give them the credit they deserved.

Johnson had a number of problems with Hume, Robertson, and Gibbon, but a brief summary would perhaps highlight the following. Johnson despised Hume's ideas, particularly his skepticism and his attacks on religion. He judged Hume's character accordingly, even though the two never met. Gibbon fared similarly in Johnson's eyes as a skeptic and an assailant of Christianity. Johnson also knew Gibbon slightly from The Club and was not impressed with him personally. In contrast, Robertson and Johnson were friends who admired each other, and Johnson praised his histories. Nevertheless, he criticized Robertson for excessively ornate prose and "cumbrous detail," claiming that he "always thought Robertson would be crushed by his own weight, – would be buried under his own ornaments" (*Life*, 2: 237). These stylistic concerns apparently limited his appreciation of Robertson's overall achievement, and Gibbon's prose was even more elaborate than Robertson's.

That Johnson never credited these historians as they deserved is ironic, because all of them created the kinds of capacious historical writing that Johnson wanted, including elements of intellectual, social, and cultural history, and even some from biography. Johnson's understanding of earlier eighteenth-century historiographical contexts showed his abilities in evaluating history and historical narrative. But with the great later eighteenth-century historical triumvirate, the problem was not that Johnson misjudged them. It was that he simply refused to judge them at all.

CHAPTER 6

Johnson and Fiction

Freya Johnston

Henry Fielding, born two years before Samuel Johnson, ended his authorial life rejecting fiction. In the preface to his final, posthumously published
work, *A Journal of a Voyage to Lisbon* (1754), Fielding suggested that he
would have admired Homer more had the greatest poet of antiquity
"written a true history of his own times in humble prose" rather than the
Iliad or the *Odyssey* – works of invention that, however astonishing, could
serve only to betray or corrupt reality. Any author worthy of veneration
would strive instead to record it.[1]

Samuel Johnson never went as far as this in his comments on and
(occasionally severe) criticisms of fiction. But nor did he ever commit
himself, as Fielding once had, to that "new species of writing" we now
call the novel, a form in which the fictional impersonation of a morally
compromised or mixed reality proved so beguiling as to stimulate the
reproofs of *Rambler* 4 (1750).[2] Johnson nowhere mentions in this essay
that he has Fielding or his greatest work of fiction in mind, but Mr
Rambler's criticisms of the modern novel – that "It is . . . not a sufficient
vindication of a character, that it is drawn as it appears," and that fiction
should strive "to increase prudence without impairing virtue" (*Rambler*, 1:
22) – are usually taken as directed toward *The History of Tom Jones,
a Foundling* (1749):

> Many writers, for the sake of following nature, so mingle good and bad
> qualities in their principal personages, that they are both equally

[1] Henry Fielding, *The Journal of a Voyage to Lisbon, Shamela, and Occasional Writings*, ed.
Martin Battestin with Sheridan W. Baker and Hugh Amory (Oxford: Clarendon Press, 2008), pp.
548–49.
[2] As Alan D. McKillop notes, "From Fielding himself comes the idea of the 'new species' which makes
the title of the pamphlet attractive, and the pamphleteer follows the novelist in combining the idea of
the new kind of writing with the idea of the author as law-giver in this kind." *An Essay on the New
Species of Writing Founded by Mr. Fielding*, ed. and introd. Alan D. McKillop (Los Angeles: William
Andrews Clark Memorial Library, 1962), p. 2.

conspicuous; and as we accompany them through their adventures with delight, and are led by degrees to interest ourselves in their favour, we lose the abhorrence of their faults, because they do not hinder our pleasure, or, perhaps, regard them with some kindness for being united with so much merit. (*Rambler*, 1: 23)

Here, Johnson makes his decisive entrance into one of the most vehemently contested aspects of the eighteenth-century novel: should its characters, plausible resemblances of human beings as they truly are, each combine good and bad qualities, or do such characters, if they are represented as morally ambiguous compounds, pose an unacceptable threat to their (typically young) readers? Is it the task of these fictions merely to reflect the world as it is, or should they also aspire to improve their audience? In the great theatrical and judicial arenas of the eighteenth-century novel, in which rival versions of the truth compete for the public's favor, Johnson took seriously the threat that vice would prove a more compelling and persuasive actor than virtue.

And yet, commenting on the closely related genre of biography (a name that is sometimes given to novels themselves, as comparably realistic portraits of individuals),[3] he differed from himself on this matter, arguing at one point for the exclusion of bad qualities from an individual portrait on the same basis as that on which he had argued in *Rambler* 4, while on another occasion – replying to James Boswell's suggestion that "in writing a life, a man's peculiarities should be mentioned, because they mark his character" – making quite the opposite case:

> JOHNSON. "Sir, there is no doubt as to peculiarities: the question is, whether a man's vices should be mentioned; for instance, whether it should be mentioned that Addison and Parnell drank too freely: for people will probably more easily indulge in drinking from knowing this; so that more ill may be done by the example, than good by telling the whole truth." Here was an instance of his varying from himself in talk; for when Lord Hailes and he sat one morning calmly conversing in my house at Edinburgh, I well remember that Dr. Johnson maintained, that "If a man is to write *A Panegyrick*, he may keep vices out of sight; but if he professes to write *A Life*, he must represent it really as it was:" and when I objected to the danger of telling that Parnell drank to excess, he said, that "it would produce an instructive caution to avoid drinking, when it was seen, that even the learning and genius of Parnell could be debased by it." And in the Hebrides

---

[3] The author of *An Essay on the New Species of Writing* (1751) hails Fielding as "the Founder of this new Biography" and as having "introduc'd this new kind of Biography" (pp. 12, 16).

he maintained, as appears from my "Journal," that a man's intimate friend should mention his faults, if he writes his life. (*Life*, 3: 154–55)

The coexistence of diametrically opposed views on this central question – the force and influence of example – carries over from Johnson's conversation into his writing. His longest work of fiction not only entertains contrary or inconsistent opinions on the same subject, it also reflects upon the human causes of such contrariness and inconsistency. In *The Prince of Abissinia. A Tale* (1759), later known as *The History of Rasselas, Prince of Abyssinia*, the princess explains to her brother that: "We differ from ourselves just as we differ from each other, when we see only part of the question, as in the multifarious relations of politicks and morality" (*Rasselas*, 105). If the critic will inevitably vary in his or her responses to a question that cannot yield a single correct answer, the novelistic character – however unambiguously he or she is introduced – can also seem to change sides in the course of those "multifarious relations" that, taken together, comprise an eighteenth-century novel. Fielding's Mr. Allworthy may initially appear to fulfill the exacting criteria that Johnson requires in *Rambler* 4 of a novelistic hero – namely, that he exhibit "the most perfect idea of virtue; of virtue not angelical, nor above probability, for what we cannot credit we shall never imitate, but the highest and purest that humanity can reach" (*Rambler*, 1: 24). However, in the course of *Tom Jones*, Mr. Allworthy, "a human Being replete with Benevolence, meditating in what manner he might render himself most acceptable to his Creator, by doing most Good to his Creatures," repeatedly proves to be a poor judge of character, both harsh and impulsive in his reactions to other people's apparent wrongdoing. In his case, as in Tom's, Fielding desires his readers to understand that "A single bad Act no more constitutes a Villain in Life, than a single bad Part on the Stage," and that we should therefore "never" be "hasty to condemn."[4] If Johnson in one mood might have thought this meant that the inclusion of bad qualities or habits in prose narratives fostered the reader's indulgence of those same vices, in another mood he would have endorsed Fielding's conclusion that

> nothing can be of more moral Use than the Imperfections which are seen in Examples of this Kind; since such form a Kind of Surprize, more apt to affect and dwell upon our Minds, than the Faults of very vicious and wicked Persons. The Foibles and Vices of Men in whom there is great Mixture of

---

[4] Henry Fielding, *The History of Tom Jones, A Foundling*, ed. Martin C. Battestin and Fredson Bowers, 2 vols. (Oxford: Clarendon Press, 1974), 1: 43, 329.

Good, become more glaring Objects, from the Virtues which contrast them, and shew their Deformity; and when we find such Vices attended with their evil Consequence to our favourite Characters, we are not only taught to shun them for our own Sake, but to hate them for the Mischiefs they have already brought on those we love. (*Tom Jones*, 1: 527)

To follow nature in the sense that Johnson typically ascribes to that word, which is to say "truth" or "reality," is generally reckoned to be a good thing – as in the *Preface to Shakespeare* (1765), which praises "the poet of *nature*; the poet that holds up to his readers a faithful *mirrour* of manners and of life," as contrasted with the metaphysical poets, whose "fictions were often violent and unnatural" (*Shakespeare*, 1: 62; *Life of Cowley*, *Lives*, 1: 38). For Johnson, however, fidelity to the world can never be enough on its own. Even in a realistic work of fiction, committed to showing life as it truly is, the author is "at liberty, tho' not to invent, yet to select objects," and he or she is especially responsible for making the right choice of material in novels, the kind of reading that serves as "introductions into life" for young people (*Rambler*, 1: 22, 21). Such works of fiction are typically "the entertainment of minds unfurnished with ideas, and therefore easily susceptible of impressions; not fixed by principles, and therefore easily following the current of fancy; not informed by experience, and consequently open to every false suggestion and partial account" (*Rambler*, 1: 21). Readers of this kind may be led by one kind of fiction into another, far more disastrous variety; namely, a lifelong misapprehension of the world. In all of the many genres in which he elected to write, Johnson's concern remained primarily for the moral and mental health of the wavering, vulnerable, and easily distracted reader. That entailed vigilantly attending to the borderline between truth and falsehood.

Arguments about the motives and uses of fiction – understood in its broadest sense as "The act of feigning or inventing," as he defines it in his *Dictionary* (1755) – may well be as old as literature itself. The originality of Johnson's contribution to such debates lies not so much in his critical response to the novel as a genre (although his comments upon the relative merits of Samuel Richardson, Henry Fielding, and Frances Burney are often richly suggestive) as in his powerfully riven sense of the imagination. On the one hand, it is a creative resource, an index of human ingenuity and achievement; on the other, it is a dangerous, alluring competitor with truth for control of the human psyche.[5] The contest between fiction and truth is itself the subject of many novels – or "histories," as they were often styled in this period (the full titles of *Clarissa*, *Tom Jones*, and of later editions of

[5] See R. C. Reynolds, "Johnson on Fielding," *College Literature*, 13:2 (1986): 157–67.

Rasselas, among many other works of eighteenth-century fiction, all contain the word *History*).[6] Johnson, whose "attention to veracity was without
equal or example," was perhaps suggesting as much when he remarked of
Richardson's heroine Clarissa Harlowe that "there is always something she
prefers to truth" (Hester Lynch Piozzi, *Anecdotes of the Late Samuel
Johnson, LL.D, in the Last Twenty Years of his Life* [1786], in *JM*, 1: 297).

Johnson cherished the capacity he identified in Richardson, especially as
contrasted with Fielding, to demonstrate "knowledge of the heart." The
price for such knowledge was, admittedly, quite high: "If you were to read
Richardson for the story, your impatience would be so much fretted that
you would hang yourself. But you must read him for the sentiment, and
consider the story as only giving occasion to the sentiment" (*Life*, 2: 175).
By "sentiment," Johnson meant something like the thoughts or morals
contained in Richardson's work, to which the plot or story must be
considered subordinate. This foregrounding of "sentiment" suggests an
approach to realistic fiction that might prevent young readers from becoming utterly absorbed in an all-too-plausible imaginary world, and therefore
also counter any threat to their capacity to distinguish between right and
wrong (although the fondness expressed by many readers for the villainous
Lovelace suggests that Richardson was not entirely successful on this
score).[7] Another reason that Johnson accords to plot less importance
than "sentiment" in Richardson is that his fiction is written in epistolary
form. All events are therefore reported by the same agents who are involved
in them. This kind of writing gains in immediacy and intimacy in the sense
that each correspondent is narrating a story in which he or she is also
playing a part, and the outcome of which is unknown to the characters
themselves; at the same time, it loses momentum in the sense that everything we are reading is a minutely detailed retrospective account of
something that has already happened (even if only moments ago).

---

[6] When Johnson told the printer William Strahan about *Rasselas* on January 20, 1759, he had decided
neither upon the hero's name nor the title of his work, which he referred to as "The choice of Life or
The History of – Prince of Abissinia" (*Letters*, 1: 178). The first (1759), second (1759), third (1760),
fourth (1766), fifth (1775), and sixth (1783) editions all bore the title *The Prince of Abissinia. A Tale*. In
Strahan's ledgers, the second edition is called "Rasselas Prince of Abissinia" and "Rasselas" (*Rasselas*,
p. xxv). Even if the book was by that stage widely known as *Rasselas*, the name of the hero – like the
label of *History* – was not included in the formal title until after Johnson's death: *The History of
Rasselas, Prince of Abissinia. A Tale* was published by Harrison and Co. in 1787. Meanwhile, the
French translation by Octavie Belot had styled itself *Histoire de Rasselas, Prince d'Abissinie*
(Amsterdam: Prault Fils, 1760).

[7] On rival interpretations of Lovelace and *Clarissa*, see William Beatty Warner, *Reading "Clarissa": The
Struggles of Interpretation* (New Haven: Yale University Press, 1979).

The proliferation of literary forms impersonated, adopted, and exploded by fiction in Johnson's lifetime was such that he could define the novel in his *Dictionary* as "A small tale, generally of love" in the same decade in which *The History of Sir Charles Grandison* (1753) was published – a decidedly large tale primarily concerned with the moral life in which love plays only one part.[8] Richardson might with good reason have disputed in relation to his own work the term "novel," and Johnson's *Dictionary* signals his own deprecating attitude toward merely entertaining fictional tales such as that produced by many of Richardson's contemporaries and sucessors. In later life, however, he proved remarkably and delightedly susceptible to Burney's epistolary fiction *Evelina, or the History of a Young Lady's Entrance into the World* (1778), comparing her characters favorably with those of Fielding (whose Amelia, however, remained the best heroine of the lot).[9]

Johnson himself published long and short works of prose fiction – *The Vision of Theodor* (1748); allegorical tales in *The Rambler* (1750–52); *The History of Rasselas* (1759); and a fairy tale, *The Fountains* (1766). He issued critical statements about fiction in journalism and reviews, in the *Lives of the Poets* (1779–81), and in discussions subsequently reported in Boswell's *Life of Johnson* (1791). In writing and in conversation, he was alert to the philosophical and ethical aspects of fiction and to its necessary origins in and dependence upon "nature," "reality," and "truth." In all these contexts, including that of his own fictional writing, fiction is often itself put on trial. In the same year in which he published his novelistic history or oriental tale, *Rasselas*, Johnson pronounced in the voice of Mr. Idler (*Idler* number 84) that fiction was something to be outgrown:

> from the time of life when fancy begins to be over-ruled by reason and corrected by experience, the most artful tale raises little curiosity when it is known to be false; tho' it may, perhaps, be sometimes read as a model of a neat or elegant stile, not for the sake of knowing what it contains, but how it is written; or those that are weary of themselves may have recourse to it as a pleasing dream, of which, when they awake, they voluntarily dismiss the images from their minds. (*Idler*, 262)

---

[8] The citations provided in Johnson's *Dictionary* for sense 1 of "NOVEL" underscore its contemptible nature: (1) "Nothing of a foreign nature; like the trifling *novels* which Ariosto inserted in his poems. *Dryden*." (2) "Her mangl'd fame in barb'rous pastime lost, / The coxcomb's *novel* and the drunkard's toast. *Prior*."

[9] Chauncey Brewster Tinker (ed.), *Dr. Johnson and Fanny Burney: Being the Johnsonian Passages from the Works of Mme. D'Arbley* (Westport, CT: Greenwood Press, 1911), p. 32. "Fielding's Amelia was the most pleasing heroine of all the romances" (*Anecdotes of the Late Samuel Johnson, JM*, 1: 297).

As in the *Preface to Shakespeare*, so in this periodical essay Johnson's cool appraisal of fiction's limited ability to influence the human mind – other than as a stylistic model or temporary distraction – gives little sense of the force he elsewhere attributed to stories or images that succeed in creating the impression of truth and reality. If the dreamers who indulge in the pleasures of an "artful tale" are in this instance able "voluntarily" to dismiss it from their minds when they awake, the self-deluding and solitary thinker in *Rasselas* ends up enslaved by "the power of fiction," chained to a life in which "fictions . . . operate as realities, false opinions fasten upon the mind, and life passes in dreams of rapture or of anguish" (*Rasselas*, 152). In this character's case, "fiction" is being deployed in the sense of "deception" or "hallucination," but the general implication of the terrible influence of such fictions upon the mind is intimately related to how and what we read; to our own credulity and habits of thinking, as well as to the character, skills, and motives of the author. Novels such as *Don Quixote* (1605–15) and *The Female Quixote* (1752), the latter written by Johnson's friend Charlotte Lennox, are fictions that concern themselves with the dangers of fiction in both the general and particular senses – delusion and literature – at once taking seriously and sending up the idea that readers of romance may end up misreading the real world.

Given his habitual impatience with long books (he "hardly ever read any poem to an end"; *Life*, 1: 70), it is surprising not only that Johnson seems to have reached the final page of *Clarissa* – though suspicions might be aroused on that score by the claim that "it was not the two *last*, but the two *first* volumes of Clarissa that he prized" (*Anecdotes of the Late Samuel Johnson*; *JM*, 1: 282) – but also that the three books he nominated as the only ones to be "wished longer" by their readers are all substantial works of prose fiction: *Don Quixote, Robinson Crusoe* (1719), and *Pilgrim's Progress* (1678–84) (*Anecdotes of the Late Samuel Johnson; JM*, 1: 332).[10] We know from Thomas Percy that another of the books that Johnson had no trouble getting to the end of was "the old Spanish romance of FELIXMARTE OF HIRCANIA, in folio, which he read quite through" (*Life*, 3: 49). It is relevant both to Johnson's criticisms of the novel and to the conduct of his fictional compositions that Percy mentions this in the context of there being something troubling to Johnson about his absorption in such wild, protracted tales: "I have heard him attribute to these extravagant

---

[10] Of *Paradise Lost* Johnson remarked, in contrast: "None ever wished it longer than it is. Its perusal is a duty rather than a pleasure" (*Lives*, 1: 196).

fictions that unsettled turn of mind which prevented his ever fixing in any profession" (*Life*, 3: 49).

Neither Percy nor Boswell elaborates upon this brief anecdote. But the underlying connection between a love of fiction, an unsettled mind, and the failure to make a decisive choice of profession may be one reason for the repeatedly invoked "choice of life" in this book; indeed, "The Choice of Life" was in January 1759 one of Johnson's preferred names for his tale (*Rasselas*, 51, 56, 81, 111, 161, 175; the phrase "choice of life" is sometimes italicized when it occurs within chapters, as if to bring out its titular possibilities).[11] It may also help to explain why this fictional quest ultimately goes nowhere, ending in a "conclusion, in which nothing is concluded" (*Rasselas*, 175). The story unites authority with desultoriness, its decisive command of human psychology and ethics combining with a lack of resolution at its close.

Boswell thought that, had Johnson "written nothing else," *Rasselas* "would have rendered his name immortal in the world of literature" (*Life*, 1: 341). Many readers at the time of the work's first appearance, and ever since, have found it consoling and disheartening in equal measure; at least two of them were driven to compose sequels in which everything is firmly worked out for the best.[12] Toward the end of the tale, the astronomer's point – that he is unable to say what might be the right choice of life, but he can say for sure that he has made the wrong one himself – sums up the work's pervasive sense of human frailty, errancy, and inadequacy (*Rasselas*, 161). Yet that sense is as often the engine of comedy in the story as it is of instruction or despondency, and the astronomer is successfully restored from a state of madness to sanity; he makes friends, he finds himself busily involved with and respected by other people, and he gradually comes to reconcile himself to the world. The prince and his companions acquire a knowledge of life and of themselves in the course of their sometimes bruising, sometimes funny encounters with other flawed human beings, many of whom have designs on them.

If Johnson's tale reads less like a continuous prose narrative than as a series of moral essays along the lines of *The Rambler*, that is perhaps due in part to the work's occasional nature. Johnson claimed, we are told, to have written *Rasselas* "in the evenings of one week," sending it to the printers "in portions as it was written" so that "with the profits he might

---

[11] *Letters*, 1: 178 (Johnson to William Strahan, January 20, 1759). See above, n6.
[12] See Jessica Richard, "'I Am Equally Weary of Confinement': Women Writers and *Rasselas* from *Dinarbus* to *Jane Eyre*," *Tulsa Studies in Women's Literature*, 22:2 (2003): 335–56.

defray the expense of his mother's funeral" (*Life*, 1: 341; see also *Rasselas*, xxi–xxiii). If this account of the work's origins and motivations is accurate, that too might partly explain the open-endedness of Johnson's episodic narrative, and perhaps also what some readers have diagnosed as its bleakness. Yet it is far from clear that the story directly reflects Johnson's personal feelings or circumstances at the time of his mother's death, even if those circumstances are what finally compelled him to write and publish it. To judge by his fondness for oriental fictions in *The Rambler* and *The Idler*, he may well have been meditating a work of this kind for years.[13]

When Johnson seized the opportunity to read *Rasselas* again in 1781, apparently for the first time since it had been published more than two decades earlier, it was with rapt enjoyment, "avidity," and approval, a response which seems to imply his own appreciation of the work as a composite and continuous whole, as well as that his opinions about fiction and life had not changed much since its initial appearance (*Life*, 4: 156). Percy's language of fixity ("I have heard him attribute to these extravagant fictions that unsettled turn of mind which prevented his ever fixing in any profession") appears in this anecdote again, only in this case happily: his friend was reading "his own 'Prince of Abyssinia,'" says Boswell, "on which he seemed to be intensely fixed" (*Life*, 4: 156). At the end of the book the travelers, having surveyed the world and spoken to many people, as well as having frequently debated with one another, remain unable to "fix" upon anything (the verb is applied to the prince in the last chapter, on page 176). The older characters, Imlac and the astronomer, may be more passive than the rest, being "contented to be driven along the stream of life without directing their course to any particular port" (*Rasselas*, 176). But every one of the cast has by now learned that none of their wishes can be obtained. They resolve to make their way back to Abyssinia – the place from which boredom and disgust had originally provoked most of them to escape. But it is by no means clear that they will act on this resolution, nor that (if they do so) they can or will be readmitted to "the prison of pleasure" that is the Happy Valley (*Rasselas*, 164).

Leopold Damrosch, writing about *Rasselas*, proposed that "Johnson insists on the gulf between art and life. Art is a kind of delusion, a substitute for reality and often an illicit improvement upon it."[14]

---

[13] See *Ramblers* 38, 65, 190, 204, 205; *Idlers* 75, 99.
[14] Leopold Damrosch, Jr., "Johnson's *Rasselas*: Limits of Wisdom, Limits of Art," in Douglas Lane Patey and Timothy Keegan (eds.), *Augustan Studies: Essays in Honor of Irvin Ehrenpreis* (Newark: University of Delaware Press, 1986), pp. 205–14, 210.

Johnson's attitude to fiction, in the inter-related senses of self-deception and artistic invention, ranges from (at its most disturbed) the portrait of the astronomer in *Rasselas* to the doggedly untroubled description of tragedy in the *Preface to Shakespeare*:

> It will be asked, how the drama moves, if it is not credited. It is credited with all the credit due to a drama. It is credited, whenever it moves, as a just picture of a real original; as representing to the auditor what he would himself feel, if he were to do or suffer what is there feigned to be suffered or to be done. The reflection that strikes the heart is not, that the evils before us are real evils, but that they are evils to which we ourselves may be exposed. If there be any fallacy, it is not that we fancy the players, but that we fancy ourselves unhappy for a moment; but we rather lament the possibility than suppose the presence of misery, as a mother weeps over her babe, when she remembers that death may take it from her. The delight of tragedy proceeds from our consciousness of fiction. (*Shakespeare*, 1: 78)

This appraisal of "our consciousness of fiction" offers a far more sanguine, down-to-earth assessment than Johnson typically formulates of the human capacity to remain aware that pictures of "a real original" are just that. Yet even in this determinedly level-headed, assertive context – "It will be . . . it is not . . . It is . . . It is . . . it is not" – his imagination works to conjure up the figure of a mother who is herself imagining the (realistic) possibility of her baby's death. Watching a tragedy, we remain fully aware, Johnson insists, that fiction is fiction and life is life. By way of contrast, here is Imlac on the solitary astronomer, who has gradually fooled himself into the fantastical belief that he controls the weather. When his young companions begin to laugh at the astronomer's folly, they are brought up short:

> To indulge the power of fiction, and send imagination out upon the wing, is often the sport of those who delight too much in silent speculation. When we are alone we are not always busy; the labour of excogitation is too violent to last long; the ardour of enquiry will sometimes give way to idleness or satiety. He who has nothing external that can divert him, must find pleasure in his own thoughts, and must conceive himself what he is not; for who is pleased with what he is? He then expatiates in boundless futurity, and culls from all imaginable conditions that which for the present moment he should most desire, amuses his desires with impossible enjoyments, and confers upon his pride unattainable dominion. The mind dances from scene to scene, unites all pleasures in all combinations, and riots in delights which nature and fortune, with all their bounty, cannot bestow. . . . By degrees the reign of fancy is confirmed; she grows first imperious, and in time despotick. Then fictions begin to operate as realities, false opinions fasten upon the mind, and life passes in dreams of rapture or of anguish. (*Rasselas*, 151–52)

What begins as amusement ends as imprisonment. Chastened by this exposition, Nekayah, Pekuah, and Rasselas all forswear their imaginative recreations – a promise which is as impossible to keep as any other that is made in the tale. One reason for the astronomer's case being taken so much more seriously than that of a member of the stage audience in the *Preface to Shakespeare* is that the solitary reader or thinker always strikes Johnson as an inherently more vulnerable and pitiable figure than the spectator who is one of a crowd. The origins of this feeling, like his fondness for romance, lie in childhood; specifically, in Johnson's reaction to *Hamlet* as a child at home in Lichfield: "he read Shakspeare at a period so early, that the speech of the Ghost in Hamlet terrified him when he was alone" (*Life*, 1: 70); "when he was about nine years old, having got the play of Hamlet in his hand, and reading it quietly in his father's kitchen, he kept on steadily enough till, coming to the Ghost scene, he suddenly hurried upstairs to the street door that he might see people about him" (*Anecdotes of the Late Samuel Johnson*; *JM*, 1: 158).

Human credulity, including and sometimes especially the capacity for self-delusion, is at stake in Johnson's perpetual striving to maintain a distinction between fiction and reality. At the lower end of the scale is the affectation that leads people to try to pass themselves off as something that they are not. Considering this subject in *Rambler* 21, Johnson concludes:

> If we therefore compare the value of the praise obtained by fictitious excellence, even while the cheat is yet undiscovered, with that kindness which every man may suit by his virtue, and that esteem to which most men may rise by common understanding steadily and honestly applied, we shall find that when from the adscititious happiness all the deductions are made by fear and casualty, there will remain nothing equiponderant to the security of truth. (*Rambler*, 1: 115)

Whatever compliments may be gained by pretense, by assuming a "fictitious excellence" of character, are worthless by comparison with the praise we deserve. Another version of this point – the ultimate super-iority of truth to fiction – is reached in the *Preface to Shakespeare*. Here, it is phrased in terms of "stability" rather than "security," but in both cases Johnson contrives that "truth" should have and be the last word: "The irregular combinations of fanciful invention may delight a-while, by that novelty of which the common satiety of life sends us all in quest; but the pleasures of sudden wonder are soon exhausted, and the mind can only repose on the stability of truth" (*Shakespeare*, 1: 61–62).

In the end, the primary task of literature is not to produce a mere simulacrum of reality but to direct its creative, fictional powers to activate the nascent or stagnant moral life, to awaken us to things as they are. The point is demonstrated in *Rambler* 96 (1751), itself a work of fiction, which culminates in the triumphant union of truth with its apparent enemy. Johnson's comic allegory sees the daughter of Jupiter and Wisdom personified as a rather bossy, spoiled, and vengeful teenager who does not meet with the applause she demands of her audience:

> Truth, who, when she first descended from the heavenly palaces, expected to have been received by universal acclamation, cherished with kindness, heard with obedience, and invited to spread her influence from province to province, now found that, wherever she came, she must force her passage. Every intellect was precluded by Prejudice, and every heart preoccupied by Passion. (*Rambler*, 2: 152)

In a new twist on a very old story about literature – that it copies nature – Truth comes to learn from and then to impersonate Falsehood, at which point her name becomes Fiction. She is compelled to do this because of the natural resistance of the human mind to sheer, unadorned reality:

> The Muses wove in the loom of Pallas, a loose and changeable robe, like that in which Falsehood captivated her admirers; with this they invested Truth, and named her Fiction. She now went out again to conquer with more success; for when she demanded entrance of the Passions, they often mistook her for Falsehood, and delivered up their charge; but when she had once taken possession, she was soon disrobed by Reason, and shone out, in her original form, with native effulgence and resistless dignity. (*Rambler*, 2: 152)

Robed in the guise of Fiction, Truth dupes human beings into admitting her to their hearts and minds. They cease to be frightened of her and begin rather to desire her; not because they have become any better, but because she has learned the art of seduction. Truth is more alluring when dressed than naked. But the moment she gains control of her newly acquiescent human victim, fiction can be discarded.

CHAPTER 7

Johnson and Gender

Samara Anne Cahill

Perhaps no eighteenth-century author has been better served by changing attitudes to gender in the twentieth and twenty-first centuries than Samuel Johnson. Known as a misogynist for most of the twentieth century – largely due to anecdotes from James Boswell's canonical *Life of Samuel Johnson* (1791), such as "a woman's preaching is like a dog's walking on his hinder legs. It is not done well; but you are surprized to find it done at all" (*Life*, 1: 463) – Johnson has been slowly recuperated by scholars since the end of the 1970s. During the mid-1980s, particularly due to the annual journal *The Age of Johnson*, scholars increasingly examined, discussed, and revised Johnson's reputation as a misogynist until, by the early 1990s, the scholarly consensus held Johnson to be a progressive, if representative, man of his time who supported women through patronage, mentorship, and his own work.[1] This consensus was solidified by the end of the 1990s with the publication of Kathleen Nulton Kemmerer's *"A Neutral Being between the Sexes": Samuel Johnson's Sexual Politics* and Eithne Henson's essay "Johnson and the condition of women" in *The Cambridge Companion to Samuel Johnson* (1997).[2] From the perspective of the twenty-first century, Johnson's previous reputation was the product of the historical preeminence of Boswell's biography and its portrayal of a masculinist Johnson of the Club and London streets to the exclusion of accounts of Johnson's life

[1] See Charmaine Wellington, "Dr. Johnson's Attitude toward the Education of Women," *New Rambler* 18 (1977): 49–55; Isobel Grundy, "Samuel Johnson as Patron of Women," *AJ*, 1 (1987): 59–77; Donald Greene, "The Logia of Samuel Johnson and the Quest for Historical Johnson," *AJ*, 3 (1990): 1–33; James G. Basker, "Dancing Dogs, Women Preachers and the Myth of Johnson's Misogyny," *AJ*, 3 (1990): 63–90; Margaret Anne Doody, "Dear Miss Boothby," *London Review of Books*, 14:21 (1992): 10–11; Annette Wheeler Cafarelli, "Johnson and Women: Demasculinizing Literary History," *AJ*, 5 (1992): 61–114; and all the articles in the *South Central Review*, Special issue: "Johnson and Gender," 9:4 (1992).
[2] Kathleen Nulton Kemmerer, *"A neutral Being between the Sexes": Samuel Johnson's Sexual Politics* (Lewisburg, PA: Bucknell University Press, 1998) and Eithne Henson, "Johnson and the Condition of Women," in *Companion*, pp. 67–84.

94

by female friends and mentees such as Hester Thrale Piozzi, Frances Burney, and Hannah More. Boswell's own fraught attitudes to women, and how his bias might have informed his representation of the elderly Johnson, were largely ignored until the late twentieth century. (Thomas Babington Macaulay's indebtedness to Boswell in his characterization of Johnson as an extreme conservative Tory hardly helped Johnson's reputation.[3]) There is now a wealth of evidence that Johnson was, in fact, unusually supportive of women, their intellects, their professional literary ambitions, and their education.[4] This capsule history brings us to the present day in the scholarship on Samuel Johnson and women.

But women are not the only ones with a gender, nor is "gender" an uncontested concept in twenty-first century scholarship. Indeed, to use the touchstone of Ana Frietas de Boe and Abby Coykendall's collection *Heteronormativity in Eighteenth-Century Literature and Culture*, sex, gender, and sexuality should all be considered contested concepts since heteronormativity, as

> [The "regime of the normal"] sets the conditions for who does – or who does not – count as normally and rightfully human by producing and policing three interwoven categories of difference: sex (dichotomous male/female embodiment), gender (asymmetrically socialized roles, characteristics, or behaviors), and sexuality (the expectation, even obligation, to form heteroerotic attractions culminating in marriage, reproduction, and kinship).[5]

Indeed, they conclude that heteronormativity "congeals into a fully fomented hegemony by the end of the eighteenth century" (p. 14). De Boe and Coykendall and their contributors show the stakes of the cultural logic of heteronormativity in eighteenth-century England and our own twenty-first-century context.

While this chapter will attend to gender, it will not further consider queer and trans eighteenth-century studies since the latter fields currently tend either to ignore Johnson or to focus on members of his social network, such as Boswell or the Bluestockings. Nevertheless, potential developments are on the horizon; indeed, Julia Ftacek's application of the concept of "chirality" to transgender eighteenth-century studies could potentially

---

[3] See Donald Greene, "The Myth of Johnson's Misogyny: Some Addenda," *South Central Review*, 9:4 (1992): 6–17.

[4] See Julia Robertson Acker, "'No Woman is the Worse for Sense and Knowledge': Samuel Johnson and Women," University of Maryland, College Park, M.A. dissertation (2007).

[5] Ana Frietas de Boe and Abby Coykendall (eds.), *Heteronormativity in Eighteenth-Century Literature and Culture* (Basingstoke: Ashgate, 2014), pp. 7–8.

enrich Johnson studies, too.[6] Complicating the sex/gender distinction provides an insight into Johnson's own complex and intersectional attitude to gender – intersectional because informed by its intersection with one or more other vectors, including race, class, ethnicity, sexuality, or religion.[7]

This approach to Johnson's intersectional attitude to gender requires a few acknowledgments to be made first: (1) Johnson was an apparently heterosexual man who was sensitively attuned to the degree to which heterosexual men benefited from their status as such; (2) Johnson took heteronormativity to be natural while recognizing the injustices to which women were subject; and (3) Johnson's (complex and evolving) support of women did not preclude him from participating in nonintersectional discourses that privileged Christian women and men at the expense of other groups.[8]

One of these discourses was the displacement of critiques of Western patriarchy onto stereotypes of an "Eastern," and often Muslim, Other, usually the stereotype of the barbaric, lascivious Muslim man. This "feminist orientalism," grounded in Christian chauvinism, was common among the women of Johnson's acquaintance and Johnson found this displacement useful in his defenses of women's education.[9] I will return to the issue of feminist orientalism – which relies on a contradistinction between stereotypically conceived Christian and Muslim masculinities – but foundationally I wish to emphasize that Johnson saw women's nature as progressive and evolving rather than given and static, and that this argument is supported by a cross-genre view of his work, including the tragedy *Irene* (1749), the periodical *The Rambler* (1750–2), *A Dictionary of*

---

[6] Julia Ftacek, "Egg Hatching; Or, Letting the Eighteenth Century Be Trans," *Eighteenth-Century Fiction*, 33:4 (2021): 577–80. See also Thomas A. King, "How (Not) to Queer Boswell," in Chris Mounsey and Caroline Gonda (eds.), *Queer People: Negotiations and Expressions of Homosexuality, 1700–1800* (Lewisburg, PA: Bucknell University Press, 2007), pp. 114–58; Susan Lanser, "Bluestocking Sapphism and the Economies of Desire," *Huntington Library Quarterly*, 65:1–2 (2002): 257–75; and Declan Kavanagh, *Effeminate Years: Literature, Politics, and Aesthetics in Mid-Eighteenth-Century Britain* (Lewisburg, PA: Bucknell University Press, 2017).

[7] Kimberlé Williams Crenshaw, "Demarginalizing the Intersection of Race and Sex: A Black Feminist Critique of Antidiscrimination Doctrine, Feminist Theory and Antiracist Politics," *University of Chicago Legal Forum*, 1 (1989): 139–67.

[8] For Johnson's sometimes troubling portrayal of mothers, particularly the Countess of Macclesfield, the putative mother of Richard Savage, whose life he wrote (1744), see Toni O'Shaughnessy Bowers, "Critical Complicities: Savage Mothers, Johnson's Mother, and the Containment of Maternal Difference," *AJ*, 5 (1992): 115–46, and Felicity Nussbaum, "'Savage' Mothers: Narratives of Maternity in the Mid-Eighteenth-Century," *Cultural Critique*, 20 (1991–2): 123–51.

[9] The term "feminist orientalism" was coined by Joyce Zonana in "The Sultan and the Slave: Feminist Orientalism and the Structure of 'Jane Eyre,'" *Signs*, 18:3 (1993): 592–617. I discuss feminist orientalism at length in *Intelligent Souls? Feminist Orientalism in Eighteenth-Century English Literature* (Lewisburg, PA: Bucknell University Press, 2019).

the English Language (1755), the philosophical oriental tale *Rasselas* (1759), and the *Life of Milton* (1779).

Johnson on Sex and Gender

The conjunction of three definitions from Johnson's *Dictionary of the English Language* leads to a telling conclusion. First, Johnson acknowledges that in everyday usage "sex" and "gender" could be interchangeable terms. He defines "SEX" as "The property by which any animal is male or female" (Def. 1), yet "GENDER" may refer to "A sex" (Def. 2). Second, the inclusion of the verb "TO WOMAN" (v.a, "To make pliant like a woman") indicates that female biology could be separated from conventionally feminine behavior. In other words, Johnson acknowledges that sex and gender are considered equivalent in daily usage, but he also acknowledges that gendered behavior does not necessarily map onto biological sex.

Johnson's denotative distinction between biological sex and socialized behavior means that women's education is crucial for their personal moral development. This conclusion is borne out in Johnson's fictional writings, and it is thus worth considering his gendering of genre. In his philosophical novel *Rasselas* (1759), Johnson presents a group of privileged travelers, Monophysite Christians, on a quest to discover what constitutes the happy life.[10] Bored with living in the isolated comfort of Abyssinia's Happy Valley, the eponymous prince sets out to see the world with his sister, the Princess Nekayah, her faithful servant, Pekuah, and their guide, Imlac, a philosopher poet. The travelers observe different levels of society in several different countries but do not find the "happy life" by the time the tale concludes.

Rasselas owes a debt to the increasingly popular genre of the "oriental tale," which tended to involve elements of fantasy, magic, and exotic travel. Yet these were exactly the elements of "wonder" that Johnson excluded from his consideration of modern fiction (what we would today call the realist novel) in *Rambler* 4, published on Saturday March 31, 1750 (*Rambler*, 1: 19). Johnson drew a generational and generic line between the woman-centered and woman-authored French and, later, English fiction of the 1660s–1720s – Madeleine de Scudéry's ten-volume romance *Clélie* (1654–61), Penelope Aubin's hermit-populated *The Noble Slaves*

---

[10] On the protagonists of *Rasselas* as "Monophysite African Christians," see Thomas Keymer, "Introduction," in Samuel Johnson, *The History of Rasselas, Prince of Abyssinia* (Oxford: Oxford University Press, 2009), pp. xxi (ix–xxxiv).

(1722), and Elizabeth Singer Rowe's supernatural didactic *Friendship in Death* (1728), for example – and the male-authored novels of the 1740s by Henry Fielding and, particularly, by Samuel Richardson, whom Johnson described in *Rambler* 97 as "an author from whom the age has received greater favours, who has enlarged the knowledge of human nature, and taught the passions to move at the command of virtue" (*Rambler*, 2: 153). Richardson, for his part, began his guest-authored *Rambler* 97 with a comparison of *The Rambler* and its influential predecessor periodical *The Spectator* (1711–12), hoping that *The Rambler* might show to "the rising generation" of "the better half of the human species [women]" what the "fashionable follies" of their mothers were, just as *The Spectator* showed the "fashionable follies" of their grandmother's generation (*Rambler*, 2: 153). Both Richardson and Johnson, then, saw a gendered, generational, and generic distinction between "women's" prose fiction and the male-authored periodicals and prose fiction of the novel.

Johnson on Romance

Johnson distinguished the contemporaneous fiction favored by "the present generation" of readers in the 1740s and 1750s from the works of the 1720s and earlier because current fiction was able to "exhibit life in its true state, diversified only by accidents that daily happen in the world, and influenced by passions and qualities which are really to be found in conversing with mankind"; it was able to "keep up curiosity without the help of wonder." By "wonder," Johnson meant that the new realist fiction was, as he says in *Rambler* 4, "therefore precluded from the machines and expedients of the heroic romance" including "giants," "a hermit and a wood," "imaginary castles," and "a battle and a shipwreck" (*Rambler*, 1: 19). Though Johnson considered this non-wondrous fiction to be "the comedy of romance," he distinguished realist fiction from the "heroic romance" because the latter is "produced without fear of criticism, without the toil of study, without knowledge of nature, or acquaintance with life" (*Rambler*, 1: 19).[11] To write a work of realist fiction, by contrast, requires,

---

[11] For "realist fiction," see Ian Watt's influential (and much debated) analysis of "realism" as the distinguishing characteristic of the novel: Ian Watt, *The Rise of the Novel: Studies in Defoe, Richardson, and Fielding* (London: Chatto & Windus, 1957). For an analysis of Johnson's view of the realist novel, see Mark Kinkead-Weekes, "Johnson on 'The Rise of the Novel'," in Isobel Grundy (ed.), *Samuel Johnson: New Critical Essays* (London: Vision; and Totowa, NJ: Barnes & Noble, 1984), pp. 70–85. On the oriental tale and the realist novel, see Srinivas Aravamudan, *Enlightenment Orientalism: Resisting the Rise of the Novel* (Chicago, IL: University of Chicago Press, 2012), pp. 1–30.

"together with that learning which is to be gained from books, that experience which can never be attained by solitary diligence, but must arise from general converse, and accurate observation of the living world." He concludes that these "performances have ... little indulgence, and therefore more difficulty" (*Rambler*, 1: 20), since anyone with experience and knowledge of ordinary life may judge what may happen to anyone on any day. It seems logical that if Johnson were to undertake a work of creative writing, then, he would conform to his own theory of realism.

Yet Johnson did not. In his two major works of fiction – *Irene* and *Rasselas* – Johnson reworked feminist orientalist tropes already associated with women writers and transferred the consideration of "life in its true state" from England to Constantinople and North Africa, respectively. Why would Johnson need an "Eastern" backdrop to consider the "accidents" of women's education that "daily happen in the world" of eighteenth-century England? There are at least three (overlapping) possibilities: the "East" is a *speculum mundi*; the "East" is an example of hybrid novelization; and the "East" is the displacement characteristic of feminist orientalism. All three acknowledge that the "East" is an oblique way of exploring domestic concerns.

In Kevin Berland's view, writers of oriental tales "used the east as a *speculum mundi* reflecting an image of the west, made just a little strange by the infusion of exotic contexts, but in the end resolving – as the reader possesses the text in its entirety – into something familiar."[12] Alternately, Brean Hammond and Shaun Regan modify Bakhtin's concept of "novelization" to "refer to a cultural process which, we will argue, took place in post-1660 England, making for the mingling and mixing of different literary modes within and between all the major genres," which eventually led to "the gradual domestication of the literary agenda."[13] In this view, *Rasselas*, which is notoriously difficult to place within a specific genre, would be a hybrid outlier that attends to English domestic concerns but not in a domestic context; *Irene* would be an example of a novelized tragedy – formally a drama but exploring the "'novelistic' topic" of women's education and therefore, according to Hammond and Regan, participating in the "particular ideological agendas" characteristic of the novel.[14]

---

[12] Kevin Berland, "The Paradise Garden and the Imaginary East: Alterity and Reflexivity in British Orientalist Romances," *The Eighteenth-Century Novel*, 2 (2002): 137–59, 155.

[13] Brean Hammond and Shaun Regan, *Making the Novel: Fiction and Society in Britain, 1660–1789* (Basingstoke: Palgrave Macmillan, 2006), pp. 21, 24.

[14] Hammond and Regan, *Making the Novel*, pp. 24–25.

The third possibility, and the one upon which I focus, is feminist orientalism. In *Irene* and *Rasselas*, Johnson divides women into two contrasting representative examples of "learned" behavior – conventional feminine "pliancy" or cowardice, and conventional masculine courage. By dramatizing how women's education causes women to behave in one of these two ways, Johnson not only shows that one *becomes* rather than is born a woman, but also that it is possible "to woman" women and, therefore, logically, for women *not* to be conventionally "womanly."[15] However, in detaching biological women from socially gendered "womanly" behavior, Johnson problematically contradistinguishes Christian and Muslim masculinities in a way that valorizes Christianity at the expense of Islam while nonetheless defending (Christian) women's moral agency.

Gender and Education in *Irene* and *Rasselas*

In *Rasselas*, the travelers – Prince Rasselas, his sister Nekayah, her servant Pekuah, and Imlac – learn about the world, various philosophies, and themselves as they encounter strange lands and foreign customs when they depart the "Happy Valley" in Abyssinia to investigate the nature of happiness. *Rasselas* includes a number of episodes dealing with women's (and others') education, but perhaps the most intriguing one occurs when Pekuah is kidnapped outside the pyramids near Cairo by Arabian bandits (chapters 33, 38–39). Pekuah is held in the harem of the Arab chieftain for several months before being ransomed by her companions.

Nekayah, as Rasselas's sister, is an elite woman in a way that Pekuah is not. Though friendly, the two women are not of the same social standing, nor do they have the same expectations or privileges. Up to this point in the tale, Johnson had seemed to establish a conventional class distinction between the intrepid Nekayah and the cowardly Pekuah, who is kidnapped because her fear of entering the pyramids separated her from the rest of the group. Yet it is precisely Pekuah's cowardice that reveals how wise she is capable of being. The separation enabled by her cowardice galvanizes Pekuah into conquering her fear: in the harem, away from Nekayah, she takes on a leadership role among the other kidnapped women and sets them an example of courage, resourcefulness, and ingenuity.

---

[15] My phrasing of course plays on Simone de Beauvoir's famous sentence "One is not born, but rather becomes, a woman." Simone de Beauvoir, *The Second Sex* (New York: Vintage Books, 1973), p. 301.

Readers might expect the abduction to initiate an episode of sexual trauma characteristic of the prose fiction of writers such as Penelope Aubin and Elizabeth Singer Rowe.[16] However, according to Thomas Keymer, "wherever Johnson looks to be on the cusp of a cliché of oriental fiction, his next move is to overturn generic expectations or frustrate readerly desires"; moreover, the Arab chieftain "turns out to be a world-weary Johnsonian melancholic."[17] This significant intervention in the portrayal of the stereotypical sexual barbarity of the harem patriarch, however, does not extend to the women of the harem. Pekuah describes them to Nekayah after she is ransomed:

> The diversions of the women ... were only childish play, by which the mind, accustomed to stronger operations, could not be kept busy. I could do all which they delighted in doing by powers merely sensitive, while my intellectual faculties were flown to Cairo. . . .
>   Nor was much satisfaction to be hoped from their conversation: for of what could they be expected to talk? They had seen nothing; for they had lived, from early youth, in that narrow spot: of what they had not seen they could have no knowledge, for they could not read. They had no ideas but of the few things that were within their view, and had hardly names for any thing but their clothes and their food. (*Rasselas*, 139–40)

The emphasis here is on Pekuah's moral and intellectual superiority – she considers her "mind" to be "accustomed to stronger operations" than the minds of the women of the harem due to their illiteracy and confinement. Pekuah's attractiveness of mind and conversational abilities perhaps echo the most famous raconteuse of world literature, a woman who must also use her wits to survive the harem – the Scheherazade of Antoine Galland's *The Arabian Nights Entertainments* (1704–17), the translation of which was extremely popular in eighteenth-century England.[18]

In contrast to Scheherazade and Pekuah, the women of the Arab chieftain's harem are childish and intellectually "narrow" because they are grounded in only the sensory and the frivolous – even their vocabulary is stunted (they only have "names" for their clothes and food). Pekuah and Nekayah (one a servant, one a princess, in a demonstration of Johnson's

---

[16] Penelope Aubin, *The Strange Adventures of the Count de Vinevil and His Family* (1721), *The Noble Slaves* (1722), and *The Life and Adventures of the Young Count Albertus* (1728); and Elizabeth Singer Rowe, *Friendship in Death* (1728).
[17] Keymer, "Introduction," p. xxiv.
[18] For an analysis of the harem as a "chronotope" where time stands still through Scheherazade's storytelling, see Ros Ballaster, *Fabulous Orients: Fictions of the East in England, 1662–1785* (Oxford: Oxford University Press, 2005), p. 11.

sympathy for women of various social strata) are both distinguished by
their investment in rationality and education (they both have names for
many things and many ideas); but this intersectional defense of women's
education across class (or, rather, status) barriers becomes nonintersectional when Muslim religious difference is considered.

In *Rasselas*, the inextricable meshing of intellectual development and
moral education is put into sharp relief by the contrast between Pekuah
(who learns to set a good example of courage when thrown on her own
resources) and the enervated women of the Arab harem. Johnson also
explored the connection between moral and intellectual rigor in the
relationship between Irene and Aspasia in his only drama, *Irene* (1749).
Set against the religio-political backdrop of the conquest of
Constantinople by Mehmed II in 1453, *Irene* juxtaposes the fates of
Aspasia, a stalwart Christian heroine fortified by a "masculine" education,
with Irene, a more traditionally educated woman who converts to Islam.

At the dramatic center of *Irene* is a fictional account of the seduction of the
Greek heroine, Irene, by the Ottoman conqueror of Constantinople (the
sultan is called "Mahomet" in the play, though the historical figure was
Mehmed II). Following the conquest of Constantinople (modern-day
Istanbul), a band of Greek soldiers struggles to overthrow Mahomet while
their captured friends, Aspasia and Irene, resist the advances of the stereotypically amorous conqueror. Both women are intelligent, pious Christians, yet
Aspasia's education has been more rigorous than Irene's. Mahomet at first falls
in love with Aspasia, but she is so stalwart in her rejection of him that he soon
turns to the more accommodating Irene, described as being "Of equal beauty,
but of softer mien, / Fear in her eye, submission on her tongue" (*Irene*, I. ii,
119–20; *Poems*, 124). Irene is a conventionally feminine woman – softer, more
pliant, and ultimately guilty of the apostasy Aspasia's integrity avoids. Aspasia
tries to persuade Irene that female softness – pliancy and cowardice – are
learned, not natural, behaviors. As Aspasia has already trained herself to fight
cowardice, she warns Irene:

> The weakness we lament, our selves create,
> Instructed from our infant years to court
> With counterfeited fears the aid of man;
> We learn to shudder at the rustling Breeze,
> Start at the Light, and tremble in the Dark;
> Till Affectation, rip'ning to belief,
> And Folly, frighted at her own chimeras,
> Habitual cowardice usurps the soul.
>
> (*Irene*, II. i, 26–33; *Poems*, 134)

For Aspasia, cowardice is a moral failing – a usurpation of the soul – but one that only women are taught and habituated to: a man would never be trained or "instructed" to counterfeit weakness. Irene, however, balks at this notion of female courage. She tells Aspasia:

> Not all like thee can brave the shocks of fate,
> Thy Soul by nature great, enlarg'd by knowledge,
> Soars unencumber'd with our idle cares,
> And all Aspasia but her beauty's Man.

> (*Irene*, II. i, 34–37; *Poems*, 134)

Irene identifies the main difference between the two women as one of education, though interestingly Irene chooses to individualize the comparison rather than acknowledge Aspasia's critique of the systemic problem of women's conventional "feminine" education. While admitting that Aspasia's position is one that is "enlarg'd by knowledge," Irene insists that it is Aspasia's individual soul that makes her great and that everything about Aspasia – except for her outward, conventionally feminine "beauty" – is manly. This is an astonishing complication of the more contemporary concept of "gender identity" as socialized. Further, given the fates of the two women – Aspasia escapes with her Greek lover Demetrius while Irene is unjustly executed by Mahomet – Johnson unambiguously endorses Aspasia's position that women's conventional femininity is not only artificial but also morally and physically destructive.

Though well-intentioned, Irene fundamentally erred in believing that she could control the future or trust Mahomet's promise that she would have the power to protect anyone. Indeed, she cannot even protect herself from the false charge of having betrayed Mahomet – he orders her to be strangled before she can explain or defend herself. Aspasia, on the other hand, though she and Demetrius are vulnerable refugees at the play's conclusion, has at least avoided Irene's "pangs of guilt" (*Irene*, III. ix, 132; *Poems*, 168).

Here I want to draw out several implications of Johnson's portrayal of gendered behavior. First, Johnson unambiguously blames bad education for conventionally "womanly" traits like pliancy and cowardice in the face of moral challenge. Women are moral agents and are therefore not naturally pliant or cowardly – these are learned and gendered behaviors. Second, Johnson likewise acknowledges differences among men based on different socializations. Third, unfortunately, Johnson uses the stereotypical "Muslim" setting of the harem to register the gendered differences among Christian men and women – and even between himself and other Christian men.

Life of Milton

Johnson's defense of women's education at the expense of Islam was not limited to his fiction. Indeed, Johnson used the example of the bad education of women in the harem against a fellow Englishman with whom he politically disagreed. As he says in the *Life of Milton*:

> It has been observed, that they who most loudly clamour for liberty do not most liberally grant it. What we know of Milton's character in domestick relations, is, that he was severe and arbitrary. His family consisted of women; and there appears in his books something like a Turkish contempt of females, as subordinate and inferior beings. That his own daughters might not break the ranks, he suffered them to be depressed by a mean and penurious education. He thought women made only for obedience, and man only for rebellion. (*Lives*, 1: 171)

Here, Johnson uses a trope of feminist orientalism outside of his fiction, suggesting that the feminist orientalist displacement of the "Eastern" locales did have a domestic use. The co-constitution of political opponents and stereotypical Muslim masculinity shows how easily a progressive view of women's education could slip into a political and Christian chauvinism that dispensed with (political) opponents by associating them with regressive "Turkish" attitudes.

Is it possible that Johnson influenced the feminist orientalism of the women whom he supported as mentor, patron, or friend? Charlotte Lennox published an essay in her compendium *The Lady's Museum* (1760–1) in which she argues that to "prohibit women entirely from learning is treating them with the same indignity that Mahomet did, who, to render them voluptuous, denied them souls."[19] Furthermore, Hannah More contended, "How much . . . is it to be regretted, that the British ladies should ever sit down contented to polish, when they are able to reform, to entertain, when they might instruct, and to dazzle for an hour, when they are candidates for eternity."[20] Like other eighteenth-century women writers, she too meshes a stereotype of Muslim doctrine with the intellectual marginalization of

---

[19] Charlotte Lennox, *The Lady's Museum. By the Author of The Female Quixote*, 2 vols. (London: J. Newbery and J. Coote, 1760–1), 1: 9.
[20] Hannah More, *Essays on Various Subjects, Principally Designed for Young Ladies* (London: J. Wilkie and T. Cadell, 1777), p. 19.

women: "UNDER the dispensation of Mahomet's law, indeed, these mental excellencies cannot be expected, because the women are shut out from all opportunities of instruction, and excluded from the endearing pleasures of a delightful and equal society."[21] More quotes from Mahomet's speech in *Irene* to assert that what she takes to be Muslim doctrine truly prevents women from developing their rational faculties. As the sultan initially tells Irene, women are made for men's pleasure, their bodies are the source of that pleasure, and their minds and souls require no cultivation: "Form'd to delight, and happy by delighting, / Heav'n has reserv'd no future paradise," but "bids them rove the paths of bliss, secure / Of total death, and careless of hereafter" (*Irene*, II. vii, 16–19; *Poems*, 146).[22] More does not acknowledge Mahomet's later conviction that Irene has persuaded him to change his mind (though, again, his new belief that women have souls does not prevent him from summarily executing Irene).

As James Basker has pointed out in his survey of the "radical affinities" of Mary Wollstonecraft and Johnson, Wollstonecraft included a selection from *Irene* in her educational anthology *The Female Reader* (1789). And perhaps Wollstonecraft had Johnson's *Life of Milton* in mind when she wrote of Milton's agreement with the "mussulman's creed" in his depiction of Eve in *Paradise Lost* (1667):

> I cannot comprehend his meaning, unless, in the true Mahometan strain, he meant to deprive us of souls, and insinuate that we were beings only designed by sweet attractive grace, and docile blind obedience, to gratify the senses of man when he can no longer soar on the wing of contemplation.[23]

Wollstonecraft is very much building on Johnson here. Her alignment of mere gracefulness, docility, and sensuousness with badly educated women is an echo of *Irene*, just as her exclusion of conventionally feminine women from "soar[ing]" intellectually echoes the description of Aspasia: "Thy Soul by Nature great, enlarg'd by Knowledge, / Soars unencumber'd with our idle Cares" (*Irene*, II. i, 35–36; *Poems*, 134). Basker remarks that Wollstonecraft had "an unusually deep and extensive" familiarity with "virtually every one of Johnson's works," from which she included five selections in her anthology.[24] Nor was Wollstonecraft alone. According to

[21] More, *Essays*, pp. 19–20.   [22] More includes this quotation from *Irene* in *Essays*, p. 21.
[23] Mary Wollstonecraft, *A Vindication of the Rights of Men* with *A Vindication of the Rights of Woman and Hints*, ed. Sylvana Tomaselli (Cambridge: Cambridge University Press, 2001), p. 87.
[24] James G. Basker, "Radical Affinities: Mary Wollstonecraft and Samuel Johnson," in Alvaro Ribeiro, SJ and James G. Basker (eds.), *Tradition in Transition: Women Writers, Marginal Texts, and the Eighteenth-Century Canon* (Oxford: Clarendon Press, 1996), pp. 41–55, 47.

Jessica Richard, both conservative and, like Wollstonecraft, more radical women readers in the eighteenth and nineteenth centuries perceived that *Rasselas* "authorizes a restless craving for liberty, interrogates the social order without resolving or settling the questions it raises, and implies a sense of the injustice of women's suffering."[25]

Is Johnson the primary influence on his female acquaintances' attitudes to Islam? No. Only Wollstonecraft's text was written after the publication of the *Life of Milton*. And even if all these women were familiar with *Irene*, as Hannah More and James Boswell certainly were, this particular discursive strand of feminist orientalism – seeing women's education and Muslim doctrine as diametrically and irreconcilably opposed – had been calcifying in Englishwomen's writing since the late 1690s. But Johnson's use of feminist orientalist tropes also used by Elizabeth Singer Rowe, Penelope Aubin, Charlotte Lennox, Hannah More, and Mary Wollstonecraft demonstrates that he both contributed to and reinforced a kind of writing largely identified with women in the eighteenth century. This fact complicates Johnson's characterization of female-centered romance as obsolete – he clearly had no difficulty endorsing women-centered tropes that recognized the socialized nature of gender. Thus, while Johnson disparaged the female-centered writing of late-seventeenth to early-eighteenth-century romance, this does not necessarily mean that he disparaged women's writing; indeed, he borrowed (and admittedly reworked) female-identified tropes in two works of fiction and at least one work of literary criticism.

Conclusion

Johnson repeatedly demonstrated that he believed that women were moral agents and that the conventionally "feminine" education described and rejected by Aspasia in *Irene* could only lead to pliancy, softness, and cowardice. Irene is a woman who *chooses* to be "womaned"; Aspasia, and Nekayah and Pekuah in *Rasselas*, are women who choose to be otherwise. In other words, while being invested in the heteronormative framework described by de Boe and Coykendall, Johnson nevertheless cleaved biological sex from social gender by focusing on the moral disadvantages of Englishwomen's

---

[25] Jessica Richard, "'I Am Equally Weary of Confinement': Women Writers and *Rasselas* from *Dinarbas* to *Jane Eyre*," *Tulsa Studies in Women's Literature*, 22:2 (2003): 335–56.

conventional education. The displacement of women's education to an "Eastern" setting enabled Johnson to valorize Christian masculinity (Demetrius, Rasselas) at the expense of Muslim masculinity (Mahomet, the Arab chieftain), while dramatizing for women the consequences of a "womanly" education.

CHAPTER 8

Johnson, Race, and Slavery

Nicholas Hudson

The period of Johnson's life witnessed historic changes in the way the British and Europeans understood racial difference and the practice of subjugating and enslaving non-Western people. From the writing of Linnaeus, Buffon, and others, including Johnson's friend Oliver Goldsmith, Europeans developed a system of racial classification that ultimately divided humankind into four to six "races" on ostensibly "scientific" grounds. The British slave trade reached its peak after the 1713 treaty with Spain, the "Asiento," which gave Britain extensive control of the importation of Africans to its prosperous colonies in America and the Caribbean. Yet this practice also sparked a backlash against slavery that began during the last twenty or so years of Johnson's life and that culminated, shortly after his death, in the abolitionist campaign, the West's first great human rights movement. On these issues, Johnson's scattered written and spoken comments present a clear and consistent picture. Johnson abhorred the slavery of Africans and other peoples with unwavering and passionate indignation. He appears to have been unswayed by recent racial divisions of humankind, remaining convinced of the common humanity of all people on earth, whom he regarded as driven by the same passions, endowed with the same intelligence, and possessing the same rights to liberty and independence.

There is, then, much to admire about Johnson's attitudes to race and slavery. Notwithstanding, there are other questions that we must consider in our evaluation of Johnson's thought on these issues. Johnson's opinions on slavery consist largely of dispersed and anonymous commentary, much of which would have been unknown to us without Boswell's record of his life. Johnson's failure to undertake a stronger and more public intervention into the rising protest against slavery in the 1770s and early 1780s presents a problem, for this issue had been brought forcefully to public attention by trials concerning two escaped slaves, James Somerset and Joseph Knight. Other major figures such as Adam Smith, William Warburton, and John

Wesley were making their opposition to slavery and the slave trade clear and public in ways that Johnson did not. How should we explain this reticence? I will suggest that Johnson was held back by competing political concerns about the disruptive use of "natural rights" in support of other causes that he strongly opposed at exactly the same time, notably the radicalism inspired by John Wilkes and the American Revolution.

As made clear in recent accounts of the roots of British abolitionism, distaste for slavery and the slave trade in the general public long preceded the actual campaign to abolish these practices in the 1780s.[1] Abolitionists were able to build on widespread disgust at the idea that Britain, the supposed land of liberty, engaged in slavery, which nonetheless seemed a distant colonial institution protected by powerful vested interests. In *The Negro's & Indians Advocate* (1680), for example, Morgan Godwyn argued for the baptism and Christian indoctrination of slaves, who included at that time both Africans and indigenous Americans. He nonetheless had to confront the assumption that a "Negro" was "*no Man*," a task he undertook by insisting on Africans' capacity to perform well in positions of responsibility even on plantations.[2] Although Godwyn clearly disdained slavery, he saw not the shadow of possibility that this practice might be ended. Yet Godwyn's discomfort with slavery was not unusual. Though pious and orthodox enough to please Samuel Richardson, the popular novelist Penelope Aubin condemned slavery through the voice of her eponymous heroine in *The Life of Charlotta du Pont*:

> The selling human Creatures, is a Crime my Soul abhors; and Wealth so got, ne'er thrives. Tho he is black, yet the Almighty made him as well as us, and Christianity ne'er taught us Cruelty: We ought to visit those Countreys to convert, not buy our Fellow-Creatures, to enslave and use them as if we were Devils, or They not Men.[3]

In what is evidently the first English tract entirely devoted to condemning colonial slavery, *An Essay Concerning Slavery* (1746), the anonymous author set about "proving Slavery to be contrary to the Law of God and Nature," appealing to the natural law theories of Samuel Pufendorf and John Locke.[4] Like Godwyn, however, this author expressed no hope that slavery

---

[1] See Christopher Leslie Brown, *Moral Capital: Foundations of British Abolitionism* (Chapel Hill: University of North Carolina Press, 2006).
[2] Morgan Godwyn, *The Negro's & Indians Advocate* (London: J.D., 1680), pp. 3, 12–13.
[3] Penelope Aubin, *The Life of Charlotta du Pont* (London: A. Bettesworth, 1723), p. 89.
[4] *An Essay Concerning Slavery* (London: Charles Corbitt, 1746), p. 2.

could be abolished, devoting most of this tract instead to advising how this system could be made more humane.

Building into the 1750s and 1760s, attacks on the enslavement of Africans mounted among many prominent philosophers and divines. In *Discourses on All the Principle Branches of Natural Religion and Social Virtue* (1749–52), the popular Baptist preacher James Foster condemned slavery as contrary to the principles of Christianity, though he framed his argument as a *"private protest"* against an immovable atrocity.[5] The Scottish philosopher Francis Hutcheson attacked slavery in *A System of Moral Philosophy*,[6] as did Adam Smith in his *Theory of Moral Sentiments*:

> Fortune never exerted more cruelly her empire over mankind, than when she subjected those nations of heroes to the refuse of the jails of Europe, to wretches who possess the virtue neither of the countries they come from, nor of those which they go to, and whose levity, brutality, and baseness, so justly expose them to the contempt of the vanquished.[7]

Smith went on, in *The Wealth of Nations* (1776), to argue that slavery was in fact a highly inefficient form of labor that could be sustained only in highly profitable industries such the production of sugar and tobacco.[8] With the outbreak of the Seven Years War in the American colonies, along with rising discontent among the colonists themselves, public antagonism against colonial slavery became more widespread and pronounced in the 1760s. In *Two Dialogues on the Man-Trade* (1760), signed by J. Philmore, the author condemned slavery as unchristian and contrary to British values, provoking a disdainful rebuke in *The Monthly Review* for attempting to undermine the nation's commerce.[9] This author nonetheless had allies among elite establishment figures: in a sermon delivered before the Society for the Propagation of the Gospel in Foreign Parts in 1766, William Warburton, Bishop of Gloucester, asserted that the enslavement of "our BRETHREN both of Nature and Grace, shocks all feelings of

---

[5] James Foster, *Discourses on All the Principle Branches of Natural Religion and Social Virtue*, 2 vols. (London and Edinburgh: Mr. Noon et al., 1749–52), 2: 158.
[6] Francis Hutcheson, *A System of Moral Philosophy*, 2 vols. (London: R. and A. Foulis and A. Millar; Glasgow: T. Longman, 1755), 2: 202–11.
[7] Adam Smith, *The Theory of Moral Sentiments* (London: A. Millar; Edinburgh: A. Kincaid and J. Bell, 1759), p. 403.
[8] See Adam Smith, *An Inquiry into the Nature and Causes of the Wealth of Nations*, 2 vols. (London: W. Strahan and T. Cadell, 1776), 1: 147.
[9] J. Philmore, *Two Dialogues on the Man-Trade* (London: J. Waugh et al., 1760), p. 65; *Monthly Review*, 24 (February 1761): 160–61.

humanity, and the dictates of common sense."[10] In the background to these pronouncements, Granville Sharp began his heroic efforts to prove and enforce the illegality of slavery under English law. In 1765 he successfully took up the case of Jonathan Strong, whose former master in Barbados had attempted to resume his ownership in England. In 1771, Sharp championed the similar case of Thomas Lewis all the way to the court of Lord Chief Justice Mansfield, setting the scene for the landmark case of *Somerset v. Stewart* in 1772.

Mansfield's ruling in the Somerset case is of special interest to readers of Johnson because his major statement on slavery, dictated to Boswell in 1777, concerned the parallel case of a Jamaican slave, Joseph Knight, who attempted to escape the clutches of his vaunted master in Scotland. Before examining this dictation, we should consider its legal and philosophical context. Typical of jurists in the eighteenth century, Mansfield had equivocated on the status of slaves brought to England. Although he pronounced slavery "odious," Mansfield also wished to protect the rights of property. In the Thomas Lewis case, he found a loophole that allowed him to avoid making a decision on these conflicting considerations, for Lewis had been previously freed and was not technically a "slave." There was no such loophole available in the Somerset case, for Stewart had his receipt for purchasing Somerset before carrying him to England. When Stewart then attempted to detain Somerset, who had absconded, Sharp brought forward a writ of *habeas corpus*, forcing Mansfield to make the decision on the legality of slavery that he had previously evaded. Although natural law theorists such as Grotius, Pufendorf, and Locke had condemned slavery in general, they had offered certain exceptions to this rule: a person might be enslaved in exchange for his or her life in war, willingly sell himself or herself into slavery, or inherit the enslaved status of parents. In the first volume of his *Commentaries on the Laws of England* (1765), Sir William Blackstone rejected all these exceptions yet also prevaricated, indicating that a slave-owner's supposed property was protected by the same law that secured a master's jurisdiction over an apprentice.[11] Mansfield did not reach for this equivocation or the other supposed exceptions to the law against slavery. He felt obliged to set Somerset free, acknowledging that there was no law in England to

[10] William Warburton, *A Sermon Preached before the Incorporated Society for the Propagation of the Gospel in Foreign Parts* (London: E. Owen and T. Harrison, 1766), p. 26.
[11] See Sir William Blackstone, *Commentaries on the Laws of England*, 4 vols. (London: Clarendon Press, 1765–9), 1: 410–15.

overrule a writ of *habeas corpus* even in the case of a person enslaved elsewhere.[12]

As this trial revealed, there were two issues at play in considerations of slavery into the 1770s. The first was the moral issue of the generally "odious" nature of slavery and the slave trade, a question that concerned the status of Africans or indigenous non-Europeans as fellow human beings rather than as objects or beasts who could be owned. Yet this issue did not automatically translate into an opinion about the legality of slavery in "positive" law – that is, whether even a morally objectionable practice might be made legal by the laws of a certain country or colony. Mansfield did not rule that slavery was always illegal because it was immoral but only that it was illegal in English law. On the first issue of morality, Johnson's contempt for the enslavement of non-Europeans was clear, emotional, and consistent throughout his life. In an early unsigned work, his *Life of Francis Drake*, renowned Elizabethan sea captain and privateer, published in *The Gentleman's Magazine* in 1740 and 1741, Johnson dwelled at length on Drake's humane and cordial relationships with African and indigenous peoples. In Panama, for example, Drake formed an alliance against the Spanish with the "Symerons, or fugitive negroes, who having escaped from the tyranny of their masters . . . asserted their natural right to liberty and independence" (*BW*, 98). The timing of this statement was significant, for it undermined patriotic fervor provoked by the Spanish boarding of British slave vessels that led to the War of Jenkins's Ear (1739–48). Though anonymously, Johnson contrasted a great British naval hero with the activities of supposed patriots in the modern Caribbean. In his similarly unsigned introduction to John Newbery's collection *The World Displayed* (1759), Johnson decried the random murder of Africans by the Portuguese in the fifteenth century. He directly related this barbarity to the dehumanizing of slaves in the British colonies:

> We are openly told, that they had the less scruple concerning their treatment of the savage people, because they scarcely considered them as distinct from beasts; and indeed the practice of all European nations, and among others of the English barbarians that cultivate the southern islands of America proves, that this opinion, however absurd and foolish, however wicked and injurious, still continues to prevail. Interest and pride harden the heart, and it is vain to dispute against avarice and power. (*Demand*, 442).

---

[12] See Norman S. Poser, *Lord Mansfield: Justice in the Age of Reason* (Montreal: McGill-Queen's University Press, 2013), pp. 286–98.

These statements on non-European people suggest that Johnson was totally unaffected by the beginnings of what would become the racial "science" of the nineteenth century. The racial division of humankind was first proposed in 1684 by François Bernier, who distinguished between five "Espèces ou Races d'homme" [species or races of man] – Europeans, Africans, Tartars, Lapps and Americans.[13] A version of this taxonomy was developed by Linnaeus in *Systema Naturae* (1735–58) and then pursued in great detail by the Comte de Buffon in his *Histoire Naturelle* (1749), the first work where "race" begins to replace the more conventional "species" or "variety." The many natural philosophers influenced by Buffon and Linneaus included Johnson's friend Goldsmith in *An History of the Earth and Animated Nature* (1774). Professedly indebted to Buffon, Goldsmith ascribed dark complexions to a "degeneracy" of an original whiteness, postulating that this appearance corresponded with a deeper degeneration of intellectual faculties. As Goldsmith wrote of dark-skinned peoples, "As their persons are thus naturally deformed ... their minds are equally incapable of strong exertions."[14] Johnson's various statements, on the contrary, never doubt that humans of whatever geographical origin or skin-color possess the same intelligence and essential motivations.

Predictably, the new racial doctrines supplied a convenient line of argument for proponents of slavery and the slave trade following Mansfield's reluctant ruling in 1772. Neither Buffon nor Goldsmith in fact denied the common humanity of non-white people. Polygenism, or belief in the multiple origins of humankind, remained for the time being a minority position of writers like Voltaire and Lord Kames. Edward Long pursued the polygenist thesis with vicious enthusiasm in *The History of Jamaica* (1774) because it contradicted the principle that Africans were, as Warburton put it, "BRETHREN" deserving of the same natural rights as white people. Nonetheless, monogenist forms of racial thinking could also be used by pro-slavery authors like Samuel Estwick in response to the Mansfield ruling. Even if "Negroes" were humans, Estwick argued, they were "an inferior race of people" who could be justly enslaved and needed harsh correction to discipline their incorrigibly "dark" souls.[15] Johnson appeared to view this whole debate over racial origins and classification as

---

[13] Francois Bernier, "Nouvelle division de la terre, par les differentes espèces ou races d'homme qui l'habitent," *Journal des Sçavans*, 12 (1684): 148.
[14] Oliver Goldsmith, *An History of the Earth and Animated Nature*, 8 vols. (London: J. Nourse, 1774), 2: 228.
[15] Samuel Estwick, *Considerations on the Negroe Cause, So Called* (London: J. Dodsley, 1773), pp. 80–82.

trivial and obnoxious. In June 1763, Boswell witnessed Johnson arguing with an "Irishman" in an eating-house over the cause of dark skin. "This matter has been much canvased among naturalists," Johnson observed, "but has never been brought to a certain issue," evidently so infuriating the Irishman that Johnson walked away (*Life*, I: 401). Hester Piozzi's inference, in *Anecdotes of the Late Samuel Johnson, LL.D* (1786), that Johnson regarded "negroes" as "a race naturally inferior," contradicted her own observations on Johnson's education of Francis Barber, whom he treated as an adopted son and finally made him his principal heir (*JM*, I: 292). Surrounded by the intensified climate of racial thinking in the 1780s, Piozzi was evidently projecting her own views onto Johnson.

But what of the legal issues surrounding slavery? As noted, even authors and judges who found slavery morally "odious" or contrary to natural rights conceded that there might be certain exceptions to this rule or that slavery could be made "legal" by "positive" law. In fact, Johnson himself seemed to concede these possibilities in his 1777 dictation to Boswell. Boswell had been enlisted as an assistant to John Maclaurin, an advocate for Joseph Knight, a former slave who had absconded from his master who in turn sued for Knight's return in the Scottish Court of Sessions. When Boswell approached Johnson for advice on this case, Johnson dictated a carefully worded argument defending Knight's right to be released from captivity. In the context of the times, however, it is a highly restrained and measured legal argument. Although "men in their original state were equal," Johnson reasoned, an individual might forfeit his equality or freedom "by a crime." This loss of freedom could not, however, descend to that individual's children. The laws of Jamaica by which Knight had been enslaved, he went on, "are merely positive; and apparently injurious to the rights of mankind." Johnson nonetheless carefully limited this reference to "the rights of mankind," clarifying his meaning in this way: "whoever is exposed to sale is condemned to slavery without appeal." In other words, the question was not that slavery was always contrary to "the rights of mankind" but rather that Knight had been afforded no *appeal*. Under Scottish law, Johnson argued, it should be up to the supposed slave-owner Wedderburn to prove that Knight had forfeited his freedom legally: "That the defendant has by any act forfeited the rights of nature we require to be proved."

This argument thus gave up a great deal to the possibility of legal slavery, at least as sanctioned by positive law. While lamenting that "moral right should ever give way to political convenience," Johnson offered a curious excuse for the moral deviance of Jamaican law: "temptations of interest are sometimes too strong for human virtue." His main position was that there was no such "temptation" or "political convenience" in Knight's case, for his enslavement would benefit no one in the British Isles except Wedderburn (*Life*, 3: 202–3). One wonders what research Johnson may have done on Scottish law or legal philosophy. If, for example, he had consulted George Wallace, he would have found that this author denied all excuses for slavery as "absurd." Wallace argued that no law could contravene the laws of nature infringed by slavery, and that a judge should rule accordingly: "Are any laws as binding as the eternal laws of justice? Is it doubtful, whether a judge ought to pay a greater regard to them, than to the arbitrary and inhuman usages, which prevail in a distant land?"[16] Indeed, Wallace's position was close to the final judgment of the Court of Sessions in the Knight case, for its ruling was much stronger than Mansfield's in the Somerset case. The Scottish judges affirmed the absolute repugnance of slavery to both natural and Scottish law, Boswell's own father, Lord Auchinleck, writing an impassioned judgment to this effect.[17] Johnson's reasoning was more like Francis Hutcheson's, who conceded the possibility of legal slavery under certain conditions, but insisted that the onus was always on the slave-owner to prove that these conditions had been met: "He who detains another by force in slavery, is always bound to prove his title . . . . The violent possessor must in all cases shew his title, especially where the old proprietor is well known. In this case, each man is the original proprietor of his own liberty."[18] Besides their agreement, in Johnson's words, that "the defendant has by any act forfeited the rights of nature we require to be proved," both Hutcheson and Johnson stressed that enslavement is essentially an act of "violence." As Johnson stated, Knight "is certainly subject to no law, but that of violence" (*Life*, 3: 203). Violence was in some cases permissible, but this needed to be proved.

Why did Johnson so carefully measure his defense of Knight's right to freedom? This question is significant because advocates of the slave industry were becoming increasingly efficient at finding loopholes in the law to justify their practices. An example of this advocacy was Boswell himself. Following Johnson's dictation, Boswell acknowledged that his friend "perhaps, was in the right" on "this particular case." Nevertheless, by 1791, when he published *The Life of Johnson*, Boswell took a stand against

---

[16] George Wallace, *A System of the Principles of the Law of Scotland* (London: A. Millar, D. Wilson and T. Durham; Edinburgh: G. Hamilton and J. Balfour, 1760), p. 96.

[17] See Iain Whyte, *Scotland and the Abolition of Black Slavery, 1756–1838* (Edinburgh: Edinburgh University Press, 2006), p. 9.

[18] Hutcheson, *A System of Moral Philosophy*, 2: 210–11.

the bill in Parliament to abolish the slave trade, led by William Wilberforce. According to Boswell, "The vast body of Planters, Merchants, and others, whose properties are involved in this trade," had underestimated the strength of the abolitionist campaign because of "the insignificance of the zealots who vainly took the lead in it." It was true that "some men of superior abilities" had supported this "wild and dangerous" cause, but they had been incited by "a love of temporary popularity" or "a love of general mischief" (*Life*, 3: 200). As for Johnson, his more general hatred of slavery was "owing to prejudice, and imperfect or false information." Showing "zeal without knowledge," he had failed to consider the serious economic damage that would be caused by abolishing the slave trade, which was in any event "humanely regulated." Indeed, slave traders were doing Africans a favor by freeing them from "intolerable bondage in their own country" and introducing them to civilization and Christianity (*Life*, 3: 203–4).

It is notable that Boswell was taking a page out of Johnson's own style of reasoning. On many occasions, Johnson had denounced skeptics like Hume as vainly seeking popularity rather than truth. (In a widely cited note in his 1748 essay "Of National Characters," Hume had in fact pronounced that "negroes" were "naturally inferior to the whites" on the evidence that there was "No ingenious manufactures amongst them, no arts, no sciences.")[19] Nonetheless, no issue so clearly showed the differences between Boswell and Johnson as their attitudes toward slavery. Boswell recognized that Johnson's dictated statement did not reflect his broader and more emotional hostility to colonial slavery. He recalled a story of Johnson's toasting "the next insurrection of the negroes in the West Indies" before "some very grave men at Oxford" (*Life*, 2: 200). This anecdote might mislead us. In fact, there is no reason to assume that "grave men" at Oxford would be any less opposed to slavery than Johnson was. As Boswell indicated, the primary advocates for the slave trade were those with vested interests in the plantation industry, a significant segment of the mercantile "middle-class." Hostility to the slave trade was a broad bipartisan cause, forging a peculiar alliance between advocates of wide political reform, like Sharp or Thomas Day (coauthor of the Rousseau-inspired poem of 1773, "The Dying Negro"), and people with otherwise conservative attitudes like Warburton, Wilberforce, Hannah More, and indeed Johnson himself. It evidently pleased Boswell

[19] David Hume, *Essays, Moral, Political, and Literary*, ed. E. F. Miller (Indianapolis, IN: Liberty Press, 1987), p. 208, n10.

to think that he was taking the sensible or "grave" position on slavery and was on the side of powerful planters and merchants against "insignificant" zealots for abolition. What he truly revealed about himself was a deference to wealth and prestige that formed no part of Johnson's character or political reasoning.

Johnson's failure to speak in stronger and more unqualified terms in his dictation to Boswell on the Knight case might indeed be explained by the limited nature of the task at hand. As shown by the Vinerian lectures on the history of the English law that Johnson cowrote (1767–73) with Robert Chambers, the Vinerian Chair of English Law at Oxford, he was a knowledgeable and skilled legal writer who wished to provide Boswell with a watertight argument for Joseph Knight's freedom. Johnson demonstrated his more passionate commitment to the cause of anti-slavery in his subsequent inquiries to Boswell about the Court of Session's decision and in his joy at their affirmation of the illegality of slavery in Scotland (see *Letters*, 3: 42, 104). Notwithstanding, we need to consider why Johnson did not write more publicly and forcefully on the issue of slavery.

This is a real question for, as we have considered, the issue of colonial slavery was rising to public attention in the 1770s, particularly in the aftermath of the Somerset case. The issue of slavery went to the heart of Britain's changing national identity, particularly its emergent imperialism and capitalism, like no other. As pointed out by Sharp and other critics of slavery, it was contradictory for Britons to proclaim that they "never will be slaves" and yet enslave others.[20] This phrase from James Thomson's "Rule, Britannia!" was written in 1740 during the War of Jenkins's Ear, when the public had been whipped into patriotic fervor by the depredation of British slave vessels. Some authors were noticing the contradiction. In the words of the author of *An Essay concerning Slavery* (1746), "that the generous Free Briton, who knows the Value of Liberty, who prizes it above life . . . that he should be instrumental in depriving others of a Blessing he would not part with but with life . . . this doth surprise, grieve and torment me!"[21] What Granville Sharp called "ranting expressions in praise of liberty" in the American colonies also deeply angered Johnson.[22] As Johnson observed in *Idler* 11 (1758), "slavery is now no where more patiently endured, than in countries once inhabited by the zealots of liberty" (*Idler*, 37). Johnson's most resonant line against slavery appears near the end of his diatribe

[20] James Thomson and David Mallet, *Alfred: An Opera* (London: A. Millar, 1740), p. 20.
[21] Anon., *An Essay concerning Slavery* (London: Charles Corbett, 1746), p. 27.
[22] Granville Sharp, *A Representation of the Injustice and Dangerous Tendency of Tolerating Slavery* (London: Benjamin White and Robert Horsfield, 1769), p. 81.

against American rebellion in *Taxation no Tyranny* (1775): "how is it we hear the loudest yelps for liberty among the drivers of negroes?" (*PW*, 454). In fairness to Americans, many saw the same contradiction. These included the Quaker abolitionist Anthony Benezet and the admirable Benjamin Rush, a signer of the Declaration of Independence, who declared that he wished to erect a "TEMPLE OF AFRICAN LIBERTY IN AMERICA."[23]

Johnson was nonetheless keen-minded and detected a danger to his own political positions by wholeheartedly supporting the natural rights of humankind. Nowhere did Johnson more frequently refer to natural rights – as he does in statements about slavery in the *Life of Drake* – than in his dictation to Boswell about the Knight case. In his statements on rebellion in America, on the contrary, and in his attacks on rising British political radicalism, as in his pamphlet against John Wilkes, *The False Alarm* (1770), Johnson never refers to natural rights in a positive way. He knew that both Wilkes and American rebels relied heavily on the idea of natural rights in their claims against royal or parliamentary authority. In *The False Alarm*, Johnson referred instead "to the great law of social necessity ... All government supposes subjects, all authority implied obedience. To suppose in one the right to command what another has the right to refuse is absurd and contradictory" (*PW*, 325). In the Vinerian law lectures, Chambers denied that we have access to "eternal and archetypal law." Without the Christian revelation, the ancients could only determine that law should have a general tendency to the social good.[24] Chambers and Johnson agreed with Granville Sharp that the form of servitude practiced in Medieval England, villenage, was defunct and irrelevant to modern English law. The Vinerian lectures nonetheless ascribe the obsolescence of villenage not to the progress of reason but to the influence of Christianity and the refinement of social manners. The great good of a civil society was indeed "safety of *person* and *personal liberty*." Yet Chambers and Johnson had little to say about personal liberty beyond the sanctity of *habeas corpus*, the main protection against unauthorized physical seizure.[25] As Johnson told Boswell in 1769, "The *habeas corpus* is the single advantage which our government has over that of other countries" (*Life*, 2: 73). *Habeas corpus* was indeed the legislation pivotal to Sharp's case on behalf of Lewis and Somerset, finally obliging Mansfield

---

[23] Benjamin Rush, *An Address to the Inhabitants of the British Settlements in America* (Philadelphia: John Dunlap, 1773), p. 6.
[24] Sir Robert Chambers, *A Course of Lectures on the English Law 1767–1773*, ed. Thomas M. Curley, 2 vols. (Madison: University of Wisconsin Press, 1986), 1: 84–5.
[25] Chambers, *A Course of Lectures* 2: 102, 6–7, 14.

to rule that the right to personal freedom could not be denied even a former slave. Yet Johnson nowhere suggested during this period of Wilkite disruption and American rebellion that the natural right to personal liberty could be extended further to justify defying the authority of the crown, making seditious statements, or refusing to pay taxes without parliamentary representation.

This then was Johnson's dilemma in the period of the Somerset and the Knight cases, widely publicized events that first put colonial slavery and the slave trade on trial. On the one hand, he despised slavery and ardently supported the rights of all people to resist subjugation by European colonizers, whom he generally portrayed as unauthorized invaders motivated solely by the lust for power and money. Jamaica, he wrote in *An Introduction to the Political State of Great-Britain* (1756), "continues to this day a place of great wealth and great wickedness, a den of tyrants, and a dungeon of slaves" (*PW*, 137). On the other hand, by the 1770s Johnson was preoccupied by the use of natural rights to justify dissent that he considered disruptive and seditious. It was indeed possible for writers of this time to hold conservative or moderate opinions on other social or political questions and yet oppose slavery with great conviction. John Wesley, for example, was a man whom Johnson liked and respected. Despite his controversial leadership of the Methodist movement, Wesley never left the Church of England and was understood as a Tory on most issues. In 1774, Wesley nonetheless declared that "I absolutely deny all Slave-holding to be consistent with any degree of even natural Justice."[26] Johnson would have sympathized with Wesley's belief that slavery was contrary to the teachings of Christianity. Given Johnson's abhorrence of the general behavior of colonizers, he would also have agreed that it was better that the Caribbean islands be "sunk in the depths of the sea"[27] rather than be cultivated by slaves. Nonetheless, Johnson's dictation to Boswell on the Knight case suggests that he wished to keep his objections to slavery confined to a fairly narrow legal compass, a behind-the-scenes advocacy rather than a public stand. Other opponents to the slave trade were indeed extending their agitation for rights to other issues. Granville Sharp also wrote on behalf of a widened political franchise. He approached Johnson for support for his campaign against the impressment of sailors, a major radical cause, but evidently found little sympathy.[28]

---

[26] John Wesley, *Thoughts Concerning Slavery* (London: R. Hawes, 1774), p. 17.
[27] Wesley, *Thoughts Concerning Slavery*, p. 20.
[28] See Edward Charles Lascelles, *Granville Sharp and the Freedom of Slaves in England* (Oxford: Oxford University Press, 1928), p. 92.

Johnson may also have believed, like many opponents to slavery before the 1780s, that this was a futile cause. As he observed in his introduction to Newbery's *The World Displayed*, "Interest and pride will harden the heart, and it is vain to dispute against avarice and power" (*Demand*, 442). The investors in the slave trade and colonial plantations wielded a powerful influence in Parliament. George III showed no inclination to challenge their practices. Notwithstanding, skeptics about the possibility of abolishing the slave trade, and eventually colonial slavery, turned out to be wrong. One possible fruit of the final loss of the American colonies in September 1783, when Britain officially ended the war, was that the nation no longer needed to protect its financial stakes in American colonial plantations. Only the Caribbean islands were left. Beginning in the year of Johnson's death with James Ramsay's *Essay on the Treatment and Conversion of African Slaves in the British Sugar Colonies* (1784), abolitionism picked up as a broad public cause, leading to petitions that amassed hundreds of thousands of signatures and a popular boycott of sugar. Even in this relatively undemocratic nation, public pressure finally prevailed, though it took until 1807 for Parliament to finally abolish the slave trade.

One can only believe that Johnson, if he had lived longer, would have ardently supported this cause and even written publicly on its behalf. Many leading abolitionists, like Wilberforce and More, had no interest in supporting other kinds of "liberty." Even Edmund Burke, who had dithered about improving the conditions of slaves, finally backed Wilberforce's bill for abolition, though with abiding doubts about its practicality.[29] There can be no doubt of Johnson's personal and emotional commitment to antislavery, as well as his disinterest in new "scientific" theories promoting a hierarchy of "races." He was an unreformed and unwavering believer in the common humanity and common rights of all people, whatever their origin or color. His failure to write more publicly on slavery in the 1770s is regrettable, for he was still highly active and influential as a writer. Here was an issue of fundamental importance that had caught the public's attention like never before. He was nonetheless preoccupied by other claims to "rights" that he regarded as specious and contrary to social order. Ironically, it was left to Boswell, a defender of the slave trade, to hand down the fullest record of Johnson's hatred of slavery and belief in the equality of all human beings.

---

[29] See Peter James Marshall, *Edmund Burke and the British Empire in the West Indies: Wealth, Power and Slavery* (Oxford: Oxford University Press, 2019), pp. 202–22.

CHAPTER 9

Johnson's Politics

Clement Hawes

We know, or think we know, that Samuel Johnson – in terms of domestic British politics – adhered to the Tory side of things. That he long detested the Whigs and their ministers, who held exclusive power from 1715 to 1760, seems self-evident. His remarks to others in his close circle make clear his frequent outbursts of curmudgeonly wit against the Whigs. That these performances are sometimes playful – the stylized enactment of an attitude – raises, as one comes to understand Johnson's provocative conversation, the crucial matter of tone. "The first Whig," Johnson quipped to Boswell in 1778, "was the Devil" (*Life*, 3: 326). This amusing pedigree is delivered with a smile at his own excess. But how should we specify his seriously considered political commitments? Did his views flow from commitments to the standard Tory causes – that is, to the monarch over parliament, to the Anglican Church over every rival body of Protestant worshippers, and to the power of great landlords? Was Johnson a settled conservative, publicly occupying a position on the right side of the British political spectrum? Might he have been a Jacobite?

Even at first glance, "Tory" seems an ill-fitting label to affix to Johnson's body of writings. A strong case has been made for a Johnson who held and voiced a great many forward-looking opinions: opposition to debtor's prison, for example, and to the death penalty, and to the abuse of French prisoners of war. In opposing slavery as such, he anticipates by several decades the founding in 1787 of the Society for the Purpose of Effecting the Abolition of the Slave Trade. In noting that "No man is by nature the property of another" (*Life*, 3: 203) – in a legal brief drafted on the situation of an escaped slave, Joseph Knight – Johnson gives the lie to any rationale for intergenerational slavery or racist "Black Codes." He refers to Jamaica, in "An Introduction to the Political State of Great Britain" (1756), as "a place of great wealth, and dreadful wickedness, a den of tyrants, and a dungeon of slaves" (*PW*, 137). He opposed the government's licensing of the stage under Prime Minister Walpole. He expresses consistent awareness of the terrible experience of the poor. Johnson expresses constant opposition to the abuses of the powerful, from exploitative and bullying landlords in the countryside to overbearing parents. In two consecutive essays in *The Rambler* (numbers 170 and 171), Johnson dares to write in the first-person voice of a female sex worker, "Misella," whose calculated seduction by a wealthy older cousin has relegated her to the streets. All this far exceeds the label of "Tory." But to stop at this point would be still to miss Samuel Johnson's greatest political contribution.

We see the full force of Johnson's intellect in his acts of political reframing. The most substantial issues of Johnson's day would involve the British nation, at war with France, and the expansion of the British empire. And it is indeed at the scale of empire that Johnson would make his most telling political interventions. No other eighteenth-century British intellectual questions the *Great* in Great Britain with anything like Johnson's acuity and force. Later mocked as "Little Englandism," Johnson's stance represents a critical and penetrating perspective on an expansionist Britain. But it is *how* Johnson achieves this perspective that reveals the most about his revisionary mode of political thought.

The very meaning of a "national" affair changes when it is circumscribed as an imperial event. This power of contextualizing reveals a key link between Johnson's provocative conversation and his even more penetrating written words: his persistent intellectual habit of *reframing*. He would have known Plutarch's story of Alexander's cutting of the Gordian knot – a beautiful example of reframing a problem – and he is often most acute when he changes the commonplace boundaries of a topic. Sometimes those boundaries, as the charged association between commerce and slavery suggests, indicate where moral decency has been hideously warped by the motive of profit. And sometimes those boundaries, as such conceptual rubrics as *nation* and *empire* suggest, can be literal and geographical. Our attempt to comprehend Johnson's politics must take more fully into account his radical and persistent opposition to British imperial aggression. Although Johnson seldom misses an opportunity to bash the Whigs, he often achieves the most political cogency and power by reframing domestic politics altogether.

The limitations of labels derived from domestic politics can be seen in Johnson's sympathy for Scots Highlanders. This sympathy has led a few historians to speculate that he was a closet Jacobite, still supporting the long-dethroned Stuart family. His published respect for the Jacobite Flora Macdonald after his trip with Boswell to the Isle of Skye (1773) is evident in the description of her as "a name that will be mentioned in history, and if courage and fidelity be virtues, mentioned with honour" (*Journey*, 67). For Johnson, however, this regard had more to do with Macdonald's honor and bravery than with a belated political allegiance to the Stuart dynasty. He was well aware, moreover, that the impoverished Celtic Highlands had experienced a mode of internal colonialism that involved aggression not only by England but by lowland Scots as well. There is an anti-colonial subtext to Johnson's sympathies for the Highlands, now tapped as a source of recruits for the British army. Johnson tunes in to the humiliating deprivation of their traditional dress:

> Their pride has been crushed by the heavy hand of a vindictive conqueror, whose severities have been followed by laws, which, though they cannot be called cruel, have produced much discontent, because they operate upon the surface of life, and make every eye bear witness to subjection. To be compelled to a new dress has always been found painful. (*Journey*, 89)

British military domination had yielded mostly alienation rather than gradual absorption into Hanoverian Britishness. In starkly reframing this situation in terms of conquest, Johnson reveals the bitter dynamics of being ruled from without.

Johnson's reframing of the Highlanders as victims of internal colonialism illustrates his compelling and habitual reworking of conventionally national perspectives. Did this flow from Jacobite loyalties? The question of Jacobitism is, at best, one attempt to grapple with Johnson's obvious distance from eighteenth-century political norms. Had he been a Jacobite, that allegiance would have been illegal, and so unsayable directly, and so closeted, and so impossible to ever verify. Jacobitism could only be expressed by way of coded hints, and detecting it now requires a hermeneutics of hypervigilant suspicion. Scanning for clues can be a risky approach: one does not wish to succumb to critical paranoia. After the Battle of Culloden (1746) and after the so-called Highland Clearances had gotten underway (1750), Jacobitism was a dead letter. The Battle of Culloden, the last gasp of Jacobite resistance, was the final dynastic war in British history. Invading from Scotland, the Jacobites got within sixty miles of London and were then chased back to the Highlands. The Clearances were a mode of ethnic cleansing, as the brutal euphemism has it; and George II and his uncle, William Augustus, the Duke of Cumberland, had decided to take down militarily both Highlands culture and its infrastructure. In devastating the Highlands, Cumberland – the so-called "Butcher of Culloden" – won the war and lost the peace. A decided crack in Hanoverian hegemony remained. However, Johnson's own considerable distance from Hanoverian politics – far from being the flailing of a Jacobite dinosaur – was not nostalgic. He was oriented to questions of British expansion. For Britain, future wars would be national or imperial rather than dynastic.

In recontextualizing so many forms of British domination by way of a sustained anti-imperial critique, Johnson straddles cosmopolitanism and a very qualified nationalism. Many enthusiasts for a modern vernacular literature in eighteenth-century Britain, such as the poet and playwright James Thomson (1700–48), manifest a vehement British cultural nationalism. Thomson is a sterling example of Whig culture and its triumphalist historiography. He was very well known for *The Seasons* (1730), a long descriptive poem, and also for "Rule, Britannia!," the bellicose anthem that exhorts the British navy to "rule the waves." That Thomson penned a long poem celebrating the progress of "liberty" again exemplifies his eager alignment of muse and nation. Here are the first seven lines from Part V of "Liberty," where the speaker is Liberty personified:

> HERE interposing, as the GODDESS paus'd, –
> Oh blest BRITANNIA! in THY Presence blest,
> THOU Guardian of Mankind! whence spring, alone,
> All human Grandeur, Happiness and Fame:
> For Toil, by THEE protected, feels no Pain;
> The poor Man's Lot with Milk and Honey flows;
> And, gilded with Thy Rays, even Death looks gay.[1]

In his *Life of Thomson* (1780), in the *Lives of the Poets*, Johnson makes the following comment about this poem, for which his enthusiasm is notably tepid:

> At this time a long course of opposition to Sir Robert Walpole had filled the nation with clamours for liberty, of which no man felt the want, and with care for liberty, which was not in danger. Thomson, in his travels on the continent, found or fancied so many evils arising from the tyranny of other governments, that he resolved to write a very long poem, in five parts, upon Liberty. (*Lives*, 3: 1283)

Thomson's poem is shadowboxing with a Catholic and absolutist threat. The ostensible progress of liberty exemplifies what Herbert Butterfield in 1931 termed "The Whig interpretation of history."[2] The mythic march of progress in Thomson's poem, as liberty unfolds across the ages to reach

---

[1] James Thomson, *The Prospect: Being the Fifth Part of Liberty. A Poem* (London: A. Millar, 1736), ll. 1–7.
[2] As per his influential book, *The Whig Interpretation of History* (London: G. Bell, 1931).

more and more British people, finds in the past a logic of improvement in the political life of the nation. This is teleological history with a vengeance – it is quite precisely an invented tradition – and the rising trajectory of history validates the present British nation as such. In "The Bravery of the English Common Soldiers" (1760), Johnson offers a contrarian view: "Liberty is, to the lowest rank of every nation, little more than the choice of working or starving; and this choice is, I suppose, equally allowed in every country" (*PW*, 283). So much for the unique blessings of English liberty! And so much, likewise, for the notion that Johnson's critiques emerge from the monarchist right.

In eighteenth-century Britain, the other powerful camp from which Johnson might theoretically have emerged is cosmopolitanism. Overt cosmopolitans, such as Lady Mary Wortley Montagu (1689–1762), in her *Turkish Embassy Letters* (written 1717, published 1763), however, are unapologetic elitists who – while bonding easily and comfortably with foreign elites – regard local cultures as beneath their notice. Johnson adds a new and snobbery-free chapter to cosmopolitan traditions. He sustains a delicate balance between respect for the local and for the variegated greater world.

Rather than choose between cosmopolitanism and vernacular accessibility, Johnson calibrates his political choices to embrace both. His difference from Thomson is telling. Thomson's full-throated cultural nationalism was commonplace by the later eighteenth century, and some intellectuals went to the length of promoting various peasant poets as homegrown, unschooled alternatives to the classical tradition. In such a moment, Johnson would thus take considerable fire for his calculated irreverence in his edition of and critical preface to such a major luminary as Shakespeare. Other nations had produced equally great authors – so Johnson thought – not least Cervantes, whose influence is ubiquitous in seventeenth- and eighteenth-century English writing. This is not a Tory refusal of democracy, but a repudiation of national chauvinism. Over and over again, a considered rejection of literary nationalism shapes Johnson's deliberate literary provocations. His analysis of Spanish influences upon English poets such as Samuel Butler (1613–80), whose mock-heroic *Hudibras* (1674–8) draws on *Don Quixote*, pointedly refuses any reification of national culture.

Perhaps the best example of Johnson's way of reframing domestic politics can be found in his principled opposition to the Seven Years War, the results of which would give Britain access to its North American settlements with negligible opposition from France. The Seven

Years War was fought between 1756 and 1763; the conflict, involving five continents, was arguably the first *world* war. Johnson's most famous intervention in the Seven Years War has to do with the battle of Quebec in 1759. Published in November of that year, *Idler* 81 assumes the point of view of a Native American chief soberly assessing the regularity and order of enemy British troops. In this speech, as throughout his *oeuvre*, Johnson recognizes indigenous claims to the land, rightly noting that disadvantageous treaties could have been achieved only through fraud or force. "[T]here was a time when our ancestors were absolute lords of the woods, the meadows and the lakes," the chief begins, but then "a new race of men entered our country from the great ocean. . . . Those invaders ranged over the continent, slaughtering in their rage those that resisted, and those that submitted, in their mirth" (*Idler*, 252, 253). The results for survivors were horrific:

> Of those that remained, some were buried in caverns, and condemned to dig metals for their masters; some were employed in tilling the ground, of which foreign tyrants devour the produce; and when the sword and the mines have destroyed the natives, they supply their place by human beings of another colour, brought from some distant country to perish here under toil and torture. (*Idler*, 253)

Johnson's awareness of European racism – and of the policy of using Black slaves in the new world where they would be isolated by their skin color – adds a characteristic range to his anti-imperial intervention. "Mines and caverns" might remind one of, say, conditions at the Bolivian silver mine at Mt. Potosi, but in fact the French enslavement of Sioux and other Native Americans in the Great Lakes region also involved slavery in the iron mines of modern-day Minnesota. While some Native Americans prospered by way of the fur trade around the Great Lakes, others – including those around Quebec – were vulnerable to being absorbed into slavery. Both the French and the English threatened the native inhabitants of North America.

Johnson likewise reframes the context of negotiations with Native Americans. For him, no legitimate treaty could be negotiated between indigenes and much better-armed invaders – plundering invaders who, in any case, would almost invariably negotiate in bad faith. Here again is the ventriloquized voice of his "petty chief":

> What reward can induce the possessor of a country to admit a stranger more powerful than himself? Fraud or terror must operate in such contracts; either they promised protection which they never have afforded, or

instruction which they never imparted . . . .. Their treaties are only to deceive, and their traffick only to defraud us. (*Idler*, 253)

That the French had been at least slightly more benign in certain ways does not escape Johnson's notice: English racism – which meant, for example, avoiding intermarriage with Indians, even those who were allies – might not only be oppressive: it could be self-defeating.

Johnson was quite willing to reframe anti-colonial violence as legitimate resistance. "But the time," says the Native American chief, "perhaps is now approaching when the pride of usurpation shall be crushed, and the cruelties of invasion shall be revenged." Johnson's evident endorsement here of "vengeance" is extremely rare in his *oeuvre*, and this appearance marks the special intensity of his anti-colonial response. His chief looks forward to the mutual destruction of the French and British forces:

> The sons of rapacity have now drawn their swords upon each other, and referred their claims to the decision of war; let us look unconcerned upon the slaughter, and remember that the death of every European delivers the country from a tyrant and a robber; for what is the claim of either nation, but the claim of the vulture to the leveret, of the tiger to the faun? (*Idler*, 254)

The charged language here – "a tyrant and a robber" – clearly defines the vast political crime underway by both European parties. The conclusion is breathtaking:

> Let them then continue to dispute their title to regions which they cannot people, to purchase by danger and blood the empty dignity of dominion over mountains which they will never climb, and rivers which they will never pass. Let us endeavour, in the mean time, to learn their discipline, and to forge their weapons; and when they shall be weakened with mutual slaughter, let us rush down upon them, force their remains to take shelter in their ships, and reign once more in our native country. (*Idler*, 254)

Perhaps in *The Wretched of the Earth* (1961), Frantz Fanon was secretly channeling Samuel Johnson and his anti-colonial ethics of self-defense. Boswell tells us about Johnson's famous toast at Oxford, "Here's to the next insurrection of the Negroes in the West Indies" (*Life*, 3: 200). Such a toast to anti-slavery violence bespeaks Johnson's capacity for authentic-ally radical views. To be sure, unlike Fanon, he did not advocate native or anti-slavery violence as a psychological means of recovering self-respect. Yet Johnson genuinely respected native sovereignty over traditionally used and occupied lands. This is to say that he disputed the "improvement" rationale used in the wake of John Locke's *Second Treatise on Government*

(1689) to seize uncultivated land in Ireland and North America. Johnson's perspective allows him to defamiliarize and reframe, quite radically, the supposed logic of colonial conflicts. Perhaps we have only begun to explore the varieties of cultural company that Samuel Johnson can keep, the constellations in which he can figure as a luminous critic of imperial practices and apologetics.

There may be some readers for whom a narrative of native victimization itself somehow smacks of a colonial trope. Native Americans in the Great Lakes region were doing well throughout the seventeenth and into the early eighteenth centuries. Indigenous people were trading with the French and benefiting from the thriving trade in beaver skins. With the Treaty of Paris (1763), Britain agreed to curtail white settlement west of the Appalachians, a promise they were unable or unwilling to keep. Pontiac, who had unified numerous Great Lakes tribes, resisted white settlers for several years after the Seven Years War – known in colonial America as the "French and Indian War" – was over. But the dynamics of continuous colonial settlement would bear out both Pontiac's resistance and Johnson's condemnations of American colonial "robbers" – a label simultaneously invoking their theft of indigenous land and their personal origins, in many cases, as convicted thieves and highwaymen who had been transported from the old to the new world. By way of transportation, England was exporting its social problems, and these colonial settlers – by way of constant westward expansion – would unloose a cascade of changes on the indigenous way of life.

A further example of Johnson's interest in reframing the domestic can be seen in an essay published in the *Universal Chronicle* on September 9, 1758, that explores the destructiveness of war in the guise of an animal fable.[3] With macabre wit, Johnson allows one to overhear a mother vulture teaching her young about the "strange ferocity" in people "which I have never observed in any other being." Since "man ... is the only beast who kills that which he does not devour," he becomes a "benefactor" to vultures, who feed off human carcasses. Sardonically, Johnson has the mother vulture sum up: "men are by some unaccountable power driven one against another, till they lose their motion, that vultures may be fed" (*Idler*, 319, 320). Thus Johnson obliquely comments on the burden of grief for casualties from abroad, the cost of the macro-politics of empire.

---

[3] This essay was originally published as *Idler* 22 in the *Universal Chronicle* but was omitted when the 103 individual *Idler* essays were published as a collection (1761), "probably," as the Yale editors suggest, "because of its misanthropic tone"; *Idler*, 317 n1.

Vultures who are eagerly watching – collapsing the human enterprise of war into a convenient slaughterhouse for carrion-eating birds – are an antidote to a complicit public language that dwells on sacrifice. Johnson's absurdism reframes resignation to mass death with laughter at human stupidity. His essay exemplifies his ability to find an anti-war angle in the midst of a grotesque war-fever.

More sharp-edged reframing can be seen in Johnson's famous resistance to the folkloric nationalism that emerged in mid-eighteenth-century Britain. This stance has long been positioned as *aesthetically* conservative. From Bishop Percy's *Reliques of Ancient English Poetry* in 1765 to Wordsworth and Coleridge's *Lyrical Ballads* in 1798, a ballad revival would unfold both new literary possibilities and new aesthetic limitations. It takes a concerted effort now to question a teleological literary history – to refuse to see this entire development, in retrospect, as artistically inevitable. Johnson, however, sensed the potentially dangerous falsification of history in such undertakings as the eighteenth-century ballad-collecting project. As he possibly intuited, a sense of *the people's* oral culture as more or less timeless leads soon enough to the logic we now identify as racial essentialism. Bishop Percy's famous collection of ballads planted a seed from which the fostering of a national culture would become intertwined with emerging categories of race. Percy has indeed been accused of racializing, anachronistically, the entire medieval period. The point, however, is not that the ballads are racist *per se*, but that Percy's presentation of them through the category of "Anglo-Saxon" is fraught. While the English never embraced the *Volk* in the terrifying mode of twentieth-century German fascism, they did incorporate a certain populism into the racial ideologies of British imperialism – an ethno-national sense of the natural sway of one "people" over others putatively lower on the ladder of progress. Johnson resists this possibility almost in advance – not merely as a conservative aesthetic reflex but also out of wariness toward the political reification of large-scale identities. This has sometimes been seen as a retrograde aesthetic obstructionism, but it is in fact a well-considered resistance to an emerging romantic nationalism. If we think of *topoi* and ballads as a sort of literary commons, Johnson shows us what to avoid as we tend them.

Johnson's intervention in the Ossian affair is of a similar nature. In 1762, James Macpherson published what he claimed was the translations from a third-century poet from the Highlands named "Ossian." Thus appeared the epic poem *Fingal*, which satisfied the hunger for a homegrown bard not trained in the classics: that is, a *British* Homer. Macpherson's "translations" were fabrications; he had no original epic poem in Scots Gaelic.

Macpherson refused any public access to his so-called originals, and Johnson, among others, correctly smelled fraud.[4] Macpherson's "Ossian" fraud cannot now be defended without special pleading that he is somehow "representing" the Gaelic people and the Gaelic language. Such a defense requires averting one's gaze from Macpherson's plundering of Irish antiquities, all in the name of a Scots-cum-British nationalism, and this is not even to mention his fraudulence and lying. Johnson would never have condoned such a falsehood – the historian Hugh Trevor-Roper's original example of an invented tradition – and both Macpherson and his poetry are symptoms of empire.

Johnson's satirical attacks on this developing romantic nationalism are both amusing and telling. His improvised burlesque of a ballad stanza, called by editors "I Put My Hat upon My Head," mocks the potential for banality and dumbing down in modern literary ballad topics:

> I put my hat upon my head
> And walk'd into the Strand,
> And there I met another man
> Who's hat was in his hand.

(*Poems*, 269)

This is brilliantly stupefying. The target for such an impromptu sally is the aesthetics of talking down to "the people." However, Johnson's "Upon the Death of Dr. Robert Levet" (1782) – as moving a poem in ballad form as one could ever find – touches us precisely because Johnson does not pretend that there is no social or educational distance between him and his rough-hewn friend and housemate, Dr. Robert Levet. Johnson's cosmopolitanism is not elitist; his democratizing spirit is not populist.

What, then, does Johnson's cosmopolitan nationalism look like? Given that his first book was a translation of the Jesuit Father Jerome Lobo's *A Voyage to Abyssinia* (1735), Johnson needed to introduce this work to a British and Protestant audience. In the preface, he expresses a universalism that constitutes his lifelong credo. The reader will "discover," Johnson writes, "what will always be discover'd by a diligent and impartial enquirer, that wherever human nature is to be found, there is a mixture of vice and virtue, a contest of passion and reason, and that the Creator doth not appear partial in his distributions, but has balanced in most countries their particular inconveniences by particular favours"

---

[4] See Clement Hawes, *The British Eighteenth Century and Global Critique* (New York: Palgrave, 2005), pp. 29–66.

(*Voyage*, 3–4). Although Johnson's own translation was from a French text, Lobo was Portuguese and thus at least indirectly associated with the Inquisition. Yet Johnson thought highly enough of Lobo's perspective to risk an anti-Catholic blowback. He inoculates himself against this, however, with a brisk paragraph attacking the Church – which, though often unreasonable, could also produce a cosmopolitan figure such as Lobo, as Johnson's choice to translate implies.

Given his anti-colonial politics, how did Johnson respond to the claims of the British Enlightenment? What reframing goes on, for Johnson, as regards a new emphasis on the faculty of reason? Both in writings and in conversation he exploited the relative openness to debate – even between aristocrats and bourgeois commoners – for which the Enlightenment remains celebrated. He contributed through his writings to the strenuous cultivation of a more informed and more engaged public. He responded to the Enlightenment's emphasis on rationality with his customary complexity – he played around with a chemistry set, for example, and he tried to make accurate empirical measurements during his journey to the Hebrides. Even so, his deeply rooted skepticism tended to check any overweening, overly general claims to progress.

Although Johnson certainly cannot be pitted against the Enlightenment, he did combat its most pernicious myth, which would fully emerge only in the nineteenth century. This is the claim to a unique "Western" rationality, which would be traced back to classical Greece. In the hands of Hegel and his lesser imitators, this genealogy would eventually become no less than a racist framing – and thus a racist rewriting – of world history, from the "Greek miracle" to industrializing Europe.[5] A rationality that is practical, speculative, and free of despotism, however, was not and never will be the special property of any continent or population. One of Johnson's most compelling approaches to the issue of rationality can be found in *Rasselas*, a novella that pointedly emphasizes the rationality of Africans, published in the year (1759) that Britain would get the upper hand in the Seven Years War. As a novella, *Rasselas* is highly unusual in foregrounding not a marriage plot but, rather, friendship and sibling affection. Its main characters are Africans: Coptic Christians who do not owe their Christianity to Europe's colonial impact on Africa. These characters, Rasselas, Imlac, Nekayah, and Pekuah, in their search for the right way to live, rationally explore a great range of topics related to the conduct of life. This pointed emphasis on African rationality, identifying the characters as worthy of respect and

[5] See Hawes, *Global Critique*, pp. 67–92.

engagement, inevitably offended subsequent British imperialists because it went against the currents of imperial expansion and its ideological justification. *Rasselas* remained a thorn in the side of Thomas Babington Macaulay, an early nineteenth-century senior civil servant in British India, and the single most influential writer of Whiggish history. In a notorious essay on Johnson, Macaulay mobilized every available trope to render Johnson as obsolete and backward-looking.[6] Similarly, the early twentieth-century historian of the British Empire, Edward Salmon, opined that "One does not look to the universal wisdom of Dr. Johnson for much of note on matters of empire."[7] Times change, however, and now, at this juncture, about seventy years after decolonization took hold, we can, after all, look to Johnson for wisdom in matters of empire, which includes the knowledge that all empires are temporary and will pass. Johnson characteristically regards any sense of permanence or invulnerability, whether cultural or political, as an illusion. We should also note that imperial ideology, to the extent that it provoked powerful opposition, was not always unchallenged. Like an embarrassing episode from one's rebellious adolescence, Johnson reminds us that a British sense of entitlement to rule vast swathes of the globe was not forever present – was not, so to speak, *natural.*

Johnson's *oeuvre* demonstrates the contingency of imperial ideology, and he may be said to have reframed the idea of patriotism. He saw direct criticism as indispensable to any worthwhile understanding of love for one's country. "Patriotism," Johnson quipped to Boswell, "is the last refuge of a scoundrel" (*Life*, 2: 348). Perhaps this famous remark in 1775 applies, in the first instance, only to William Pitt the Elder and his brand of self-described patriots. Boswell rather painfully belabors the point that Johnson was not speaking against love of one's country as such – an explanation that deflates the brilliance of the remark, which reminds us that Johnson had little patience for sentiments of nationalism. Even if it amounts to a certain poetic license, we are authorized by Johnson's whole body of writing to give this remark its full resonance. How many wretched political scoundrels have resorted to wrapping themselves in their national flags? Johnson doubtless regarded actual patriotism as rare – and doubtless it is.

Johnson's refusal to frame Milton, as he refuses to frame Shakespeare, in grand nationalistic terms, demonstrates his consistent critical attention to such matters. His most controversial biography, the *Life of Milton* (1779),

---

[6] Thomas Babington Macaulay, "Review of John Wilson Croker's Edition of Boswell's *Life of Johnson,*" *Edinburgh Review*, 54 (1831): 1–38.
[7] Edward Salmon, *The British Empire*, ed. Hugh Gunn, 12 vols. (London: W. Collins, 1924), 2: 83.

does indeed reflect Johnson's prickly distaste for the poet's Cromwellian politics. Johnson terms Milton, a defender of the 1649 regicide committed against Charles I, a "surly republican" and observes of *Paradise Lost* that "none ever wished it longer" (*Lives*, 1: 171, 195). But his various reservations about Milton's republicanism and about *Lycidas* (pastoral poetry is "easy, vulgar, and therefore disgusting"; *Lives*, 1: 176) also reiterate his refusal to create a national pantheon of untouchable and fossilized authorial icons. Moreover, he is generous in his appraisal of *Paradise Lost*, affirming it as one of the two greatest productions of the human mind. His funniest jab at Milton – calling the theologically independent poet "a sect of one" – comes after we learn that Milton "grew old without any visible worship" (*Lives*, 1: 107). A "sect of one" is iconoclastic because it encapsulates Milton's sense of himself as entirely self-originating. Milton, as Johnson clearly sees, had a sense of his own merit – an ego – to match his originality, and yet after all he gives Milton full credit for his hard-earned originality. Although Johnson makes visible his own politics in this critical biography, that politics is not after all knee-jerk Toryism. The *Life of Milton* is a multilayered and sometimes funny account of an unquestionably great author; and in it, Johnson continues his pattern of recasting British poetic demigods as imperfect and fallible creators. He shows us how to tend both the canon and the commons.

In conclusion, Johnson benefits from a comparison with the great American Enlightenment figure, Thomas Jefferson. The Eurocentrism sometimes attributed to Jefferson cannot be used to castigate Johnson, who responds more deeply, more critically, and more honestly than Jefferson to the contradiction between racism and universalism. In response to Jefferson, revolutionary America's most eloquent intellectual, Johnson asks in "Taxation No Tyranny" (1775), "how is it that we hear the loudest yelps for liberty from the drivers of Negroes" (*PW*, 454), an irony that has remained alive to this day. In comparison to Johnson's alert and unflinching political and historiographical criticism, Jefferson's would-be universal declaration that all men are created equal looks decidedly suspect and exclusionary, especially in the light of the history of the last 200 years.

How should we think of Johnson and abolition, for which he helped prepare the ground? Nineteenth-century abolition was the culmination of several decades of reformist struggle. This struggle was led in parliament by William Wilberforce (1759–1833), a leading member of the evangelical "Clapham Sect." First the British traffic in slaves was abolished (1807) and then slavery itself was abolished throughout the colonies (1833), a great victory – yet the British would largely replace the unpaid labor of African slaves in the colonies with the exploited labor of indentured laborers from India. The empire would thrive, meanwhile, on its newly achieved anti-slavery virtue, now folded into a rejuvenated imperial ideology. Wilberforce himself would go on to support "commerce, Christianity, and civilization" – the latter term marking his support for imperial expansion. Johnson benefits from this comparison as well. He was far more prescient in opposing slavery without truckling to imperial imperatives.

Johnson demonstrates the necessity of immanent critique, arising from within the terms of the object under consideration. His *oeuvre* poses questions about traditions and collective identity that remain highly pertinent. The invention and reinvention of traditions – the establishment and revision of canons in the name of one political entity or another – cannot easily be disentangled from social antagonisms, from demarcating an *us* from a *them*. Johnson is unique in the intensity with which he insists that it is more important to look at ourselves critically than merely to celebrate our national cultures.

CHAPTER 10

Johnson's Poetry

John Richetti

In *The Life of Samuel Johnson* (1791), James Boswell relates an anecdote he had heard from David Garrick about Johnson and the recently-deceased (1732) Welsh violinist Charles Claudius ("Claudy") Philips (*Life*, 1: 148). Garrick had recited for Johnson an epitaph for Philips written by a Dr. Richard Wilkes in Wolverhampton, where Philips was buried:

> Exalted soul! whose harmony could please
> The love-sick virgin, and the gouty ease:
> Could jarring discord, like Amphion move
> To beauteous order and harmonious love;
> Rest here in peace, till angels bid thee rise,
> And meet thy blessed Saviour in the skies.

Boswell records that Johnson "shook his head at these common-place funereal lines" and said to Garrick, "I think, Davy, I can make a better." And after he stirred his tea for a while, says Boswell, "he almost extempore produced the following verses":

> Philips! whose touch harmonious could remove
> The pangs of guilty pow'r, and hapless love,
> Rest here, distrest by poverty no more,
> Find here that calm thou gav'st so oft before;
> Sleep undisturb'd within this peaceful shrine,
> Till angels wake thee with a note like thine.

(Poems, 68–69)

Johnson was a young man of thirty-two when he composed these lines, which were published in 1740 and, if he is to be believed, his customary poetic method was in later life extemporaneous in exactly this manner. Just as he composed this little poem mentally and exactly before he wrote it down, he claimed that he produced his other, more elaborate poems in much the same way. Johnson told a friend that he had composed the first seventy lines of *The Vanity of Human Wishes* in Hampstead, where his wife

135

was staying for her health: "The whole number was composed before I committed a single couplet to writing" (*Life*, 2: 15; *Poems*, 90–91).

But there are other revealing, more significant features of this charming epitaph that point to Johnson's characteristic poetic manner and favorite themes in his verses. For one thing, the pretentious and irrelevant mythological allusion in Wilkes's epitaph – the story of Amphion, a son of Zeus who by his magic built the walls surrounding Thebes – is discarded in favor of some imagined but plausible and appropriate moments, small and touching scenes from Philips's life as a musician. The epitaph evokes the soothing moral and psychological effects that Johnson imagines that Philips's music provides for his audiences, as well as Johnson's sympathy for the musician's poverty, assuaged by the escape from worldly cares and rest that he says death provides. There is a teasing mystery in Johnson's choice of the afflictions that Philips's music could "remove" – "guilty power and hapless love," two situations in strikingly odd contrast to each other that illustrate Johnson's taste for moral and psychological poetic compression that is sometimes difficult to understand.

Overall, this epitaph exemplifies Johnson's poetic commitment to moral and social realism and his dislike of fanciful fictions and commonplace classical allusions, as well as his aversion to high-flown, obscure, or melodramatic diction, attitudes that we can observe not only in Johnson's poetic works but also clearly and often polemically in his literary-critical writings. The image that closes the Philips epitaph is marked, as it were, as a pleasant and poetic fiction, patently imaginary but emotionally apt, completely unaffected and natural, with the angels playing not seraphic or heavenly tunes but a human note, as Johnson's final line announces and savors the symmetry, which is just like Philips's own music. He also wrote an epitaph for Hogarth, a revision of the one Garrick wrote at the request of the painter's widow:

> The hand of art here torpid lies
>   That traced th' essential form of grace,
> Here death has clos'd the curious eyes
>   That saw the manners in the face.
> If genius warm thee, reader, stay,
>   If merit touch thee, shed a tear,
> Be vice and dulness far away
>   Great Hogarth's honour'd dust is here.
>
> (*Poems*, 268)

The Johnsonian signature can, again, be seen in this epitaph; his praise is of the painter's ability to render precisely the real. Hogarth is a figure who lived in the world he represented and who presented actual people, an artist who had, the expression is precise, "curious eyes" and who in the opening line is identified as a hand that could in his paintings render human essentials.

In 1740, in fact, Johnson composed *An Essay on Epitaphs* that appeared in *The Gentleman's Magazine.* He treated the epitaph as a literary genre that had important moral force. "As honours are paid to the dead in order to incite others to the imitation of their excellencies, the principal Intention of *epitaphs* is to perpetuate the examples of virtue, that the tomb of a good man may supply the want of his presence, and veneration for his memory produce the same effect as the observation of his life" (*BW*, 497). He goes on to conclude that "The best subject for *epitaphs* is private virtue; virtue exerted in the same circumstances in which the bulk of mankind are placed, and which, therefore, may admit of many imitators" (503). The intense moral practicality in such thoughts is striking. For Johnson, epitaphs, like more elaborate poetic forms, are instruments for actual and effective personal moral improvement, and, I would add, are more effective for their brevity and pointed assertiveness.

Johnson wrote a poem on the death of a friend that is not an epitaph, but rather an elegy. "On the Death of Dr. Robert Levet" (1782) is his most intense short poem, mourning the death of a member of his odd household, an unlicensed medical practitioner who ministered to the poor. The poem articulates with restrained eloquence Johnson's moral and religious values, evoking in its opening lines daily life as full of toil and suffering. Boswell records that Johnson recited it for him in March of the year Levet died, "with an emotion which gave [it] full effect" (*Life*, 4: 165). The opening stanza is especially revealing and powerful, as the poem is a comment on human life in general and not just Levet's:

> Condemn'd to hope's delusive mine,
>   As on we toil from day to day,
> By sudden blasts, or slow decline,
>   Our social comforts drop away.

(*Poems*, 314, ll. 1–4)

The image of human beings condemned by delusive hope to incessant toil in a dark mine is a strikingly original metaphor for ordinary life, repeated in the fifth stanza as "misery's darkest caverns," as is the picture of inevitable, sudden or slow, decline as "social comforts" leave us. As someone in his early eighties as I write this essay, I can testify to the deep pathos of Johnson's words in this elegy from my own loss of friends and family members as "social comforts" have been taken away from me by death, "dropping away," as Johnson puts it with devastating neutrality that bespeaks intense pain.

But the second stanza lightens the gloom with a luminous evocation of Levet, whose transition to the grave is a triumphant passage we are instructed to witness (where "officious" means "eager to help"):

> Well tried through many a varying year,
>   See Levet to the grave descend;
> Officious, innocent, sincere,
>   Of ev'ry friendless name the friend.
> Yet still he fills affection's eye,
>   Obscurely wise, and coarsely kind;
> Nor, letter'd arrogance, deny
>   Thy praise to merit unrefin'd.

(ll. 5–12)

There is in "affection's eye" a nearly personal reference and a suggestion of tears. The image is more affecting and avoids bathos and sentimentality for being merely a suggestion.

Johnson's view of life and death is, of course, suffused with his intense Christian beliefs, which find articulation in the seventh stanza:

> His virtues walk'd their narrow round,
>   Nor made a pause, nor left a void;
> And sure th' Eternal Master found
>   The single talent well employ'd.

(ll. 25–28)

That is to say, unlike the servant in Jesus's parable (Matthew 25: 14–30), who buried the single talent (in the biblical story, a sum of money) he had been left with and was condemned by his master for not improving it or using it, Levet has used his "talent" (in the modern sense of an ability) for the good of others within his "narrow round," which is the world of the poor and the wretched. Such a milieu is vividly evoked in the fifth stanza, in which Levet's ministrations are evoked as vigorous but modest, heroically self-effacing but effective:

> When fainting nature call'd for aid,
>   And hov'ring death prepar'd the blow,
> His vig'rous remedy display'd
>   The power of art without the show.

(ll. 13–16)

Johnson also composed many brief poems for friends, verses inspired by personal relationships and daily interactions. Occasional, usually light and humorous, verse was congenial for Johnson, as it was for many others in the period when writing *vers de société* was a treasured social skill for private, intimate occasions cultivated by the educated middle and upper classes, as opposed to published writing by professional poets. Here is a partial but representative list of such poems by Johnson: "An Ode on a Lady Leaving Her Place of Abode; Almost Impromptu" (1731), "To Miss Hickman Playing on the Spinet" (1731), " To Miss Carpenter on Her Playing upon the Harpsichord in a Room Hung with Some Flower-Pieces of Her Own Painting" (1746), "On a Lady's Presenting a Sprig of Myrtle to a Gentleman" (1747), "To Mrs. Thrale, on Her Completing Her Thirty-Fifth Year" (1777), "On Seeing a Portrait of Mrs. Montagu" (1779), "A Short Song of Congratulation" (1780), "On Hearing Miss Thrale Deliberate about Her Hat" (1780). This last was directed at Hester Thrale's daughter, Hester Maria (Queeney), and despite its light touch it sounds a moral note about inevitable mortality:

> Wear the gown, and wear the hat,
>   Snatch thy pleasures while they last;
> Hadst thou nine lives like a cat,
>   Soon those nine lives would be past.

(Poems, 306)

Such occasional poems testify to Johnson's attention in his verse to the ordinary and the quotidian and even trivial matters of life as it is lived, seen fresh and with wit and good humor to be shared by others. Such private and intimate verse celebrates simple human intercourse and the joys of friendship and sociality. It also testifies to Johnson's keen sense of humor. Here is his quatrain on Colley Cibber, the actor and (very bad) poet who became the laureate in George II's reign, a king Johnson loathed:

> Augustus still survives in Maro's [Virgil's] strain,
> And Spenser's verse prolongs Eliza's reign;
> Great George's acts let tuneful Cibber sing;
> For nature form'd the poet for the king.

(Poems, 70)

Perhaps his most amusing occasional poem is "A Short Song of Congratulation" (1780), written about the young Sir John Lade when he came of age. Lade was the son of Mrs. Thrale's sister, whose husband had left their son a large estate.

Long-expected one and twenty
    Ling'ring year at last is flown,
Pomp and pleasure, pride and plenty
    Great Sir John, are all your own.
  . . .

Wealth, Sir John, was made to wander,
    Let it wander as it will;
See the jocky, see the pander,
    Bid them come, and take their fill.

When the bonny blade carouses,
    Pockets full, and spirits high,
What are acres? What are houses?
    Only dirt, or wet or dry.

If the guardian or the mother
    Tell the woes of willful waste,
Scorn their counsel and their pother,
    You can hang or drown at last.
                    (*Poems*, 307–08, ll.1–4, 17–28)

Johnson mixes morality with mordant irony, and the Yale editors note that he recited the poem "with great spirit" in November 1784 to Boswell, who thought it "a piece of exquisite satire, conveyed in a strain of pointed vivacity and humour, and in a manner of which no other instance is to be found in Johnson's writings" (*Poems*, 306). And Lade, as it turned out, did squander his inheritance.

Johnson's views on serious, professional poetry can be seen in especially clear and ample display in two of *The Lives of the Poets* (1779–81), Milton and Gray. Although he had little patience with Milton's anti-monarchical political loyalties (he called him "an acrimonious and surly republican"), Johnson paid unreserved tribute to his poetic powers, declaring of *Paradise Lost*, "considered with respect to design, [it] may claim the first place, and with respect to performance the second among the productions of the human mind." As Johnson observes in the last sentence of the Life, Milton's epic poem "is not the greatest of heroick poems, only because it is not the first" (*Lives*, I: 171, 182), coming after Homer's *Iliad* and Virgil's *Aeneid*. But Johnson's praise for *Paradise Lost* is also remarkable in its unpretentious irony: "the want of human interest is always felt," for "its perusal is a duty rather than a pleasure." We read the poem "for instruction, retire harassed and overburdened ... we desert our master, and seek for companions" (*Lives*, I: 196). That is to say, Miltonic sublimity is thrilling but irrelevant, too far from those basic human needs that poetry is meant to serve and that are the point of the friendly and affectionate interchanges of Johnson's own occasional verses.

However, Johnson's criticism of *Lycidas* is simple and direct, intensely and shockingly negative, since there is no sublimity nor any real instruction in it. Indeed, to a modern reader, Johnson's characterization of the poem is offensively harsh: "It is not to be considered as the effusion of real passion; for passion runs not after remote allusions and obscure opinions. Passion plucks no berries from the myrtle and ivy, nor calls upon Arethuse and Mincius, nor tells of rough 'satyrs' and 'fauns with cloven heel.' Where there is leisure for fiction, there is little grief" (1: 175–76). Johnson is deeply offended by the poem's conventional pastoral fiction, which he labels "easy, vulgar, and therefore disgusting" (1: 176). His logic in making this criticism is in one sense both rigorous and comically irrefutable, as he quotes Milton's lines that dwell on the shepherd's lives of the narrator and his deceased friend: "We know that they never drove a field, and that they had no flocks to batten; and though it be allowed that the representation may be allegorical, the true meaning is so uncertain and remote, that it is never sought, because it cannot be known when it is found" (1: 177).

The stern lesson Johnson offers here and elsewhere in his criticism of poetry is recurrent. For him, poetry must speak with clarity and thereby with force in unaffected language such as men and women actually use, and poetry must seek to depict and to explore recognizable human experience. Otherwise, he argues, poetry serves no moral or educational purpose; it is meaningless and irrelevant trifling with language and unworthy of the name of poetry, which for Johnson is a high and heroic moral and intellectual calling. He even offers in the *Life of Milton* a definition of poetry as "the art of uniting pleasure with truth by calling imagination to the help of reason" (*Lives*, 1: 182–83).

In his *Life of Gray*, Johnson is even harsher as he examines that poet's odes, where in a discussion of the "Ode on a Distant Prospect of Eton College," he refers to the following lines:

> Say, Father Thames, for thou hast seen
> Full many a sprightly race
> Disporting on thy margent green
> The paths of pleasure trace,
> Who foremost now delight to cleave
> With pliant arm thy glassy wave?
> The captive linnet which enthrall?
> What idle progeny succeed

> To chase the rolling circle's speed,
> Or urge the flying ball?

(ll. 21–29)

Johnson's irritated response to these lines ridicules their use of a familiar poetic convention, an address to a personified river. He calls the passage "useless and puerile," since "Father Thames has no better means of knowing than himself . . . . Gray thought his language more poetical as it was more remote from common use" (*Lives*, 3: 1464–65). Johnson insists, somewhat solemnly, that poetry in its representations must be morally and intellectually useful, and it must obey the norms and idioms of everyday life and shared perceptions of the world, avoiding the merely fanciful and decorative, offering the moral and intellectual substance that is for him its raison d'être.

Johnson's most severe criticism of Gray, however, comes in his discussions of two odes, *The Progress of Poetry* and *The Bard*, which are especially revealing. Gray offers a picture of what Johnson calls the "mythological birth of Shakespeare":

> Far from the sun and summer-gale,
> In thy green lap was Nature's Darling laid,
> What time, where lucid Avon stray'd,
> To Him the mighty Mother did unveil
> Her aweful face
>
> . . ..
>
> This pencil take (she said) whose colours clear
> Richly paint the vernal year.

(ll. 83–87, 89–90)

Johnson concludes from contemplating passages such as this that for Gray "the real effects of his poetical power are put out of sight by the pomp of machinery," that is, by the cumbersome and embarrassing fiction that Mother Nature revealed herself to the child, Shakespeare. "Where truth is sufficient to fill the mind, fiction is worse than useless; the counterfeit debases the genuine" (*Lives*, 3: 1467). Again, Johnson's terms reaffirm his strenuous commitment as critic and poet to the clarity and reality of simple and available truth and his disdain for the artifice of "machinery," which he dramatizes as a moral and epistemological disaster in its employment of an unnecessary and, for him, ludicrous fiction.

For Johnson, *The Bard* is even guiltier of such empty artifice. As Gray explains in a prefatory "advertisement," the poem is founded on a tradition that when the English king, Edward I, conquered

Wales, he ordered all the bards to be put to death. Thus, one of these bards is imagined in the poem as defying from atop a mountain crag the invading English army. And in the second stanza, the bard speaks:

> Weave the warp, and weave the woof,
> The winding-sheet of Edward's race.
> Give ample room, and verge enough
> The characters of hell to trace.
>
> (ll. 49–52)

Johnson's contempt for these incantatory but for him incoherent verses is savage. "The 'weaving' of the 'winding sheet' he borrowed, as he owns, from the northern bards; but their texture, however, was very properly the work of female powers .... Theft is always dangerous; Gray has made weavers of his slaughtered bards, by a fiction outrageous and incongruous" (*Lives*, 3: 1469).

Johnson sums up the failings of Gray's odes at the end of his critical biography: they are "marked by glittering accumulations of ungraceful ornaments; they strike rather than please; the images are magnified by affectation; the language is laboured into harshness .... His art and his struggle are too visible, and there is too little appearance of ease and nature" (*Lives*, 3: 1470). To sum up Johnson's own poetic values we might imagine the virtuous opposites of these faults: language that pleases and is not harsh; a verbal art that is not ostentatious or strenuously difficult, and that is as coherent and as clear as good prose. In fact, Johnson notes at the very end of the *Life of Gray* that his *Elegy in a Country Churchyard* possesses the qualities of the best poetry by pleasing "the common reader," by abounding "with images which find a mirrour in every mind, and with sentiments to which every bosom returns an echo" (*Lives*, 3: 1471). Johnson the critic consistently recommends that universalized human nature and common experiences are what poetry should seek to articulate; he emphatically rejects the intense singularity of an egocentric poetic "genius" like the Gray of the odes.

Johnson's first long poem, *London*, appeared in 1738, announced as "A Poem in Imitation of the Third Satire of Juvenal," a late first and early second-century Roman satirist noted for the sharp and even savage depictions of his contemporaries. Such imitation or recreation in English of classical, especially Roman, poetry was in the eighteenth century the central and defining project of many poets. Alexander Pope, for one, wrote a series of what he entitled "Imitations" of the Roman poet, Horace. The assumption behind such poems is that the writers of ancient Rome (and of Greece) are "classic," having set the standard for the highest poetic expression and thereby lasted over the centuries. Moreover, given their antiquity, they mark, as it were, the beginning of European literary culture; for aspiring poets, their writings in the English eighteenth century were strongly felt to offer readers an understanding of a natural, unchanging order stretching back to classical antiquity. For modern poets to imitate the works of these ancient authors, to adapt their subjects to contemporary English circumstances, was to render that same Nature and to dramatize its unchanging essence. And, of course, the secondary school and university curricula made the intensive study of these ancient writers the center of their pedagogy. A profoundly learned classical scholar, Johnson was steeped in the classical languages and literature, and he wrote many Latin poems and translations from Latin and Greek poets.

London is a poem that dramatizes Johnson's fidelity to his central critical position. As the Yale editors of his poems observe, his aim was "to be immediately clear to the average reader," and, as they point out, *London* was reprinted at least twenty-three times in Johnson's lifetime (*Poems*, xvi). The poem is an eloquent, if completely conventional, satire, an attack on urban life as dangerous and dirty, frustrating for honest ambition and innocent virtue. Such a view of the corruptions of life in the metropolis leads to an exaltation of the purity and peace of country life.

> For who would leave, unbrib'd, Hibernia's land,
> Or change the rocks of Scotland for the Strand?
> There none are swept by sudden fate away,
> But all whom hunger spares, with age decay:
> Here malice, rapine, accident conspire,
> And now a rabble rages, now a fire;
> Their ambush here relentless ruffians lay,
> And here the fell attorney prowls for prey;
>
> (*Poems* 48, ll. 9–15)

In the middle of the poem, there is a rousing and defiant suggestion, and a final line in this quatrain that sums up the young Johnson's deepest feelings:

> Quick let us rise, the happy seats explore,
> And bear oppression's insolence no more.
> This mournful truth is ev'ry where confess'd
> SLOW RISES WORTH, BY POVERTY DEPRESS'D:
>
> (56, ll. 174–77)

Johnson, later in life, no longer quite the resentful and struggling young writer, became the quintessential city dweller, loving what London offered. As he famously remarked to Boswell, "when a man is tired of London, he is tired of life; for there is in London all that life can afford" (*Life*, 3: 178). I am sure that the young Sam Johnson also found London delightful, but an examination of the pains and problems of urban life is a satiric commonplace that allows him the pleasures of imitating a classical text and the prestige of matching modern and ancient urban life. One might add, to quote Johnson on what he called "lapidary inscriptions" (that is, epitaphs on gravestones), when in writing them "a man is not upon oath" (*Life*, 2: 407).

But the satire in *London* has a sharp political edge as well, and, in this regard, we can say that Johnson is more than conventional. In fact, the next year (1739), he published *Marmor Norfolciense: or An Essay on an Ancient Prophetical Inscription, in Monkish Rhyme, Lately Discover'd Near Lynn in Norfolk. By Probus Britanicus*, a satirical attack on the government headed by the chief minister, Robert Walpole. *London* is full of complaints that England has fallen from Elizabethan strength and valor and allowed Spain to dominate her, a common criticism in those years by the opposition to the Walpole government. The narrator and Thales, his friend who is about to leave London for rural peace and quiet, kneel and kiss "the consecrated earth; / In pleasing dreams the blissful age renew, / And call Britannia's glories back to view; / Behold her cross triumphant on the main, / The guard of commerce, and the dread of Spain" (49, ll. 24–28). But now, says the narrator, if we survey "The land of heroes and saints," the warrior of former days has "dwindled to a beau; / Sense, freedom, piety, refin'd away, / Of France the mimick, and of Spain the prey" (53, ll. 100, 104–06).

For all its energy and sometimes, for twenty-first century readers, its amusingly crude chauvinism, *London* is a predictable and conventional satire, a young man's poem as he contemplates the difficulties of making his way in a corrupt and decadent society. Johnson's great friend, the actor David Garrick, found *London* to be "lively and easy," but found his adaptation of Juvenal's tenth satire, *The Vanity of Human Wishes* (1748), "as hard as Greek" (*Poems*, 90). But unlike *London*, and as its title makes clear, this poem is not primarily a local and polemical political satire but a grandly universalized moral meditation, a survey, as the opening couplet announces, of mankind "from China to Peru" (*Poems*, 91, l. 2). The stern voice we hear in the poem is in the sweep and finality of its observations, authoritative, commanding, almost unearthly. Oddly enough, Johnson's dominant somber tone and unforgiving judicial pronouncements in the *Vanity* deviate from Juvenal's tenth satire, which is acerbic, slangy, and irreverent, as well as focused on the specifics, scandalous and comic, of Roman decadence in the most explicit, even scabrous language.

Johnson's voice proclaims at the beginning just how intractable and nearly impenetrable human life is, with its "busy scenes of crouded life" (92, l. 4). When readers reach line 69, they discover that the previous lines belong to a character the narrator identifies as "the sage":

> Such was the scorn that fill'd the sage's mind,
> Renew'd at ev'ry glance on humankind;
> How just that scorn ere yet thy voice declare,
> Search every state, and canvass ev'ry pray'r.
>
> (95, ll. 69–72)

The almost 300 lines of the *Vanity* which follow are a series of validations of the sage's scorn, an expansion filled out with specific and concrete instances, historical anecdotes of human folly and vanity, some British, others from European history, both modern and ancient. For example, Henry VIII's Lord Chancellor, Cardinal Wolsey, is the subject of a long passage that traces his rise to power and then his fall as "his sov'reign frowns . . . Grief aids disease, remember'd folly stings, / And his last sighs reproach the faith of kings" (*Poems*, 96, ll. 108, 119–20). So, too, the reader is asked to ponder the fate of George Villiers, first Duke of Buckingham, and Robert Harley, Earl of Oxford and Tory leader under Queen Anne: "What gave great Villiers to th' assassin's knife, / And fixed disease on Harley's closing life?" (97, ll. 129–30). Johnson's poem then looks back to similar cautionary instances of reckless hubris from ancient history, "the rapid Greek" (Alexander) and the Persian emperor Xerxes, and more recently Charles XII of Sweden, who "left the name, at which the world grew pale, / To point a moral, or adorn a tale" (102, ll. 221–22). Examples such as these multiply, ending with recent British exempla, including what has always seemed to me the cruelest couplet in English verse: "From Marlb'rough's eyes the streams of dotage flow, / And Swift expires a driv'ler and a show" (106, ll. 317–18). The Duke of Marlborough had paralytic strokes that killed him. Swift was intermittently insane before his death; his servants were said to have shown him to the curious for a fee.

Johnson's poem is rich in examples from history in its 368 lines, but it is also strikingly powerful for its intense verbal energies. The work of many of these lines is performed by a host of verbs and verbals. Consider the opening lines as setting the pace for the poem:

> Let observation with extensive view,
> Survey mankind from China to Peru;

Remark each anxious toil, each eager strife,
And watch the busy scenes of crouded life;
Then say how hope and fear, desire and hate,
O'erspread with snares the clouded maze of fate,
Where wav'ring man, betray'd by vent'rous pride,
To tread the dreary paths without a guide,
As treach'rous phantoms in the mist delude,
Shuns fancied ills, or chases airy good;
How rarely reason guides the stubborn choice,
Rules the bold hand, or prompts the suppliant voice;

(*Poems*, 91–92, ll. 1–12)

Imperative verbs begin the passage; commands to the reader – survey, remark, watch, say – and then the activities evoked are of course full of movement – anxious, eager, busy, crouded, o'erspread, wav'ring, vent'rous, tread, shuns, chases, guides, rules, prompts, sink, wings, glows, flows, stops, precipitates. Boswell tells us that Johnson was a physically strong man, courageous and active. He recounts how Johnson feared death "but he feared nothing else": "One day, at Mr. Beauclerk's house in the country, when two large dogs were fighting, he went up to them, and beat them till they separated; and at another time, when told of the danger there was that a gun might burst if charged with many balls, he put in six or seven, and fired it off against a wall" (*Life*, 2: 299). There is a strong, propulsive, and purposeful kinetic energy in this poem, and there may be a parallel between these qualities and Johnson's assertive and even pugnacious personality. For example, early on in the *Vanity* Johnson describes "the gen'ral massacre of gold" and lists several crimes inspired by avarice; "Wealth heap'd on wealth, nor truth nor safety buys, / The dangers gather as the treasures rise" (*Poems*, 92, ll. 22, 27–28). Here and elsewhere in his work, Johnson is drawn to evoking not only action but often menacing processes like these dangers that "gather," which in context gives that common verb a sinister quality. Something similar occurs a few lines later in the description of kingly and deadly rivals when the vassal is safer than the imprisoned lord: "Untouch'd his cottage, and his slumbers sound, / Tho' confiscation's vultures hover round" (93, ll. 34–35). And in *London* we hear how "a rabble rages, now a fire" and "the fell attorney prowls for prey" (48, ll. 14, 16). An early anticipation of the scholar's life is memorably evoked in the *Vanity*, in which he is cautioned to "pause awhile from letters, to be wise; / There mark what ills the scholar's life assail, / Toil, envy, want, the patron, and the jail" (99, ll. 157–60). These cautionary warnings are followed by a characteristic evocation of a slow and unjust process in the appreciation of genius:

> See nations slowly wise, and meanly just,
> To buried merit raise the tardy bust.
> If dreams yet flatter, once again attend,
> Hear Lydiat's life, and Galileo's end.
>
> (*Poems*, 99, ll. 161–64)

For an anticipation of these reflections, consider parts of the short early poem "The Young Author" (1743):

> So the young author panting for a name,
> And fir'd with pleasing hope or endless fame,
> Intrusts his happiness to human kind,
> More false, more cruel than the seas and wind.
>
> ---
>
> Swiftly he sees the imagin'd laurels spread,
> He feels th' unfading wreath surround his head;
> Warn'd by another's fate, vain youth, be wise,
> Those dreams were Settle's once and Ogilby's.
> The pamphlet spreads, incessant hisses rise,
> To some retreat the baffled writer flies.
>
> (*Poems*, 72–73, ll. 11–14, 21–26)

Johnson's poems deal deliberately in the largest and most comprehensive moral generalities; "human wishes" covers a lot of ground. But his poetic approach is to treat these generalities with a vivid and energized concrete particularity. The singular genius of his best verse lies in welding both the general and the particular, and in both cases his language is plain, even ordinary, and the more effective for its clarity. One of the most effective and indeed terrifying instances of this in *The Vanity of Human Wishes* is the prayer of the old man:

> Enlarge my life with multitude of days,
> In health, in sickness, thus the suppliant prays;
> Hides from himself his state, and shuns to know,
> That life protracted is protracted woe.
> Time hovers o'er, impatient to destroy
> And shuts up all the passages of joy.
>
> (*Poems*, 104, ll. 255–60)

Time is just about the oldest and most familiar, even banal, poetic personification one can imagine, but in these lines Johnson gives it a hideous and terrifying concreteness as it "hovers" (a word he is fond of employing for its ominous implications). And this Time operates like a demented torturer on the human body as it "shuts up all the passages of joy," which is the more powerful for not identifying those "passages." Lines like these are at the core of Johnson's poetics, with their supremely effective use of ordinary language. There is nothing difficult or obscure in these lines, but they achieve a kind of negative sublimity in their evocation of natural process at its most normal and terrible. Garrick was wrong about *The Vanity of Human Wishes*. It is not difficult, but it is disturbing in its clarity and simplicity.

CHAPTER 11

Johnson's Editions of Shakespeare

Tom Mason

Given the long years of labor that had gone into its composition, and the presence of a Preface that he must have known was more acute, penetrating, and comprehensive than anything that had appeared before, the title of Johnson's first edition of Shakespeare's plays is remarkably modest: *The Plays of William Shakespeare, in Eight Volumes, with the Corrections and Illustrations of Various Commentators; To which are added Notes by Sam. Johnson.* London, M,DCC,LXV.[1] Eighteen years earlier, William Warburton had announced his edition of "The Works of *Shakespear*" with some pomp and more confidence, proclaiming it as containing "The Genuine Text (collated with All the former Editions, and Then Corrected and Emended)." Warburton claims emphatically that the plays have been "restored from the *Blunders* of the first Editors and the *Interpolations* of the two Last," so that the text has been "settled" once and for all. Johnson, in contrast, makes no claims for the status of his text and presents himself as having merely *added* to the work of "*Various Commentators.*" Nowhere does Johnson suggest that there is anything final in this edition, and his project is most fully realized in the later editions of 1773 or 1778, which contain his last thoughts and final revisions.[2] In all editions Johnson was aided by many of his friends, particularly George Steevens, who had a prodigious memory for old

---

[1] For accounts of the Preface that establish its importance in the history of criticism, in Johnson's critical *oeuvre*, and as a piece of living criticism, see G. F. Parker, *Johnson's Shakespeare* (Oxford: Clarendon Press, 1989), and Philip Smallwood, "Shakespeare: Johnson's Poet of Nature," *Companion*, pp. 143–60.

[2] *The Plays of William Shakespeare in Ten Volumes with the Corrections and Illustrations of Various Commentators; to Which Are Added Notes by Samuel Johnson and George Steevens* (London: C. Bathurst; W. Strahan; J., F., and C. Rivington, et al., 1778), is available on Eighteenth-Century Collections Online with an appropriate library access (https://bit.ly/3EVXZy4), or freely accessible via the Hathi Trust (https://bit.ly/38UOLpD). This work is cited as "1778 edition," while the Yale edition is the default citation.

plays, and who sometimes supported and sometimes corrected Johnson's readings.

All Johnson's predecessors are allowed a voice somewhere in his volumes. His own Preface is followed by the notes that Heminge and Condell had provided for the 1623 Folio, Ben Jonson's poem "To the Memory of my Beloved, the Author Mr. William Shakespeare," Nicholas Rowe's "Life" (1709), and the prefaces to their editions of the plays of Alexander Pope (1723–5), Lewis Theobald (1733), Thomas Hanmer (1744), and William Warburton (1747). All Johnson's editions are essentially collaborative; he is in constant dialogue with his predecessors, with his readers, and, being everywhere careful not to impose his mind on that of his subject, with the plays themselves – and sometimes with the personages in those plays. His collaboration with his predecessors often takes the form of firm disagreement on matters both of detail and of principle. For example, Alexander Pope had claimed in his preface that he had performed *"the dull duty of an editor,"* a phrase that irritated Johnson into compiling a list of necessary editorial qualities that were "very different from dullness." An editor of "a corrupted piece" needs to comprehend "all possibilities of meaning" and "all possibilities of expression"; together with "his author's particular cast of thought, and turn of expression" (*Shakespeare*, 1: 95).

Having laid out these daunting demands, Johnson admits to the impossibility of their ever being met: "Conjectural criticism demands more than humanity possesses." It was commonly understood that Shakespeare's plays existed in a series of corrupted pieces and therefore presented an editor with unparalleled problems. "Mr. Pope," Johnson maintained, was the first to have discovered "the true state of Shakespeare's text" (1: 94). Pope had compared many old copies, several of which differed from the 1623 Folio in ways that could be neither reconciled nor explained. He deduced that *all* the texts, including the eighteen plays represented by the Folio alone, contained lines and passages, even scenes, that could not have passed under the corrective eye of their author, whose abilities and poetic intelligence he rated just below those of Homer, who has "ever been acknowledged the greatest of poets." All texts contained interpolations, excisions, and the misunderstandings of dull printers and ignorant actors. Pope assumed that Shakespeare was a revising writer – but it was always difficult to decide which passages had been altered by the players or the author for purely literary reasons, and which for the purposes of rapid performance. By drawing on several copies at the same time, Pope had attempted to discover the original form of each scene as it might have existed in the mind of the poet – if never on a written page.

In the Preface to his edition, Johnson intersperses his prose with phrases borrowed from the plays. So he appropriates a phrase of Othello's when elaborating on Pope's account of the state of the text, and the principal cause of that state – Shakespeare's disinclination to edit his own work: "So careless was this great poet of future fame," that "he retired to ease and plenty, while he was yet little 'declined into the vale of years,'" and before he could rescue his works "from the depravations that obscured them" (*Shakespeare*, 1: 92). Shakespeare's abilities were, by this account, neither appreciated nor comprehended by his first readers – those actors who could not remember or did not understand the plays in which they had taken part, and the scribes and compositors responsible for the reproduction of his plays. Pope provided many (sometimes comic) instances of schoolboy errors in Latin, history, grammar, and plot-continuity, which, he thought, might be attributed to the ignorance of transcribers, alongside dull jests that might be laid at the door of the players. Many lines were remetered, passages rearranged or relegated. As Johnson put it, Pope, in printing inferior passages at the bottom of the page, had "thought more of amputation than of cure" (*Shakespeare*, 1: 94), and in his own text he restored many of the rejected passages (sometimes without much confidence in their merit).

Johnson also remarked that Pope had given "reason to hope that there were means of reforming" the text of Shakespeare's plays by collation of "the old copies" (1: 94). To some extent, this method had been adopted by Lewis Theobald, whose edition appeared in 1733, and anticipated Johnson's in replacing many of the passages Pope had relegated. Theobald, as Johnson saw it, "collated the ancient copies, and rectified many errors," judging that what Theobald "did was commonly right" (1: 95–96). Johnson's general estimate of Theobald's abilities was, however, noticeably lower than that of some later editors. Theobald is described in the Preface as "a man of narrow comprehension and small acquisitions, with no native and intrinsick splendour of genius, with little of the artificial light of learning" (1: 95). Johnson reprinted many of Theobald's notes and emendations, disagreed with more, and reproduced a few of the most cantankerous as objects of mirth.

Thomas Hanmer, the next editor (1744), is described in more approbatory terms: "He had, what is the first requisite to emendatory criticism, that intuition by which the poet's intention is immediately discovered, and that dexterity of intellect which despatches its work by the easiest means" (1: 97). Hanmer's handsomely illustrated edition had contained many emendations and supplied metrical deficiencies, but often without commentary or any indication of where the change had been made. For this, and for almost everything else, Hanmer was vehemently castigated and continuously mocked by William Warburton in his edition (1747). Much space is given in Johnson's edition to refuting Warburton's emendations and speculations, on the grounds that his predecessor's great fault was an overabundance of "that confidence which presumes to do, by surveying the surface, what labour only can perform, by penetrating the bottom" (1: 98).

The "labour" Johnson is referring to here is intellectual: labor of the mind, labor of thought. He is presenting himself as one who has pondered long and deeply about every line in every play, and who, given the errors of his predecessors, approaches his task in fear and trembling:

> To dread the shore which he sees spread with wrecks, is natural to the sailor. I had before my eye, so many critical adventures ended in miscarriage, that caution was forced upon me. I encountered in every page Wit struggling with its own sophistry, and Learning confused by the multiplicity of its views. I was forced to censure those whom I admired, and could not but reflect, while I was dispossessing their emendations, how soon the same fate might happen to my own, and how many of the readings which I have corrected may be by some other editor defended and established. (*Shakespeare*, 1: 109)

The last phrases are important; Johnson's conversations with other careful readers of Shakespeare look as much toward the future as the past. In many cases, Johnson's later editions represent his rethinkings, so exemplifying the self-doubt he had expressed from the first: "As I practised conjecture more, I learned to trust it less; and after I had printed a few plays, resolved to insert none of my own readings in the text. Upon this caution I now congratulate myself, for every day encreases my doubt of my emendations" (1: 108). Many of Johnson's emendations are restorations of an earlier state of the text, replacing the (sometimes ingenious) suggestions of Pope, Theobald, Hanmer, and Warburton, even when Johnson himself is unable to offer a definitive explanation. His procedure was based on the notion that the scribes, actors, and compositors must have had a real manuscript in front of them, while the authoritative text the editors were attempting to reconstruct was purely imaginary.

Johnson's own notes are extraordinarily various in kind and in import, and it is seldom possible to draw a distinction between the purely editorial and the critical and evaluative. For Johnson it was impossible to make decisions between rival readings without some notion of the *kind* of writer Shakespeare was or of what might be going on in the mind of his personages. Johnson always has in mind the likely difficulties, pains, and pleasures of his readers, and writes frequently of pains and pleasures of his own. Shakespeare's plays are frequently quoted in Johnson's *Dictionary*, published ten years earlier. In some places in his edition of the plays, he provided simple glosses to words no longer in common currency. But he soon found that "He that will understand Shakespeare, must not be content to study him in the closet, he must look for his meaning sometimes among the sports of the field, and sometimes among the manufactures of the shop" (*Shakespeare*, 1: 86). "Of this knowledge," wrote Johnson ruefully, "every man has some, and none has much" (1: 103).

In many cases, his elucidation of complicated or confused syntax was dictated by the deduction that Shakespeare was naturally given to changing the grammar and train of imagery mid-sentence. Most characteristic are Johnson's frequent admissions of noncomprehension. On occasion he will propose a rearrangement of words but keep his proposal firmly to the footnotes beneath the unchanged text. On one passage (*Midsummer's Night's Dream*, II. i, 101–17), Johnson wrote: "After all the endeavours of the editors this passage still remains to me unintelligible" (1: 146). He wrestles with it, rearranging sixteen lines, only to conclude, "I know not what credit the reader will give to this emendation, which I do not much credit myself" (*Shakespeare*, 1: 147).

Whether explaining local difficulties or commenting on particular speeches, Johnson moves rapidly to the mind of the personage first, and only secondarily to the mind of the dramatist. King John's reproaches against Hubert, whom he suspects of murdering the boy-prince Arthur (*King John*, IV. ii, 231), are "the eruptions of a mind swelling with consciousness of a crime, and desirous of discharging its misery on another." These are "drawn" (by Shakespeare rather than the King) "*ab ipsis recessibus mentis*, from the intimate knowledge of mankind" (1: 425). The explanatory tool that Johnson likes best is paraphrase, where the words of the play mingle with his own. At times, the paraphrase becomes a comment both on the thought of Shakespeare's personage and on the human condition. When the Duke in *Measure for Measure* speaks of the insubstantiality of life as a means of reconciling Claudio with his coming death – "Thou has nor youth, nor age: / But as it were an after-dinner's sleep, / Dreaming on both" (*Measure for Measure*, III. i, 32–34) – Johnson commented:

> This is exquisitely imagined. When we are young we busy ourselves in forming schemes for succeeding time, and miss the gratifications that are before us; when we are old we amuse the languour of age with recollection of youthful pleasures or performances; so that our life, of which no part is filled with the business of the present time, resembles our dreams after dinner, when the events of the morning are mingled with the designs of the evening. (*Shakespeare*, 1: 193)

There is, in Johnson's procedures, no distinction between editorial and textual concerns, and the full range of reading experiences is clear from Johnson's notes to the scene depicting the murder of Desdemona (*Othello*, V, ii, 1–3) – which in their conclusion suggest, but do not adopt, a tiny emendation.

Othello enters the chamber where Desdemona is sleeping, apparently talking to himself:

> It is the cause, it is the cause, my soul, —
> Let me not name it to you, you chaste stars! —
> It is the cause. — (1778 edition, 10: 602).

Johnson explains:

> The abruptness of this soliloquy makes it obscure. The meaning I think is this: "I am here" (says Othello in his mind) "overwhelmed with horror. What is the reason of this perturbation? Is it want of resolution to do justice? Is it the dread of shedding blood? No; it is not the action that shocks me, but 'it is the cause, it is the cause, my soul; let me not name it to you, ye chaste stars! It is the cause.'" (*Shakespeare*, 2: 1044–45)

The telling phrase is "in his mind." Johnson assumes that the words are only partial hints of what is and has been going on in Othello's agonized, deluded interior. Johnson does not elaborate on the unspeakable cause that may not be named to the chaste stars. In later editions, his co-editor, George Steevens, added a comment moving Othello a little more toward the rational: "Othello, full of horror at the cruel action which he is about to perpetrate, seems at this instant to be seeking his justification, from representing to himself *the cause*, i.e. the greatness of the provocation he has had received" (1778 edition, 10: 602). But when Othello adds, "Yet she must die, else she'll betray more men," Steevens observed that Othello has changed tack and is now "willing to suppose himself the preventer of succeeding mischief to others" (1778 edition, 10: 602).

Later in the scene, when Desdemona repeatedly refuses to acknowledge her adultery, or the gift of her husband's handkerchief to her lover, Othello says:

> Oh perjur'd woman! Thou dost stone my heart,
> And mak'st me call, what I intend to do, —
> A murder, which I thought a sacrifice.
> I saw the hankerchief.
>
> (*Othello*, V, ii. 66–69; 1778 edition, 10: 605)

Johnson explains: "This line is difficult. 'Thou hast hardened my heart, and makest me' kill thee with the rage of a 'murderer,' when 'I thought to have sacrificed' thee to justice with the calmness of a priest striking a victim" (*Shakespeare*, 2: 1045). Othello would at this stage be maintaining his earlier resolution: "I would not kill thy unprepared spirit; / No, – Heaven forefend! – I would not kill thy soul" (*Othello*, V. ii. 31–32). But Johnson notices that "one of the elder quartos" reads, "thou dost stone *thy* heart," referring to Desdemona. Although making no change to the text itself, Johnson suspected that "stone *thy* heart" might be the right reading: "The meaning then will be, 'thou forcest me' to dismiss thee from the world in the state of the 'murdered' without preparation for death, 'when I intended' that thy punishment should have been 'a sacrifice' atoning for thy crime" (2: 1045). Othello would be transferring all guilt to Desdemona, who, in refusing to confess, had hardened her own heart, and will be self-condemned in the state which Hamlet fears for his father, unhoused, unaneled. It was presumably with this likelihood in mind that Johnson added one sentence to his note: "I am glad that I have ended my revisal of this dreadful scene. It is not to be endured" (2: 1045).

Johnson several times expresses personal pain when Shakespeare depicts the death and suffering of innocent femininity: any "gratification" the reader might feel at the "destruction of an usurper and a murderer" at the end of *Hamlet* "is abated by the untimely death of Ophelia, the young, the beautiful, the harmless, and the pious" (*Shakespeare*, 2: 1011). And Johnson, famously, recorded his reaction as a child to the ending of *King Lear*: "I was many years ago so shocked by Cordelia's death, that I know not whether I ever endured to read again the last scenes of the play till I undertook to revise them as an editor" (2: 704).

But more shocking than such "mournful distress" that "fills the heart with tenderness" is the notion that a villain may consign a suffering soul to hell. Johnson always considered matters to do with the salvation of the human soul with the utmost solemnity. When Hamlet resolves to kill his uncle "in the incestuous pleasure of his bed" so that "his soul may be as damn'd and black / As hell, whereto it goes" (*Hamlet*, III. iii, 93–94), Johnson again reacts in pain: "This speech, in which Hamlet, represented as a virtuous character, is not content with taking blood for blood, but contrives damnation for the man that he would punish, is too horrible to be read or to be uttered" (2: 990). But the moment passes and counts no more in Johnson's general estimation of *Hamlet* than the cruel death of Desdemona took anything away from his estimate of *Othello*, the "beauties" of which "impress themselves so strongly upon the attention of the reader, that they can draw no aid from critical illustration" (2: 1047). All the characters – Othello ("obdurate in his revenge"), the "cool malignity" of Iago ("silent in his resentment, subtle in his designs"), and, above all, the "soft simplicity of Desdemona, confident of merit, and conscious of innocence, her artless perseverance in her suit, and her slowness to suspect that she can be suspected" – are, equally, "such proofs of Shakespeare's skill in human nature, as, I suppose, it is vain to seek in any modern writer" (2: 1047).

That the beauties of this widely popular play speak and have spoken for themselves is of equal importance with their demonstration of and dependence on Shakespeare's exceptional "skill in human nature." The presence of testimonies from the critical past – from Ben Jonson and Dryden to Johnson's friends and fellow commentators (at their best) – is essential for Johnson's central claim for Shakespeare, in that such testimony provides the essential evidence of the plays' capacity to please. Shakespeare's plays are "read without any other reason than the desire of pleasure, and are therefore praised only as pleasure is obtained" (*Shakespeare*, 1: 61). On this well-attested pleasure Johnson can base the governing law of the Preface:

> Nothing can please many, and please long, but just representations of general nature. . . . The irregular combinations of fanciful invention may delight a-while, by that novelty of which the common satiety of life sends us all in quest; but the pleasures of sudden wonder are soon exhausted, and the mind can only repose on the stability of truth. (*Shakespeare*, 1: 61–62)

Every word in the first sentence here carries weight. For the law to hold, all the conditions must be met – in full. The work must have pleased many (not merely antiquarians) and pleased many generations; the representations should be just and true reflections of those aspects of nature that are common to, and understood by, all humanity. These conditions being met, it is possible to recall Hamlet on the purpose of playing (III. ii) and claim that "Shakespeare is above all writers, at least above all modern writers, the poet of nature; the poet that holds up to his readers a faithful mirrour of manners and of life" (1: 62).

The word "nature" had a rather different force and scope for Johnson and his contemporaries than any of the many meanings obtaining today. Pope had invoked "nature" as a goddess in suggesting that Shakespeare "is not so much an Imitator as an Instrument of Nature; and 'tis not so just to say that he speaks from her as that she speaks thro' him."[3] In the first edition of the *Dictionary* (1755), Johnson had drawn on *King Lear* for several of his "explanations" of the term, including the first: "An imaginary being supposed to preside over the material and animal world. Thou, *nature*, art my goddess; to thy law / My services are bound." When he revised the *Dictionary* in 1773, Johnson added a paraphrase from Robert Boyle's *Free Enquiry into the Received Notion of Nature* (1686), a work that suggested that a more precise phrase should replace all common uses of the word "nature." This produces an entry where the first illustration, Edmund's nature goddess, is canceled and contradicted by the last: "*Nature* is sometimes indeed commonly taken for a kind of semi-deity. In this sense it is best not to use it at all."[4] Edmund's self-dedication to "nature" involved the casting-off of every other law, human or divine. A poet of nature is not likely to be more benign, perhaps, than was Edmund to his brother, father, or Cordelia herself.

Johnson's succeeding elaborations of the central critical proposition in the Preface concentrate on the words "human" and "life":

> This therefore is the praise of Shakespeare, that his drama is the mirrour of life; that he who has mazed his imagination, in following the phantoms which other writers raise up before him, may here be cured of his delirious extasies, by reading human sentiments in human language; by scenes from which a hermit may estimate the transactions of the world, and a confessor predict the progress of the passions. (*Shakespeare*, 1: 65)

It is necessary to distinguish here between truth to general nature and truth to the surface of life. The plays are "level with life" but not life-like. Readers opening the 1765 edition of Johnson's Shakespeare were immediately met by the magic-suffused *Tempest* and *A Midsummer's Night's Dream* – and with Warburton's warm endorsements of both, quoted by Johnson:

> These two first Plays, the *Tempest* and *the Midsummer-night's Dream*, are the noblest Efforts of that sublime and amazing Imagination, peculiar to *Shakespear*, which soars above the Bound of Nature without forsaking

---

[3] Alexander Pope, *The Works of Shakespear*, 6 vols. (London: Jacob Tonson, 1725), 1: ii.
[4] *A Dictionary of the English Language*, 4th edn., rev., 2 vols. (London: W. Strahan, 1773): https://bit.ly /3KiHVIp.

Sense: or more properly, carries Nature along with him beyond her established Limits.[5]

Or, as Johnson put it in the Preface, "Shakespeare approximates the remote, and familiarizes the wonderful" so that "he has not only shewn human nature as it acts in real exigences, but as it would be found in trials, to which it cannot be exposed" (1: 65). And while Shakespeare's "scenes are occupied only by men, who act and speak as the reader thinks that he should himself have spoken or acted on the same occasion" (1: 64), Johnson concedes that readers are unlikely to find many embodiments of general nature or human sentiments in human language in many places in many plays.

This notion of the unevenness of Shakespeare's work was not contentious in the eighteenth century. Johnson's Preface is (almost) ostensibly an attempt to rise to the challenge of Pope's proposition that a full and judicious account of the strengths and weaknesses of the plays might be *the* great and most instructive work of English criticism:

> It is not my design to enter into a Criticism upon this Author; tho' to do it effectually and not superficially, would be the best occasion than any just Writer could take, to form the judgement and taste of our nation. For of all *English* Poets *Shakespear* must be confessed to be the fairest and fullest subject for Criticism, and to afford the most numerous, as well as most conspicuous instances, both of Beauties and Faults of all sorts.[6]

This critical task Johnson performed, distinguishing "not dogmatically but deliberatively" (*Shakespeare*, 1: 80) between weaknesses and strengths, between beauties and faults that he thought real and those (like the demand for unities of time and place) that he considered artificial. But where Pope had contributed to his readers' critical education by marking the best passages with apostrophes of approbation and, like Rowe, had provided a list of particular beauties, Johnson is extremely reticent of praise, believing that readers are happiest when judging for themselves.

Of the complete plays, only *King Lear*, perhaps, receives entire endorsement. In most others Johnson detects "Beauties and Faults of all sorts." Shakespeare "has scenes of undoubted and perpetual excellence" (*Shakespeare*, 1: 91), and it is to scenes that Johnson repeatedly draws attention. One scene singled out for unusual praise is that containing the last words of Katherine of Aragon in *Henry VIII*

---

[5] Samuel Johnson, *The Plays of William Shakespeare*, 8 vols. (London: J. and R. Tonson, C. Corbet, H. Woodfall, et. al., 1765), 1: 3.
[6] Pope, *Works of Shakespear*, 1: 1.

(IV. ii): "This scene is above any other part of Shakespeare's tragedies, and perhaps above any scene of any other poet tender and pathetick" (*Shakespeare*, 2: 653). Johnson's praise, however, consists of a series of negatives; the scene is "tender and pathetick" despite the lack of "gods, or fairies, or poisons, or precipices, without the help of romantick circumstances, without improbable sallies of poetical lamentation, and without any throes of tumultuous misery" (2: 653) – Johnson's remarks ignore the "romantick" circumstance suggested by a long stage direction describing an elaborate dance conducted by "Spirits of peace" whose "bright faces / Cast a thousand beams upon" Katherine, promising "eternal happiness" (1765 edition; 7: 289).

There is one other scene where Johnson's comment takes us straight back to the key terms at the heart of the Preface: "nature and truth." Act III of *The Second Part of King Henry VI* includes a short scene in which Henry Beaufort, a cardinal, is discovered in his bed "raving and staring as if he were mad," as Steevens recorded from the "old copy" (1778 edition, 6: 375), and apparently reacting to his responsibility for the murder of the Lord Protector, whom even his enemies describe as the "Good Gloucester." The cardinal's extreme reaction comes as something of a surprise. Several personages, including the queen and Suffolk, her lover, have desired Gloucester's death, and the cardinal has displayed few signs of having an inner life of any kind. But now his mind is completely adrift. He takes the king to be Death himself, to whom he immediately offers a bribe:

> If thou beest Death, I'll give thee *England*'s treasure,
> Enough to purchase such another island,
> So thou wilt let me live and feel no pain.
>
> (III. iii, 2–4)

On being told that he is in the presence of the king, the cardinal assumes he is undergoing brutal interrogation:

> Bring me unto my Trial when you will.
> Dy'd he not in his bed? where should he die?
> Can I make men live, whe'r they will or no?
> — O torture me no more, I will confess.
>
> (III. iii, 8–10)

At this point he begins to assume that Gloucester still lives:

> Alive again? Then shew me where he is;
> I'll give a thousand pound to look upon him.
>
> (III. iii, 12–13)

But when dead Gloucester does appear to him, the imagined sight is unendurable:

> — He hath no eyes, the dust hath blinded them.
> — Comb down his hair; look! Look! it stands upright,
> Like lime-twigs set to catch my winged soul!

(III. iii, 14–16)

The king beseeches the "eternal mover of the heavens" to "Look with a gentle eye upon" the dying man and to "purge this black despair," asking the guilty man to "Hold up" his hand and "'make a signal" of his "hope" (III. iii, 20–28; 1778 edition, 6: 376). But Cardinal Beaufort "dies and makes no sign."

Johnson's comment is extraordinary:

> This is one of the scenes which has been applauded by the criticks, and which will continue to be admired when prejudice shall cease, and bigotry give way to impartial examination. These are beauties that rise out of nature and of truth; the superficial reader cannot miss them, the profound can image nothing beyond them. (*Shakespeare*, 2: 591)

Everything in the scene is assumed to be immediately intelligible to the reader, including the extremely broken and agonized dying speech of the guilty cardinal, the brokenness of which Johnson has emphasized by increasing the number of dashes. The scene had been, Johnson records, applauded by the critics. Many – John Hughes, Nicholas Rowe, Ambrose Phillips – had praised it with force, all apparently understanding and appreciating the workings of a disordered mind. Rowe's account of the scene may have been to the forefront of Johnson's mind:

> Cardinal *Beaufort*, who had murder'd the Duke of *Gloucester*, is shewn in the last Agonies on his Death-Bed, with the good King praying over him. There is so much Terror in one, so much tenderness and moving Piety in the other, as must touch any one who is capable either of Fear or Pity.[7]

Others, like William Dodd, had drawn a moral: "Thus hath guilt, even in this world, its due reward, and iniquity is not suffered to go unpunished."[8] Some lines in the scene would support such a reading, particularly those spoken by Warwick: "See, how the pangs of death do make him grin!" "So bad a death argues a monstrous life" (III. iii, 24, 30). Despite Beaufort's

---

[7] Nicholas Rowe, *The Works of Mr. William Shakespear*, 6 vols. (London: Jacob Tonson, 1709), 1: xxix.
[8] William Dodd, *The Beauties of Shakespear* (London: Jacob Tonson, 1752), p. 43.

almost certain damnation at the end of the scene, Johnson found this scene beautiful rather than unendurable. His only annotation is to append a Latin distich (*"Peccantes culpare cave, nam labimur omnes, / Aut sumus, aut fuimus, vel possumus esse quod hic est"*) to one effortlessly iambic but all-encompassing line from the Christian king: "Forbear to judge, for we are sinners all" (III. iii, 31; 2: 590). The distich (reading *dampnare* where Johnson had *culpare*) is found in John Strype's *The Life of the Learned Sir John Cheke*, where it is translated:

> Condemn not thy poor Brother,
> That doth before thee lay;
> Since there is none but falls:
> I have, thou dost, all may.[9]

Johnson appears to have found beauties arising out of nature and truth in the scene as a whole – the beauty residing both in the pitying forbearance of the king as much as in the terror of the murderer.

Aberystwyth University holds a copy of Warburton's edition of the plays in which Johnson had heavily marked up this scene in *The Second Part of King Henry VI* when working on his *Dictionary*. He had given similar attention to the almost forensic description of the corpse of Duke Humphrey, whose strangulation is the cause of the cardinal's (eventual) agonies: "His face is black and full of blood, / His hands abroad display'd, as one that graspt / And *tugg'd* for life" appears in the *Dictionary* as illustrations both for *grasp* and *tug*. Most telling, perhaps, is this entry:

> To STRA'NGLE. v.a. [*strangulo*, Lat.]
> To choak; to suffocate; to kill by intercepting the breath.
> His face is black and full of blood;
> His eye-balls farther out, than when he liv'd;
> Staring full ghastly, like a *strangled* man. *Shakes. H. VI*

On this passage (*The Second Part of King Henry VI*, III. ii, 168–10), as it appeared in the Shakespeare edition, Johnson observed: "I cannot but stop a moment to observe that this horrible description is scarcely the work of any pen but Shakespeare's" (*Shakespeare*, 2: 589). There are "beauties" in the scene depicting the death of the cardinal; none are mentioned in the description of Gloucester's corpse, but both are from Shakespeare's pen: "What author of that age had the same easiness of expression and fluency of numbers?" Is general nature shown almost equally in the working of

---

[9] John Strype, *The Life of the Learned Sir John Cheke* (London: John Wyat, 1705), p. 235.

a guilt-ridden human mind, the call for forgiveness, and in the congealed blood in the "'horrible" face of a strangled man?

When Johnson wrote that this death of Beaufort "will continue to be admired when prejudice shall cease, and bigotry give way to impartial examination" (2: 591), he may have been thinking of the prejudice of Theobald and Warburton, both of whom had tended to deny Shakespeare's authorship of the plays about the reign of Henry the Sixth. But Johnson may have had larger thoughts in mind when writing of a time when prejudice and bigotry "shall cease." He wrote of Milton's *Samson Agonistes* that "It could only be by long prejudice, and the bigotry of learning, that Milton could prefer the ancient tragedies . . . to the exhibitions of the French and English stages" (*Lives*, 1: 201). Might Johnson be envisaging a time to come when a "just Writer" will have formed "the judgement and taste of our nation" (as Pope had put it), nature and truth will be recognized by all, and the beauties of Shakespeare's scenes will have overcome all bigoty and overwhelmed all prejudice? Johnson maintained that Shakespeare's "adherence to general nature has exposed him to the censure of criticks, who form their judgments upon narrower principles" (*Shakespeare*, 1: 65). The result of his own effort of always careful deliberation throughout his edition has been to counteract prejudice and bigotry as exemplified by the objections of Thomas Rymer, Voltaire, and John Dennis to Shakespeare's mingling of tragedy and comedy; contempt for the unities of time, place, and action; carelessness with chronology and local manners; and his depictions of foolish ministers and drunken kings.

CHAPTER 12

Johnson's Lives of the Poets: *A Guided Tour*

Fred Parker

The *Lives of the Poets* (1779–81), as they have come to be known, were written with fluency and pleasure, out of a lifetime's experience of the literary world and of ethical and critical reflection. For many who love Johnson, it is his finest work: penetrating, humane, funny, moving, and crackling with life. Much more than the sum of its parts, it should ideally be read and re-read entire. But it is also a difficult book for the modern reader to break into, given its length, its miscellaneous quality, its unfamiliar mixing of biography and criticism, and the historically remote figures and matters with which it deals. In what follows, my modest aim is simply to point out, like a tour-guide, some striking passages and features of the work. I hope you will be tempted to explore further; you may find even in single passages a great deal to think with and think about.

Some Criteria for Poetry

About a quarter of the way into the *Life of Cowley*, after the biographical section, you will find Johnson's account of "the metaphysical poets" (*Lives*, I: 23–29), which he gives as orientation before discussing Cowley's poetry more specifically. These few pages offer a fine introduction to Johnson's criteria for poetry, and also to the method or process of his thinking.

Johnson's criteria are plural, and he tries metaphysical poetry for its fit against various categories, in each of which it is found wanting. He begins, interestingly, with sound, where the poets are careless; then comes mimesis, forfeited to their intellectual ingenuity. Such ingenuity might seem to qualify their poetry in a different area, as "wit" – but of the strongest kind of wit they fall short:

> If by a more noble and more adequate conception that be considered as wit, which is at once natural and new, that which, though not obvious, is upon its first production, acknowledged to be just; if it be that, which he that

164

never found it, wonders how he missed; to wit of this kind the metaphysical poets have seldom risen. Their thoughts are often new, but seldom natural; they are not obvious, but neither are they just; and the reader, far from wondering that he missed them, wonders more frequently by what perverseness of industry they were ever found. (*Lives,* 1: 25)

Instead, the metaphysical wit offers "the most heterogeneous ideas … yoked by violence together," and such singularity excludes them from the next category that Johnson puts forward, the power of "representing or moving the affections":

As they were wholly employed on something unexpected and surprising, they had no regard to that uniformity of sentiment which enables us to conceive and to excite the pains and the pleasures of other minds: they never enquired what, on any occasion, they should have said or done; but wrote rather as beholders than partakers of human nature; as Beings looking upon good and evil, impassive and at leisure; as Epicurean deities making remarks on the actions of men, and the vicissitudes of life, without interest and without emotion. (*Lives,* 1: 26–27)

The "analytick" bent of mind of the metaphysical poets was likewise incompatible with Johnson's final category, the sublime – "that comprehension and expanse of thought which at once fills the whole mind, and of which the first effect is sudden astonishment, and the second rational admiration." Instead, their resort was to the fake grandeur of "hyperbole," an "amplification [that] had no limits" (*Lives,* 1: 27–28).

Notice, in all this, the plurality in Johnson's approach, experimentally trying one criterion after another. Notice too how vigorously he evokes what is being queried: ingenuity; singularity; a certain kind of disinterestedness or irony; a power to astonish without limit. His positive formulations are generated by the sense of something lacking or incomplete. Finally, notice the special kind of experience that is evoked through the recurrent semi-paradox: natural *and* new, astonishment *and* rational admiration. The best kinds of creativity are also (or feel like) moments of recognition.

After these disparaging paragraphs comes a surprise, one of those semi-reversals that show Johnson to be especially engaged. "Yet," he goes on, "to write on their plan, it was at least necessary to read and think. No man could be born a metaphysical poet, nor assume the dignity of a writer, by descriptions copied from descriptions, by imitations borrowed from imitations, by traditional imagery, and hereditary similes, by readiness of rhyme, and volubility of syllables" (*Lives,* 1: 29). Suddenly, we see why

Johnson is so interested in the metaphysicals' originality, how hugely weary he is of the merely literary, the competently poetical. Cowley and Donne think with vigor, they provide matter for the mind – even Johnson's phenomenally well-stocked mind – as few poets can. (Addison, by contrast, "thinks justly; but he thinks faintly;" *Lives*, 2: 649). This power of mind is something indispensable: even if, as the metaphysicals deploy it, it is not enough. Why is this so? "Attention has no relief; the affections are never moved; we are sometimes surprised, but never delighted" (*Lives*, 1: 72).

The ability to hold our attention is crucial; few critics write as honestly as Johnson about boredom as a determining factor in reading, about our pleasure in variety and in being held in a state of expectation (e.g., about Butler's *Hudibras*; *Lives*, 1: 218–19). But the most rewarding reading experiences are felt to go still deeper – to find "the passes of the mind" (*Lives*, 3: 1198), as he writes of Dryden's "Alexander's Feast."

Gray's "Elegy"; Commemoration

Thomas Gray is one of the most recent poets to feature in the *Lives*; his poetry – especially the bardic odes – was acclaimed by some as pointing to an exciting new direction for English poetry. Johnson saw this writing as windy and pretentious, and the critical portion of the *Life of Gray* interrogates and mocks such claims, antagonistically. But at the end of those pages he closes, out of chronology, with "An Elegy in a Country Churchyard." Here he articulates the positive standard by which he has been judging, and pivots from his previous astringency to the warmth of true communion.

> In the character of his *Elegy* I rejoice to concur with the common reader; for by the common sense of readers uncorrupted with literary prejudices, after all the refinements of subtilty and the dogmatism of learning, must be finally decided all claim to poetical honours. The *Church-yard* abounds with images which find a mirrour in every mind, and with sentiments to which every bosom returns an echo. The four stanzas beginning "Yet even these bones," are to me original: I have never seen the notions in any other place; yet he that reads them here, persuades himself that he has always felt them. Had Gray written often thus, it had been vain to blame, and useless to praise him. (*Lives*, 3: 1470–71)

That famous formulation of "the common reader" pulls together both the actual reading public, and the reader as touched in the depths of our common human nature. It is an idea that underwrites Johnson's decidedly nonspecialist standpoint throughout the *Lives*.

Notice how this goes together for Johnson with the natural-yet-new paradox: Gray's stanzas *create* the experience of memory. The poetic effect is close to the content here, for Gray's dead villagers are crying out to be remembered. If this is a specially charged passage in the *Lives*, it is so because, among other things, the *Lives of the Poets* offers itself as a work of commemoration, a memorialization of the dead. You see this particularly in those moments where Johnson inserts a passage of personal recollection, or miniature funeral eulogy – of Gilbert Walmsley in the *Life of Smith*, leading into a funeral tribute to Garrick; of Goldsmith in the *Life of Parnell* (*Lives*, 2: 532–53; 560–61). Beyond such passages, the *Lives* as a whole present themselves, more consciously than most biography, as a work of preservation, a collecting-up of such stories and anecdotes, written and oral, as have come down to Johnson's day. And the recurrent structure of the *Lives* also speaks of this: first the biographical section, then the critical discussion. This ensures that after each death, the poetry is what remains behind.

Yet though, in those four stanzas, Gray's dead cry urgently to be remembered, all they get in their country churchyard is "uncouth rhymes and shapeless sculpture" – a "frail memorial," poor substitute for true "fame and elegy." The poem does not preserve their names and speaks more of effacement than of continuance. Johnson's biographies, too, continually record their own relative failure: the facts are lost, the motives can no longer be ascertained, the reports are suspect or contradictory. We regularly hear how little, not how much, is known. This is due partly to the accidents of time, and partly to a problem that no biographer can entirely overcome, as he observes in the *Life of Addison*:

> The necessity of complying with times, and of sparing persons, is the great impediment of biography. History may be formed from permanent monuments and records; but lives can only be written from personal knowledge, which is growing every day less, and in a short time is lost for ever. What is known can seldom be immediately told; and when it might be told, it is no longer known. The delicate features of the mind, the nice discriminations of character, and the minute peculiarities of conduct, are soon obliterated. (*Lives*, 2: 637)

The sense of inevitable shortfall and loss lends both value and poignancy to the project of memorialization, as to the poets' hope that their poetry will endure.

The *Life of Savage*: Comedy

Written in a more elaborately reflective style, the *Life of Savage* was composed and first published much earlier, in 1744. It is largely biographical rather than critical, and differs from most of the other *Lives* in being written out of close personal knowledge. The coherent and cumulative account that it develops does not lend itself to a tour-guide's highlighting. It is, though, one of the most rewarding *Lives* to read through from beginning to end, both for its portrait of Richard Savage and its account of the Grub-Street world of commercial writing.

Do not, however, separate it too firmly from the other *Lives*, for it offers a sustained or emphatic version of what Johnson often does more succinctly or momentarily elsewhere. The *Life of Savage* may be described as a serious comedy, organized around the ironic disparity between Savage's intellectual powers and the actuality of his situation and achievements. Johnson accepts Savage's account of himself as the illegitimate child of aristocracy, sometimes supported but more often neglected and persecuted by the wealthy and powerful on whom he believed he had a claim. Onto this archetypal tale of a birthright denied, Johnson builds a resonant structure. Savage was a man of large ideas, remarkable intellectual capacity, and irresistibly engaging conversation. He was also utterly incapable of managing his money or his impulses, incurably in debt to others, and incapable of not taking fire at perceived slights or offenses. These qualities wrecked his life, or would have wrecked a less remarkable man's life, for Savage's self-belief and cheerful self-confidence were, despite everything, indestructible. There is in Johnson's portrait something of Dickens' Mr. Micawber, and of Shakespeare's Falstaff, although combined with a real distinction of mind. Savage's sense of his due extended beyond his alleged parentage to his assertion of "the natural dignity of wit." Thus fortified, "the insurmountable obstinacy of his spirit" (*Lives*, 2: 940), his Quixote-like unwillingness or inability to make terms with the world, was practically disastrous and often self-deluding but also compels a kind of admiration. Johnson sometimes condenses the fascinating ironies involved into a single sentence:

> It was his peculiar happiness, that he scarcely ever found a stranger, whom he did not leave a friend; but it must likewise be added, that he had not often a friend long, without obliging him to become a stranger. (*Lives*, 2: 897)

> On a bulk, in a cellar, or in a glass-house among thieves and beggars, was to the found the author of *The Wanderer*, the man of exalted sentiments, extensive views, and curious observations. (*Lives*, 2: 929)

He was remarkably retentive of his ideas, which, when once he was in possession of them, rarely forsook him; a quality which could never be communicated to his money. (*Lives*, 2: 934)

A strain of comparable comedy appears in many of the other *Lives*, as if the special case of Savage reveals ironies almost inherent in *the life of a poet*. In some cases, the poet's endeavor came to nothing, or their success proved short-lived; in all cases, poetic ambition is exposed to the mundane accidents of life and the certainty of mortality; and Johnson takes special delight in exposing literary pretension to the ironies of circumstance or event or human weakness. Thus we hear of Cowley the eloquent love-poet but timid lover; of the wild story of the great Dryden's farcical funeral; of Prior presenting an ode to a king most unlikely ever to read it; of the literary dictator Addison crippled with anxiety behind the scenes of his stoical tragedy *Cato*, or whenever some parliamentary document was required of him; of Shenstone the creator of elegant landscapes, irritated to be asked if there were fish in his water. The stronger the pretension to literary specialness, the more sharply Johnson checks it against experience of life itself. Of Pope's threat that critical ill-treatment may induce him to give up writing:

> I have heard of an ideot who used to revenge his vexations by lying all night upon the bridge. "There is nothing," says Juvenal, "that a man will not believe in his own favour." Pope had been flattered till he thought himself one of the moving powers in the system of life. When he talked of laying down his pen, those who sat round him intreated and implored, and self-love did not suffer him to suspect that they went away and laughed. (*Lives*, 3: 1116–17)

This is close to satire, and a form of karma: Johnson gives Pope a hard time partly because Pope, as satirist, wrote damningly of others, ridiculing dullness and poverty as well as vice. Savage, too, "did not wholly refrain from such satire as he afterwards thought very unjust, when he was exposed to it himself" (*Lives*, 2: 902). But in the *Lives*' wider context of life's ironies and disparities, the flashes at satire merge into a different, more inclusive mode of comedy, often mordant, sometimes rueful, often also very funny. Such humor expresses a form of critical intelligence; if poetry matters, it must survive exposure to the ironies that life supplies.

Milton

Johnson did not find Milton congenial, either as man or as poet. In the final pages of the *Life of Milton* he admires *Paradise Lost* immensely, but with an admiration that observes its distance from pleasure. He seems to have responded to its sublimity or greatness as a problematic quality that excludes more intimate involvement: Milton's images and descriptions lack "the freshness, raciness, and energy of immediate observation" (*Lives*, 1: 191). Paragraphs of unstinting praise for Milton's power of imagination, thought, and invention lead up to the following:

> But original deficience cannot be supplied. The want of human interest is always felt. *Paradise Lost* is one of the books which the reader admires and lays down, and forgets to take up again. None ever wished it longer than it is. Its perusal is a duty rather than a pleasure. We read Milton for instruction, retire harrassed and overburdened, and look elsewhere for recreation; we desert our master and seek for companions. (*Lives*, 1: 196)

This sounds damning, but in the context Johnson's reservations do not undercut his praise, although they do define its nature. When reading these pages, the reader may feel that their real tribute to Milton's poem lies in the tension they consciously exhibit, the tremendous stretching of the mind that they enforce. The last sentence of the *Life* states *Paradise Lost* to be, after Homer, the greatest of heroic poems, yet it is also a work no one willingly rereads. There is a remarkable, arguably Miltonic, capaciousness in being able to advance both claims, and in certain charged passages Johnson holds a great complexity of response in a single phrase:

> The appearances of nature, and the occurrences of life, did not satiate his appetite of greatness. To paint things as they are, requires a minute attention, and employs the memory rather than the fancy. Milton's delight was to sport in the wide regions of possibility; reality was a scene too narrow for his mind. (*Lives*, 1: 190)

A different point arises from that image of Milton as "master," and from Johnson's restive resistance to such authority. In his *Life of Philips*, he describes how Philips's low-life parody of Milton "gratifies the mind with a momentary triumph over that grandeur which hitherto held its captives in admiration" (*Lives*, 1: 344). Milton's extraordinary independence of spirit – which Johnson reproves in the republican propagandist but celebrates in the poet – seems to be at work also in Johnson, his reader. As in the other substantial *Lives*, as we shall see, it is Johnson's way, in part, to mirror what he finds.

Swift

Swift presented Johnson with another grippingly uncongenial subject. Well aware of how differently Swift could be viewed – he includes a measured eulogy by Swift's friend Patrick Delany – Johnson nevertheless offers an acerbic portrait of an acerbic figure, rigorous toward himself and others, "fond of singularity, and desirous to make a mode of happiness for himself, different from the general course of things" (*Lives*, 2: 1003; the *Life's* last word on Swift is "original"; 2: 1023). At the end of the biographical section, Johnson sets out Swift's isolation and decay with a terrible factuality that blasts the possibility of comment. This and the pages on his character that follow highlight a rigor that torments itself in denying the human weakness and dependency that it cannot entirely escape.

In all this, Johnson is trying Swift's standards upon himself. For any possible defense of his behavior toward "Vanessa," "recourse must be had to that extenuation which he so much despised, 'men are but men'" (*Lives*, 2: 996). The rigorous factuality of the account of Swift's final years mimics something of Swift's own moral and stylistic rigor, and Swift is granted no shelter from a potentially satirical, ruthlessly comedic perspective. "His asperity continually increasing, condemned him to solitude; and his resentment of solitude sharpened his asperity" (*Lives*, 2: 1007).

But where in this is the writer of genius, the brilliant ironist who fascinates modern readers? When Johnson formally turns from biography to consider Swift "as an author" (*Lives*, 2: 1010), he is drawn back within a few paragraphs to Swift's personal character. This is itself eloquent. With other poets included in the *Lives of the Poets* who earn a portrait of their "character" – Milton, Dryden, Pope – this refers above all to the mind encountered in the poetry. There are connections with the biographical portrait, but Johnson shows how personality can be transfigured through the act of writing. But in Swift's case there is no escape velocity, so to speak; his poems "are, for the most part, what their author intended" (*Lives*, 2: 1022). The single though strong exception is *A Tale of a Tub*, a work unlike anything else by Swift, to be "considered by itself," written with an energy which "he afterwards never possessed or never exerted" (*Lives*, 2: 1011).

In just one paragraph does Johnson suggest how he apprehended the subtlety of Swiftian irony, its shifting power-relations, its games with the reader:

> On all common occasions, he habitually affects a style of arrogance, and dictates rather than persuades. This authoritative and magisterial language he expected to be received as his peculiar mode of jocularity; but he apparently flattered his own arrogance by an assumed imperiousness, in which he was ironical only to the resentful, and to the submissive sufficiently serious. (*Lives*, 2: 1018)

Dryden

The *Life of Dryden* is a long and sprawling work, matching the life and *oeuvre* of its subject. The evident and immense warmth of Johnson's response is hard to ground in what he says about specific works and passages; it seems to be a question, rather, of the poetry's "general effects and ultimate result" (*Lives*, 1: 481), in the phrase that Johnson uses in preferring Dryden's translation of Virgil to more polished versions. Because of this, reading this *Life* can be a puzzle. One clue comes within the account of Dryden's critical prose, which follows the biographical section. Johnson here gives his impression of how Dryden acquired his "great stores of intellectual wealth," his abundance of sparkling ideas. He read diligently, no doubt,

> yet I rather believe that the knowledge of Dryden was gleaned from accidental intelligence and various conversation . . . by vigilance that permitted nothing to pass without notice, and a habit of reflection that suffered nothing useful to be lost. A mind like Dryden's, always curious, always active, to which every understanding was proud to be associated, and of which every one solicited the regard, by an ambitious display of himself, had a more pleasant, perhaps a nearer, way to knowledge than by the silent progress of solitary reading. . . . he was carried out, by the impetuosity of his genius, to more vivid and speedy instructors . . . his studies were rather desultory and fortuitous than constant and systematical. (*Lives*, 1: 442)

The warmth of Johnson's appreciation is communicated throughout this whole passage. To write the lives of poets is to set life alongside literature, and Johnson cannot love literature that appears merely literary – ostentatiously ingenious (Cowley and Donne, sometimes) or bookish (Milton, sometimes) or conventionally "poetical." But Dryden's fullness of matter and mind feels to be impregnated by worldly connection, "gleaned" in conversation, the product of active and various encounter and sharing, and – it is stressed – "accidental" and "fortuitous" rather than "systematical."

This last point matters especially in a work of condensed biography like the *Lives of the Poets*, which records on so many pages the effect of contingency and circumstance, the accidents of upbringing and education, patronage and politics, relationship and estrangement, and finally the great contingency of aging and death. If all writing is to some degree a repudiation of contingency, it can also be its product. Johnson notes repeatedly how poets can get lucky. Some famous lines from Denham's "Cooper's Hill" are "among those felicities which cannot be produced at will by wit and labour, but must arise unexpectedly in some hour propitious to poetry" (*Lives*, 1: 94). The best moments in Addison are "what perhaps every human excellence must be, the product of good-luck improved by genius" (*Lives*, 2: 654). *The Beggar's Opera*, Gay's tremendous success, is "this lucky piece" (*Lives*, 2: 797). Pope's brilliant insertion of the sylphs into *The Rape of the Lock* was an unrepeatable highpoint, being a combination "of skilful genius with happy casualty" (*Lives*, 2: 1060). What Johnson finds in Dryden's way of acquiring knowledge and generating thought has an openness to the "fortuitous" nature of living-in-the-world that he likes immensely: his usual vigilance against the narrowness of the literary seems to relax and drop away.

This pleasure in openness or porosity continues in the paragraphs that immediately follow, on Dryden's wonderfully style-less prose style. This has "not the formality of a settled style . . . every word seems to drop by chance, though it falls into its proper place."

> He who writes much will not easily escape a manner, such a recurrence of particular modes as may be easily noted. Dryden is always "*another and the same*," he does not exhibit a second time the same elegances in the same form, nor appears to have any art other than that of expressing with clearness what he thinks with vigour. (*Lives*, 1: 443)

Again, the whole passage is worth full consideration. "Another and the same" comes from Dryden's version of Ovid's *Metamorphoses* Book 15 (line 581) and links the magically unmannered quality of Dryden's writing with the endless mobility of the Ovidian cosmos. The phrase also suggests why creativity and translation sat in him so easily together. Although Johnson's immediate topic is the prose, these thoughts extend seamlessly to the poetry: that Dryden cannot be parodied, unlike, say, Milton or Pope, says something important about the nature of his genius.

. . . and Pope

Following on from this, another passage not to be missed comes not in the *Life of Dryden* but two-thirds of the way through the *Life of Pope*, immediately before the section in which Johnson discusses Pope's poems one by one. The biographical section of the *Life of Pope* has led into an account of Pope's character, personal and intellectual, which concludes with an extended comparison of Pope with Dryden that illuminates both writers. Johnson opens this comparison by contrasting Dryden's casualness with Pope's perfectionism; Dryden wrote

merely for the people; and when he pleased others, he contented himself. He
spent no time in struggles to rouse latent powers; he never attempted to
make that better which was already good, nor often to mend what he must
have known to be faulty. . . . when occasion or necessity called upon him, he
poured out what the present moment happened to supply. . .

   Pope was not content to satisfy; he desired to excel, and therefore always
endeavoured to do his best: he did not court the candour, but dared the
judgement of his reader, [revising his work] with indefatigable diligence, till
he had left nothing to be forgiven. (*Lives*, 3: 1188)

On the face of it, Johnson is explaining how it is that Pope's product is
often better than Dryden's. But we also feel that what Dryden loses by one
measure he gains by another. Leaving much to be forgiven, he invites his
reader's "candour" or generous kindness, which is the more readily granted
because the poetry sets out merely to please, with none of the competitive
stressfulness associated with excellence. (Johnson reminds us what Pope
rarely forgot: that to excel is to excel others.)

   It is striking in this how the judgment of poetic quality is mediated by the
kind of *personal relationship* that each body of poetry offers. Johnson speaks
at the end of this comparison of his "partial fondness for the memory of
Dryden" (*Lives*, 3: 1193), who died, of course, before Johnson was born; the
personal affection Johnson feels is for the mind he meets in the poetry.

   One more quotation from the comparison with Pope:

Of genius, that power which constitutes a poet; that quality without which
judgement is cold and knowledge is inert; that energy which collects,
combines, amplifies, and animates; the superiority must, with some hesita-
tion, be allowed to Dryden. (*Lives*, 3: 1190)

Johnson's long-standing reservations about the desire for perfection, in life
as in art, mean that he approaches Pope, who "left nothing to be forgiven,"
in a correspondingly unforgiving spirit. The pretensions, insecurities, and
pettinesses of Pope the man are probed and exposed, and the poems
scrutinized, often one by one, for points of objection. Although there is
also much to praise, we are brought, at the end, to that tentative preference
for Dryden.

   But the overall judgment conveyed by the *Life of Pope* is complex; if
Johnson is often unimpressed by Pope's claims for himself, he firmly resists
contemporary tendencies to downgrade Pope as writing a second-order kind
of poetry. Johnson vigorously denies that Pope is only a poet of "good sense":

Pope had likewise genius; a mind active, ambitious, and adventurous,
always investigating, always aspiring; in its widest searches still longing to

go forward, in its highest flights still wishing to be higher; always imagining something greater than it knows, always endeavouring more than it can do. (*Lives*, 3: 1183–4)

There is nothing inherently limited about Pope's poetic intelligence, nothing to prevent his poetry being compared with the most highly imaginative, creative work. Still, there is a noticeable difference between this account of genius and that, just quoted, which comes to mind when Dryden is in the frame. The energy which "collects, combines, amplifies, and animates" – terms primarily applied to Dryden – is at home within life, it operates on and within the materials of the world; Pope's aspiring mind is forever seeking new horizons, in a restless, insatiable discontent with the given which, we may notice, is reflected in many of his poems at the level of theme and subject. The rhythm of Johnson's sentence sympathetically evokes that restlessness, even while it also establishes an element of necessary failure or division, a potential for bathos, at its core.

The pages following, toward the end of the *Life*, take Pope's major writings one by one. Johnson is fully engaged here; every paragraph is of great interest, and anyone interested in Pope will want to weigh each observation. Let me select just a few points of interest.

Passages are singled out for high praise from right across Pope's career. We get no sense of an upward curve; he never wrote better than in *An Essay on Criticism* (1711). *Eloisa to Abelard* and *The Rape of the Lock* are other early works that get glowing praise, specifically for how they hold the imagined together with the actual.

Of the *Elegy on an Unfortunate Lady*, Johnson writes in its favor that Pope has no poem "in which the sense predominates more over the diction" (*Lives*, 3: 1197). This points up a recurrent concern: is Pope in some sense too skillful a poet, able to compensate for weakness of thought with the power of language? This surfaces particularly with the philosophical *Essay on Man*: "The reader feels his mind full, though he learns nothing" (*Lives*, 3: 1219). Johnson defends Pope's musical versification, but also says that "to attempt any further improvement of versification will be *dangerous*" (my italics). This chimes with the larger model of cultural development that he sketches in relation to Pope's translation of Homer, in which "sense" increasingly needs to be supplemented by "elegance." Writing for the eighteenth century, Pope necessarily made Homer "graceful, but lost him some of his sublimity" (*Lives*, 3: 1212–14). The whole *Lives of the Poets* describes, perhaps, a curve that has Pope close to its tipping point. (See, for example, the comparison of Prior with Butler in the *Life of Prior, Lives*, 2: 726.)

But the great highpoint in the *Life of Pope* is "that poetical wonder, the translation of the *Iliad*, a performance which no age or nation can pretend to equal" (*Lives*, 3: 1210). Here Johnson's pleasure and admiration (for once not at odds) run strong and free, like nowhere else in the *Lives*. Demurrals are registered but set decisively aside, extinguished in the magnitude of Pope's achievement. Any reader wishing to explore Johnson's lead should push Pope's *Iliad* toward the top of their reading-list.

Easily Overlooked

Johnson knew that poets can surpass themselves and picks out some works for exceptional praise which may be conveniently gathered together:

- Cowley, "The Motto" ("What shall I do?"); the ode "Of Wit"; "The Chronicle"; "On the Death of Mr Crashaw."
- Denham, "To Sir Richard Fanshaw"; "On Mr Abraham Cowley."
- Dryden, "To the Pious Memory of . . . Anne Killigrew"; "Alexander's Feast".
- Smith, "On the Death of Mr John Philips."
- Congreve's *The Mourning Bride* has "the most poetical paragraph" in all English poetry (*Lives*, 2: 748; quoted in full). The passage comes from Act 2 Scene 1, beginning "It was a fancied noise."
- Blackmore, *Creation.*
- Tickell's elegy on Addison ("If dumb too long. . .").
- Shenstone's "Pastoral Ballad," especially the first part, "Absence."

Several of these items are poems of personal tribute, which may say something about Johnson's values, or about the kind of occasion that raises poets beyond themselves.

In equally miscellaneous spirit, the helpful tour-guide can also point out the valuable discussions of particular topics to be found within the *Lives*. The vexed question of the freedom of the press is addressed in the *Life of Milton* (*Lives*, 1: 125–26). An incisive sketch of *Don Quixote* begins the account of Butler's *Hudibras* (*Lives*, 1: 215–16). The colonizing idea and impulse, and the iniquities of its practice, are addressed in connection with Savage's "On Public Spirit," halfway through that *Life* (*Lives*, 2: 923–25). And at the end of the *Life of Waller* comes Johnson's fullest theorization of his belief that "poetical devotion cannot often please" (*Lives*, 1: 313–16).

Reading for Pleasure

Johnson describes Dryden's critical writings as

> the criticism of a poet; not a dull collection of theorems, nor a rude detection of faults, which perhaps the censor was not able to have committed; but a gay and vigorous dissertation, where delight is mingled with instruction, and where the author proves his right of judgement, by his power of performance. (*Lives*, 1: 437–38)

I hope I've suggested how pleasurable, in many passages, the *Lives of the Poets* are to read, and also how central pleasure is in Johnson's thinking. This is the pleasure of connection and engagement; of language that is animated and energetic rather than dutiful or conventional, yet without being estranged from the actualities of life. One good reason for the student to explore the *Lives of the Poets* is to remember the often unacknowledged hunger for pleasure that drives our reading.

CHAPTER 13

Johnson as Biographer

Leo Damrosch

The *Lives of the Poets* are not only classics of literary criticism, they are masterpieces of biography as well. By the time he wrote them late in life, Johnson was already an experienced biographer, having published brief accounts of numerous subjects ranging from Confucius to Frederick the Great. Appearing in the *Gentleman's Magazine* and elsewhere over the years, those were journeyman work and are only modestly interesting today, apart from occasional comments that are characteristically Johnsonian, as when he called the Dutch scientist and physician Herman Boerhaave "one of those mighty capacities to whom scarce any thing appears impossible, and who think nothing worthy of their efforts but what appears insurmountable to common understandings" (*BW*, 32).

The one truly impressive work from the earlier years is the 1744 *Life of Richard Savage*, grounded in Johnson's close friendship with Savage when he was first in London. It suffers, however, from closeness to its subject. Savage somehow convinced the usually skeptical Johnson that his aristocratic birth mother was cruelly persecuting him; in reality Savage was delusional, she was not his mother, and it was he who was doing the persecuting. Still, Johnson's expressions of personal feeling are affecting. When Savage, totally broke, accepted a subsidy from friends and set off to live inexpensively in Wales, "he left London in July 1739, having taken leave with great tenderness of his friends, and parted from the author of this narrative with tears in his eyes" (*Lives*, 2: 945).

Johnson comments in *Rambler* 14, "There has often been observed a manifest and striking contrariety between the life of an author and his writings" (*Rambler*, 1: 74). By then he had already said of Savage, in a nice balance between judgment and understanding, "The reigning error of his life was, that he mistook the love for the practice of virtue, and was indeed not so much a good man, as the friend of goodness" (*Lives*, 2: 909).

Borrowing from an earlier account of Savage, Johnson was able to include a moving story about his friend's final days in debtors' prison.

The last time that the keeper saw him was on July the 31st, 1743; when Savage, seeing him at his bed-side, said, with an uncommon earnestness, "I have something to say to you, Sir;" but, after a pause, moved his hand in a melancholy manner; and, finding himself unable to recollect what he was going to communicate, said, "'Tis gone!" The keeper soon after left him; and the next morning he died. (*Lives*, 2: 963)

As conclusion, after fully acknowledging Savage's fecklessness, Johnson challenges the reader: "Those are no proper judges of his conduct, who have slumbered away their time on the down of plenty; nor will any wise man presume to say, 'Had I been in Savage's condition, I should have lived or written better than Savage'" (968).

The *Lives of the Poets* began as a commission from a consortium of forty-three booksellers (or as we would say, publishers). Johnson wrote to Boswell in 1777, "I am engaged to write little Lives, and little Prefaces, to a little edition of the English poets" (*Letters*, 3: 20). There were fifty-eight in all, many of whom were considered very minor even at the time. Johnson had no role in choosing them, though he did suggest adding a few. Whenever the poems were unimpressive, he didn't hesitate to say so. "It is reported that the juvenile compositions of Stepney 'made grey authors blush.' I know not whether his poems will appear such wonders to the present age. One cannot always easily find the reason for which the world has sometimes conspired to squander praise" (*Lives*, 1: 337).

For the *Lives*, Johnson developed a three-part structure. First came formal biography, then a general assessment of character (omitted in some of the shorter lives), and finally a critique of specific poems. In some cases Johnson shows that these embody the poet's character in a meaningful way; in others no real connection is suggested, and the three parts seem a structuring convenience rather than a mode of analysis.

By the publishers' decision, the earliest poet in the collection was Abraham Cowley, who died in 1667 – no Chaucer, Spenser, Shakespeare, or Herbert. Donne's poems were discussed in connection with Cowley, but not Donne's life. A revised version of the *Life of Savage* was also included. At various times, Johnson did think of writing the lives of Chaucer and Spenser, but like many of his projects those were never carried out.

Once he began, Johnson got carried away, and when the collection was published, he explained in it, "I have been led beyond my intention, I hope, by the honest desire of giving useful pleasure" (*Lives*, 1: 1). Entitled *Works of the English Poets*, it came out in fifty-six octavo volumes in 1779–80. In 1781, the prefaces were reissued by themselves, in ten volumes, as *Lives of the Most Eminent English Poets, with Critical*

Observations on Their Works. These soon became known as *Lives of the Poets*.

Johnson once told Boswell, "The biographical part of literature is what I love most" (*Life*, 1: 425), and in *Rambler* 60 he had sketched his own ideas about biography. "We are all prompted by the same motives, all deceived by the same fallacies, all animated by hope, obstructed by danger, entangled by desire, and seduced by pleasure . . . I have often thought that there has rarely passed a life of which a judicious and faithful narrative would not be useful." But even if similar emotions are common to everyone, good biography must also illuminate the uniqueness of individuals. "Thus Salust, the great master of nature, has not forgot, in his account of Catiline, to remark that 'his walk was now quick, and again slow,' as an indication of a mind revolving something with violent commotion" (*Rambler*, 1: 320–21).

There were few recent precedents for what Johnson was undertaking; his chief models were Plutarch and Suetonius. A significant English predecessor was Isaac Walton, whose lives of Donne and Herbert (1670) he often praised, but Walton idealizes his subjects. So did many biographers. Thomas Sprat, Johnson says, "has given the character, not the life of Cowley; for he writes with so little detail, that scarcely any thing is distinctly known, but all is shown confused and enlarged through the mist of panegyrick" (*Lives*, 1: 6). Johnson is far more open to complexities of character, and to the significance of contradictory or irrational behavior.

He worked on the *Lives*, as he admitted ruefully in his diary, "in my usual way, dilatorily and hastily, unwilling to work, and working with vigour and haste" (*DPA*, 304). Nevertheless, they are deeply meditated, and at the same time wonderfully readable and fresh. Lytton Strachey memorably praised "the easy, indolent power, the searching sense of actuality, the combined command of sanity and paradox, the immovable independence of thought . . . . As one reads, the brilliant sentences seem to come to one out of the past with the intimacy of a conversation."[1] Another early twentieth-century writer concluded, "Johnson's last and greatest work is more than a collection of facts: it is a book of wisdom and experience, a treatise on the conduct of life, a commentary on human destiny."[2] By modern standards Johnson's research was spotty, but he conducted it more conscientiously than most biographers in his own time, making use of such information as he could obtain from existing

---

[1] Lytton Strachey, *Books and Characters* (New York: Harcourt Brace, 1922), pp. 74–79.
[2] Walter Raleigh, *Six Essays on Johnson* (Oxford: Clarendon Press, 1910), p. 26.

biographies, letters, and collections such as the *Biographia Britannica* (1747–66) and Anthony Wood's *Athenae Oxoniensis* (1721). He faced a double challenge, as he noted in the *Life of Addison*: for older authors there was often little information to draw upon, and for recent ones it might be ill-advised to report everything that was known. "As the process of these narratives is now bringing me among my contemporaries, I begin to feel myself 'walking upon ashes under which the fire is not extinguished,' and coming to the time of which it will be proper rather to say 'nothing that is false, than all that is true'" (*Lives*, 2: 637).

All too often, Johnson was frustrated in his search for materials. About Edmund Smith he says, "little is known" (*Lives*, 2: 509). "Of Mr. Richard Duke I can find few memorials" (2: 536). "The brevity with which I am to write the account of Elijah Fenton is not the effect of indifference or negligence. I have sought intelligence among his relations in his native county, but have not obtained it" (2: 777). More significant, Johnson thought, was the paucity of anecdotes about the celebrated Dryden.

> Of his petty habits or slight amusements, tradition has retained little. Of the only two men whom I have found to whom he was personally known, one told me that at the house which he frequented, called Will's Coffee-house, the appeal upon any literary dispute was made to him; and the other related, that his armed chair, which in the winter had a settled and prescriptive place by the fire, was in the summer placed in the balcony, and that he called the two places his winter and his summer seat. This is all the intelligence which his two survivors afforded me. (*Lives*, 1: 434)

The joke about the summer seat was so feeble that Boswell didn't get it when Johnson mentioned it in conversation and recorded it as "summer chair" (*Life*, 3: 71).

Johnson once remarked, "I love anecdotes" (*Boswell's Scotland*, 22); he had stored up many in his capacious memory and filled the *Lives of the Poets* with them, as when he describes Bishop Thomas Sprat and a colleague preaching before the House of Commons, where the listeners expressed approval by humming loudly. "Bishop Burnet sat down to enjoy it, and rubbed his face with his handkerchief. When Sprat preached, he likewise was honoured with the like animating 'hum'; but he stretched out his hand to the congregation, and cried, 'Peace, peace, I pray you, peace.' This I was told in my youth by my father, an old man, who had been no careless observer of the passages of those times" (*Lives*, 2: 551).

When Addison's *Cato* was first staged in 1713, "The author, as Mrs. Porter long afterwards related, wandered through the whole exhibition behind the

scenes with restless and unappeasable solicitude" (2: 621). Johnson knew
Mary Porter, who had been an actress in the play that night. She had died in
1767, and Johnson's father Michael as long ago as 1731, but both examples
suggest how long Johnson's memory was when recalling anecdotes for use in
the *Lives of the Poets*.

From Joseph Spence's reminiscences of Pope (*Observations, Anecdotes,
and Characters of Books and Men*, published posthumously in 1820),
Johnson borrowed an anecdote that perfectly captures the Earl of
Oxford's tendency, as Queen Anne's chief minister, to let people down.
When the playwright Nicholas Rowe sought a government appointment,
"Oxford enjoined him to study Spanish; and when, some time afterwards,
he came again, and said that he had mastered it, dismissed him with this
congratulation, 'Then, Sir, I envy you the pleasure of reading *Don Quixot*
in the original'" (*Life of Rowe*; *Lives*, 2: 585–86).

Occasionally, Johnson permits himself a personal note, as he had
done in the *Life of Savage*. Half a century previously he had heard
anecdotes about Edmund Smith from Gilbert Walmesley, a Lichfield
lawyer who gave him valuable encouragement. After repeating these
Johnson adds,

> Of Gilbert Walmsley, thus presented to my mind, let me indulge myself in
> the remembrance. I knew him very early; he was one of the first friends that
> literature procured me, and I hope that at least my gratitude made me
> worthy of his notice.
>
> He was of an advanced age, and I was only not a boy; yet he never received
> my notions with contempt. He was a Whig, with all the virulence and
> malevolence of his party; yet difference of opinion did not keep us apart.
> I honoured him, and he endured me. (*Life of Smith*; *Lives*, 2: 532–33)

Recalling the hours spent at Walmesley's convivial table prompts Johnson
to mention that David Garrick was there too, "whom I hoped to have
gratified with this character of our common friend: but what are the hopes
of man! I am disappointed by that stroke of death, which has eclipsed the
gaiety of nations, and impoverished the publick stock of harmless pleasure"
(*Lives*, 2: 532–33).

Beyond the anecdotes, the *Lives* are filled with penetrating judgments.
For example, when the death of Queen Anne brought down Oxford's
ministry, "Not knowing what to do, he did nothing; and with the fate of
a double-dealer, at last he lost his power, but kept his enemies" (*Life of
Swift*; *Lives*, 2: 985). And on Addison's fondness for alcohol, "From the
coffee-house he went again to a tavern, where he often sat late, and drank

too much wine. In the bottle, discontent seeks for comfort, cowardice for courage, and bashfulness for confidence" (*Lives*, 2: 645).

The *Lives* are flavored throughout by Johnson's wit, often the vehicle by which his judgments are delivered, as in this account of seventeenth-century Puritans:

> Much therefore of that humour which transported the last century with merriment is lost to us, who do not know the sour solemnity, the sullen superstition, the gloomy moroseness, and the stubborn scruples of the ancient Puritans; or, if we knew them, derive our information only from books, or from tradition, have never had them before our eyes, and cannot but by recollection and study understand the lines in which they are satirised. Our grandfathers knew the picture from the life; we judge of the life by contemplating the picture ... We have never been witnesses of animosities excited by the use of minced pies and plumb porridge; nor seen with what abhorrence those who could eat them at all other times of the year would shrink from them in December. An old Puritan, who was alive in my childhood, being at one of the feasts of the church invited by a neighbour to partake his cheer, told him, that if he would treat him at an alehouse with beer, brewed for all times and seasons, he should accept his kindness, but would have none of his superstitious meats or drinks. (*Life of Butler*, *Lives*, 1: 221–23)

All along there are pithy formulations that reveal new insights. Dryden had "a mind better formed to reason than to feel" (*Lives*, 1: 460). Edmund Waller "doubtless praised some whom he would have been afraid to marry; and perhaps married one whom he would have been ashamed to praise" (1: 269).

Four major lives stand out: those of Milton, Swift, Dryden, and Pope. The *Life of Cowley* is impressive too, but mainly for its analysis of the metaphysical poets, which has been called "possibly the most famous digression in the history of criticism,"[3] and which occasioned some of T. S. Eliot's canonical critical propositions.[4]

The most unsatisfying of the four is the *Life of Swift*, since Johnson had a jaundiced view of Swift the man, and not much respect for the writer. Of the existing biographies, he relied mainly on an ungenerous memoir by the Earl of Orrery (1751), and too little on more balanced accounts by Patrick Delany (1754) and Deane Swift (1755). (The important biography by

---

[3] Robert Folkenflik, *Samuel Johnson, Biographer* (Ithaca, NY: Cornell University Press, 1978), p. 109.
[4] T. S. Eliot, "The Metaphysical Poets," *in Selected Essays* (London: Faber and Faber, 1972 [1921]), pp. 281–91.

Swift's godson Thomas Sheridan didn't come out until 1784, the year of Johnson's death.)

Johnson did admire the *Tale of a Tub* but claimed provocatively that nothing else by Swift came close to it: "His *Tale of a Tub* has little resemblance to his other pieces. It exhibits a vehemence and rapidity of mind, a copiousness of images, and vivacity of diction, such as he afterwards never possessed, or never exerted" (*Lives*, 2: 1011). As for *Gulliver's Travels*, Johnson manages to damn it with faint praise: "The part which gave least pleasure was that which describes the Flying Island, and that which gave most disgust must be the history of the Houyhnhnms" (2: 1001). Johnson does not mention the *Modest Proposal*.

On Swift's character Johnson was likewise unsympathetic, but he did bring out significant traits, such as compulsive cleanliness: "He had a kind of muddy complexion, which, though he washed himself with oriental scrupulosity, did not look clear" (2: 1014). And although Johnson might have been expected to endorse the tradition that Swift only pretended to religious faith, he dismissed that charge with shrewd insight. "The suspicions of his irreligion proceeded in a great measure from his dread of hypocrisy; instead of wishing to seem better, he delighted in seeming worse than he was" (*Lives*, 2: 1014). Swift's closest friends indeed saw him that way. The politician and political philosopher Viscount Bolingbroke (who was not himself religious) called him an inverted hypocrite, *hypocrite renversé*.

On Swift's role as Irish patriot, Johnson is deeply admiring, at a time when anti-Irish prejudice was common in England. He describes with approval the success of the *Drapier's Letters* (1735) in blocking an attempt to debase Irish coinage, and he honors Swift's achievement in helping to forge a national consciousness. "In the succeeding reign [of George I] he delivered Ireland from plunder and oppression; and shewed that wit, confederated with truth, had such force as authority was unable to resist. He said truly of himself, that Ireland 'was his debtor'" (2: 1010–11).

Swift, like Johnson, was a conservative Tory. Milton was altogether different, a militant Puritan who worked for Oliver Cromwell and was fortunate, after the Restoration, not to be executed for having defended the execution of Charles I. Johnson manages to evade that issue by understanding Milton's politics not as principled commitment, but instead as a defect of character.

> His political notions were those of an acrimonious and surly republican . . .
> Milton's republicanism was, I am afraid, founded in an envious hatred of

greatness, and a sullen desire of independence; in petulance, impatient of controul, and pride disdainful of superiority. He hated monarchs in the state, and prelates in the church; for he hated all whom he was required to obey. It is to be suspected that his predominant desire was to destroy rather than establish, and that he felt not so much the love of liberty as repugnance to authority. (*Life of Milton; Lives*, 1: 171)

This evaluation suggests implications for Milton's family life, given that he treated his wives and daughters severely "as subordinate and inferior beings." Johnson makes a further point, however, when he adds that Milton "thought woman made only for obedience, and man only for rebellion" (1: 171). Before the Fall man too was obedient, as he should have been. Rebelliousness like Milton's thus recapitulates Satan's rebellion against the Almighty.

But however sternly Johnson judges Milton the man, he describes *Paradise Lost* as a supreme achievement, essentially separating the man from the work. That too raises problems for biography. Given Milton's well-known heretical beliefs, it seems implausible to declare, as Johnson does, that the theology in the poem is totally orthodox. And there is an important way in which he might indeed have drawn a connection between life and art:

To make Satan speak as a rebel, without any such expressions as might taint the reader's imagination, was indeed one of the great difficulties in Milton's undertaking, and I cannot but think that he has extricated himself with great happiness. There is in Satan's speeches little that can give pain to a pious ear. The language of rebellion cannot be the same with that of obedience. (*Lives*, 1: 186)

Many critics have argued that Milton's rebellious spirit was precisely what empowered his depiction of Satan, and some have agreed with Blake that he was of the Devil's party without knowing it. If such an interpretation ever occurred to Johnson, he clearly suppressed it. For him, "truth" was immutable and not subject to debate.

In the end, however, Johnson's estimation of Milton is generous, and he emphasizes achievement won against great odds by force of character and will. "His great works were performed under discountenance, and in blindness, but difficulties vanished at his touch; he was born for whatever is arduous, and his work is not the greatest of heroick poems, only because it is not the first." That is to say, Milton is surpassed only by Homer and Virgil.

Fancy can hardly forbear to conjecture with what temper Milton surveyed the silent progress of his work, and marked his reputation stealing its way in a kind of subterraneous current through fear and silence. I cannot but conceive him calm and confident, little disappointed, not at all dejected, relying on his own merit with steady consciousness, and waiting, without impatience, the vicissitudes of opinion, and the impartiality of a future generation. (*Lives*, 1: 160)

This is a moral hero, admirable especially since unlike Johnson, who worked by fits and starts to meet occasional demands, Milton put his entire effort into a single masterpiece and felt sure that future readers would value it as it deserved.

Less nobly resolute was Dryden, whose shifting religious and political allegiances were much criticized in his own time and later. Here Johnson is surprisingly tolerant. He acknowledges that Dryden's conversion to Catholicism, at a time when he knew that it would please Charles II, must appear self-interested. Yet Johnson chooses not to blame him:

> It is natural to hope that a comprehensive is likewise an elevated soul, and that whoever is wise is also honest. I am willing to believe that Dryden, having employed his mind, active as it was, upon different studies, and filled it, capacious as it was, with other materials, came unprovided to the controversy, and wanted rather skill to discover the right than virtue to maintain it. But enquiries into the heart are not for man; we must now leave him to his Judge. (*Life of Dryden*; *Lives*, 1: 408)

This exonerates Dryden by suggesting improbably that he just hadn't thought enough about it.

In the literary arena, where Dryden quarreled endlessly with critics and rivals, Johnson's judgment is severe. On one such occasion, "Dryden could not now repress these emotions, which he called indignation, and others jealousy; but wrote upon the play and the dedication such criticism as malignant impatience could pour out in haste" (1: 374). Yet even if Dryden disgraced himself in controversies, it was he and not his opponents whose name would be remembered. One of those was Elkanah Settle, considered at the time a worthy rival, but soon forgotten.

> Such are the revolutions of fame, or such is the prevalence of fashion, that the man whose works have not yet been thought to deserve the care of collecting them; who died forgotten in an hospital; and whose latter years were spent in contriving shows for fairs, and carrying an elegy or epithalamium, of which the beginning and end were occasionally varied, but the intermediate parts were always the same, to every house where there was a funeral or a wedding; might, with truth, have had inscribed upon his stone, Here lies the Rival and Antagonist of Dryden. (*Lives*, 1: 406–7)

This is very much in the satiric spirit of Johnson's *Vanity of Human Wishes*.

Another character flaw, as Johnson perceives it, was Dryden's abject flattery of patrons. On one of his works Johnson says, "This composition is addressed to the Princess of Modena, then Dutchess of York, in a strain of flattery which disgraces genius, and which it was wonderful that any man that knew the meaning of his own words could use without self-detestation" (1: 392–93). And on the dedications taken as a whole, "When once he has undertaken the task of praise, he no longer retains shame in himself, nor supposes it in his patron" (1: 426).

Dryden's great achievement, in Johnson's view, was to have perfected the heroic couplet. "What was said of Rome, adorned by Augustus, may be applied by an easy metaphor to English poetry embellished by Dryden, *lateritiam invenit, marmoream reliquit*, he found it brick, and he left it marble" (1: 494). But against this achievement Johnson sets the carelessness with which he used this poetic form. "Dryden was no rigid judge of his own pages; he seldom struggled after supreme excellence, but snatched in haste what was within his reach, and when he could content others was himself contented. He did not keep present to his mind an idea of pure perfection, nor compare his works, such as they were, with what they might be made" (1: 489–90).

Altogether different, in this way as in others, was Alexander Pope, the subject of the last of the major *Lives*. Still regarded in Johnson's time as the greatest modern poet, even if some critics were beginning to depreciate his work, Pope had praised Johnson's *London* when it came out, and he was remembered well by many people Johnson knew.

As with Milton, Johnson sees the poet as greater than the man. Lifelong physical disability cannot excuse his high-handed behavior toward his friends and their servants.

> The indulgence and accommodation which his sickness required, had taught him all the unpleasing and unsocial qualities of a valetudinary man. He expected that every thing should give way to his ease or humour, as a child, whose parents will not hear her cry, has an unresisted dominion in the nursery. . . . The reputation which his friendship gave, procured him many invitations; but he was a very troublesome inmate. He brought no servant, and had so many wants, that a numerous attendance was scarcely able to supply them. Wherever he was, he left no room for another, because he exacted the attention and employed the activity of the whole family. . . . In all his intercourse with mankind, he had great delight in artifice, and endeavoured to attain all his purposes by indirect and unsuspected methods. "He hardly drank tea without a stratagem." (*Lives*, 3: 1165–68)

The quotation is from Edward Young's *Love of Fame: The Universal Passion*, which Johnson called "a very great performance" (*Life of Young, Lives*, 3: 1424).

As with Dryden's quarrels, so with Pope's. Johnson, who generally ignored his own critics, deplored any willingness to descend to their level. "Pope confessed his own pain by his anger; but he gave no pain to those who had provoked him. He was able to hurt none but himself" (3: 1154). On this, Johnson adds an anecdote that he had from the painter Jonathan Richardson:

> I have heard Mr. Richardson relate, that he attended his father the painter on a visit, when one of Cibber's pamphlets came into the hands of Pope, who said, "These things are my diversion." They sat by him while he perused it, and saw his features writhen with anguish; and young Richardson said to his father, when they returned, that he hoped to be preserved from such diversion as had been that day the lot of Pope. (*Lives*, 3: 1155)

Pope's letters were available in print, and might have seemed a valuable source of insight, but Johnson is robustly skeptical about them. Even if Pope believed he was being perfectly sincere when he wrote them, "Very few can boast of hearts which they dare lay open to themselves, and of which, by whatever accident exposed, they do not shun a distinct and continued view; and, certainly, what we hide from ourselves we do not shew to our friends." It was not simple hypocrisy, then, but a subtler avoidance of self-knowledge. "To charge those favourable representations, which men give of their own minds, with the guilt of hypocritical falshood, would shew more severity than knowledge. The writer commonly believes himself" (3: 1174).

The *Essay on Man* has been much admired by modern scholars, but Johnson, for whom its ideas and argument were deeply familiar, saw the poem as an amateurish effort to philosophize by someone who had little talent for it. "Having exalted himself into the chair of wisdom, he tells us much that every man knows, and much that he does not know himself.... The reader feels his mind full, though he learns nothing; and when he meets it in its new array, no longer knows the talk of his mother and his nurse" (3: 1218–19).

Pope's true greatness lies not in arguments and ideas, but in "incessant and unwearied diligence" (*Lives*, 3: 1184) to revise and improve every single line of verse, both in meaning and in harmony of sounds. Society, not philosophy, was his proper theme, in *The Rape of the Lock*, the *Epistle to*

Arbuthnot, and the imitations of Horace. Similarly, Pope's translation of Homer had been criticized for making the ancient epic sound elegantly English, but Johnson had no patience with that: "Pope wrote for his own age and his own nation: he knew that it was necessary to colour the images and point the sentiments of his author; he therefore made him graceful, but lost him some of his sublimity" (3: 1214).

A high point of the *Lives* is a comparison between Dryden and Pope – a fair comparison since they were working in the same poetic mode. This was a recognized genre that went back to Longinus's comparison between Demosthenes and Cicero, and had been picked up by Pope himself in the Preface to his translation of the *Iliad*: "Homer, like the Nile, pours out his riches with a boundless overflow; Virgil, like a river in its banks, with a gentle and constant stream."[5] What Johnson is comparing is not just poems, but two kinds of mind, one daring and risk-taking, the other cautious and perfectionist. The daring kind appeals more directly to Johnson, but he does full justice to both. The splendid set-piece deserves to be quoted at length:

> Of genius, that power which constitutes a poet; that quality without which judgement is cold and knowledge is inert; that energy which collects, combines, amplifies, and animates; the superiority must, with some hesitation, be allowed to Dryden. It is not to be inferred that of this poetical vigour Pope had only a little, because Dryden had more; for every other writer since Milton must give place to Pope; and even of Dryden it must be said, that if he has brighter paragraphs, he has not better poems. Dryden's performances were always hasty, either excited by some external occasion, or extorted by domestick necessity; he composed without consideration, and published without correction. What his mind could supply at call, or gather in one excursion, was all that he sought, and all that he gave. The dilatory caution of Pope enabled him to condense his sentiments, to multiply his images, and to accumulate all that study might produce, or chance might supply. If the flights of Dryden therefore are higher, Pope continues longer on the wing. If of Dryden's fire the blaze is brighter, of Pope's the heat is more regular and constant. Dryden often surpasses expectation, and Pope never falls below it. Dryden is read with frequent astonishment, and Pope with perpetual delight. (*Life of Pope*; *Lives*, 3: 1190–92)

Johnson's prose style is periodic, deploying balanced clauses, parallelisms, and antitheses to bring important distinctions to light. And unlike Pope's simple analogy, in the Preface to Homer, between two kinds of rivers, the

[5] *The Iliad of Homer* (1715), ed. Maynard Mack, in Alexander Pope, *The Twickenham Edition of the Works of Alexander Pope*, ed. John Butt et al., 11 vols. in 12 (London: Methuen, 1938–68), 7: 12.

multiplied analogies in the passage above are a compliment to an attentive reader, who is invited to slow down and ponder what they imply.

Johnson concludes, "If the reader should suspect me, as I suspect myself, of some partial fondness for the memory of Dryden, let him not too hastily condemn me; for meditation and enquiry may, perhaps, shew him the reasonableness of my determination" (*Life of Pope*; *Lives*, 3: 1190–93).

My subject in this chapter has been Johnson as biographer, not as critic, but in the end the two are inseparable. It is temperament and qualities of mind, not just skill with words, that create poems worth reading. To achieve that, a poet must establish complicity with readers, making them eager for what he is giving them. Even *Paradise Lost*, deeply though Johnson admires it, can't always be said to do that. As is quoted elsewhere in this volume, "The want of human interest is always felt. *Paradise Lost* is one of the books which the reader admires and lays down, and forgets to take up again. None ever wished it longer than it is. Its perusal is a duty rather than a pleasure. We read Milton for instruction, retire harrassed and overburdened, and look elsewhere for recreation; we desert our master, and seek for companions" (*Life of Milton*; *Lives*, 1: 196).

It is here, in Johnson's view, that Dryden triumphs, with his soaring flights and intense blaze. And it is in the *Life of Dryden* that he pays tribute to the pleasure that the greatest writers create:

> Works of imagination excel by their allurement and delight; by their power of attracting and detaining the attention. That book is good in vain, which the reader throws away. He only is the master, who keeps the mind in pleasing captivity; whose pages are perused with eagerness, and in hope of new pleasure are perused again; and whose conclusion is perceived with an eye of sorrow, such as the traveller casts upon departing day. (1: 481)

That eloquent formulation may easily be applied to the *Lives of the Poets*.

CHAPTER 14

Johnson and Travel

Anne M. Thell

When we think about Samuel Johnson, we tend to locate him firmly within the world of objects. We imagine the weight of his massive *Dictionary*, thumping open to reveal thousands of diaphanous pages. Or his black boot kicking a rock with audible impact, as proof of the obduracy of the material world ("I refute it thus!"). And we picture the massy man himself, as he lumbers through narrow streets or clanks the giant locks on his Bolt Court door. We do this, I suspect, not just because of Johnson's pragmatic materialism – his empiricist faith in the material world and his wariness of illusion – or his oft-documented physical stature, but also as a means of concretizing his monumental *presence* in the eighteenth century and beyond. We like picturing Johnson kicking a rock because this appeals to our desire for simplicity and embeddedness: man, boot, rock. Such images are satisfyingly tangible and seem, however paradoxically, to distill reality from fiction or hearsay.

Johnson's lifelong interest in travel and travel writing falls neatly within this materialist framework, as the author understood travel as a crucial means to test universal values and to sift fantasy from reality. When we travel, we compare our assumptions and preconceptions against the real world and track the inevitable incongruities. As Johnson emphasizes, reality is often intractable to our hopes, fancies, or desires, and we must therefore constantly readjust our beliefs, or "enlarge our knowledge and rectify our opinions" (*Idler* 97, 298). Johnson was deeply invested in travel, as we see in the commentary that evolves across his prefaces and introductions, periodical essays, conversations and letters, and his own travelogues, both fictional and documentary. But Johnson's enduring interest in travel also reveals a more complex engagement with the material world – and Lockean empiricism more broadly – than we often recognize, and his attitude toward the genre is more complicated, more critical and probing, than we might expect. Travel signified to Johnson much more than an edifying experience or an opportunity to collect and verify information. For him, travel enables a mode of perception that combats habituation, sharpening our observational powers; permits access to comparative knowledge, which produces meaning and value; and allows us to assess our bodies and minds as we perceive, digest, and retain experiential knowledge. Facilitating a comparative intellectual paradigm, and foregrounding epistemology, travel is, for Johnson, a habit of mind that leverages distance and scale to produce a critical posture – the ability to "soar aloft, and take in wide views" – that underpins his thinking far beyond his travel texts (*Rambler* 43; 1: 233).

In a symmetry that mirrors the patterns embedded in his writing, Johnson launched and concluded his long and prolific writing career with accounts of travel. Among his earliest published prose, the preface to his translation of Father Jerónimo Lobo's *A Voyage to Abyssinia* (1735) celebrates Lobo's account as "curious and entertaining" as well as "judicious and instructive," and commends its author for consulting "his senses not his imagination" (*Voyage*, 3). Just a few years later, Johnson published a review of Jean-Baptiste Du Halde's *Description of China* (1738) that foregrounds its comparative value, or the "comparison which every reader naturally makes, between the ideas which he receives from the relation, and those which were familiar to him before" (*PW*, 15). In both these early appraisals, Johnson formulates what he will later concretize as one of the travel writer's fundamental goals, to "enable readers to compare their condition with that of others" (*Idler* 97, 300) or to explore "novelty" versus what "is in every place the same" (*PW*, 16), while also envisioning travel as an empiricist testing of what we think we know. One of Johnson's final works, *A Journey to the Western Islands of Scotland* (1775), is both a travelogue and an experiment with genre that probes the traditions of travel and life writing, cultural history, and historiography. Rather than simply demonstrating his ideals, or documenting details of place and people, Johnson's own travel texts – including both *A Journey* and his widely read novella *The History of Rasselas, Prince of Abissinia* (1759) – tend to erode the observational confidence and the aggregative impulses that so often underpin the travel genre. These works engage but also critique the form's primary conceits and assumptions to consider underlying questions about our capacity to observe otherness, the reliability of sensory experience, and the formal patterns that capture, or fail to capture, the messy business of human life. Like much of his *oeuvre*, then, Johnson's travel writing has a radical edge that interrogates even as it employs generic convention.

Between the 1730s and 1770s, Johnson exhibited a sustained, critical interest in travel and its varied articulations in print. In 1740, for instance, he helped to generate support for Commodore George Anson's famous – and ill-fated – privateering venture by releasing biographies of Robert Blake and Francis Drake on the eve of Anson's departure.[1] In 1757, he wrote a preface to Sir William Chambers's *Designs of Chinese Buildings, Furniture, Dresses, Machines, and Utensils*, and in 1759 he provided a critical introduction to John Newbery's massive, twenty-volume collection, *The World Displayed, or, A Curious Collection of Voyages and Travels*. Commentary on travel appears frequently in his periodical writings, *The Rambler* (1750–2), *The Adventurer* (1752–4), and *The Idler* (1758–60). In *Idler* 97, for instance, the author famously bemoans the observational and stylistic failures of "narratives of travellers," who tend to forget that "the great object of remark is human life" (298). Johnson urged Warren Hastings to systematically study Indian culture via an exhaustive checklist (*Letters*, 2: 135–37), and he, like many others, was fascinated by the Pacific voyages of Captain James Cook (1768–71, 1772–5, and 1776–80) (*Letters*, 3: 50). While he never met Cook, he became lifelong friends with Cook's shipmate, esteemed botanist Sir Joseph Banks, who eventually served as a pallbearer at Johnson's funeral. Once we become aware of its varied tenors, in fact, the concept of travel appears everywhere across Johnson's work, even in seemingly unlikely places, such as his early poem *London* (1738), which describes urban blight but also wanderlust and the fine gradients between reality and fantasy. We might even turn to his *Dictionary*, where we find "a metalanguage," to borrow Lynda Mugglestone's term, about travel, sensory experience, and the apprehension of knowledge.[2] Many of Johnson's recurrent metaphors are likewise rooted in travel, notably the "extensive view" that opens *The Vanity of Human Wishes* and triggers both comparative valuation and a relativist cosmopolitanism (*Poems*, 91).

Johnson had a lot to say about travel and exploration, and he also wrote in an age obsessed with travel, as mobility and cultural contact accelerated alongside new naval technologies, global trade routes, and Britain's more advanced colonial ventures. Famously, though, Johnson himself did not have the opportunity to travel that would have been afforded to – even expected of – young men of a certain class. As part of their education,

[1] Two decades later, Johnson's attitude changed, and he wrote an epigram denouncing the navigator, "On Lord Anson" (c. 1760) (*Poems*, 256–57).

[2] Lynda Mugglestone, "Conflicted Representations: Language, Lexicography, and Johnson's 'Langscape' of War," *Eighteenth-Century Literature*, 44:3 (2020): 75–95.

wealthy young men routinely undertook "The Grand Tour," a well-trodden Continental path through France and Italy that focused on classical learning and art, while men of lesser means might see the world as a sailor or privateer. Johnson did travel to some extent: He journeyed into Wales with Hester Thrale in 1744, through Scotland with James Boswell in 1773, and to France in 1775 with Hester and Henry Thrale and Joseph Baretti. But he was acutely aware that he lacked the more extensive travel experience of many of his contemporaries. This perceived deficiency – his position among the ranks of those who "are curious to know what is done or suffered in distant countries" (*Idler* 97, 299) – made Johnson even more conscious of the dynamics of *reading* about travel and of the contingency of secondhand knowledge more generally. Across his life, Johnson believed it crucial to "enlarge [our] notions by books or conversation" (*Rambler* 169; 3: 131), as all experience stimulates the mind and triggers complex thinking: "Every new scene impresses new ideas, enriches the imagination, and enlarges the power of reason, by new topicks of comparison" (*Letters*, 2: 232). Yet Johnson maintained a healthy skepticism in regard to the veracity, skill, and insight of any given author. He was especially attuned to the pitfalls of the travel genre, which could so easily deceive readers, and, even when genuine, often consisted of enumeration "without reflection" (*Idler* 97, 299).

Ever the self-aware reader and writer, Johnson understood that style and genre have vital epistemological functions that far exceed the ornamental. He viewed writing as an intellectual *process* that helps to organize and to synthesize lived experience (including travel experience). He therefore preferred travel literature that tended toward the polished and elevated, such as the travelogues of Joseph Addison, Charles Burney, and Patrick Brydone,[3] who all gravitate toward the neoclassical ideals of eighteenth-century *belles lettres*. Inasmuch as Johnson admired Baconian science and recommended empiricism to travelers – observation, mensuration, and record-keeping ("More nicety ... is better" [*Journey*, 146]) – in travel *writing*, he did not advocate the raw inventory of particulars, or the scientific "plain style," as recommended by the early Royal Society and employed across the century by eager "sons of enterprize" (*Idler* 97, 300). Instead, he was drawn to thoughtful, stylized accounts that might be seen to combine the humanist standards of the Renaissance, the empiricist rigor of natural history, and the period's various literary developments (the periodical essay, formal realism, neoclassicism). Travelers were not often

---

[3] For Johnson's ranked list of travelogues, see *Life*, 2: 345–46.

accomplished authors, as Johnson diagnosed: "Those whose lot it is to ramble can seldom write, and those who know how to write very seldom ramble" (*Letters*, 1: 348). As he also knew, this incompetence leads to not just stylistic but epistemological failures: careful writing – the strategic combination of observation and reflection, authenticity and elegance, novelty and familiarity – orders and assimilates an otherwise bewildering onslaught of sensory data. Instead of "numbering the streaks of the tulip" (*Rasselas*, 43), a practice that typifies and satirizes "the minute enumerations" of scientific writing, Johnson's "useful traveller" must engage intellect and imagination to reveal insights about "human life" (*Idler* 97, 298).

Johnson was thus attuned to both the promise and the perils of the travel genre, as well as the underlying questions it raises about the reliability of perception, memory, and induction. For instance, Cook's historic voyages aroused Johnson's interest but also his censure; as Ian Donaldson comments, Johnson "observed this cult of observation, with a mixture of curiosity and disdain," and was disappointed that Cook's men failed to learn native languages and to gather more detailed information about Polynesian culture.[4] For him, there was "very little of intellectual" value in the "South Sea" accounts, and he recognized, in Boswell's words, that much of what these travelers related "must be conjecture": "every thing intellectual, every thing abstract," was only "darkly guessed" (*Life*, 3: 7–8). Certainly, for Johnson perception is vital to cognition and our senses connect us concretely to the material world; similarly, he generally commended the advances of experimental science. But he also tended to describe the observation of external phenomena as a first and less important step in the larger process of "intellection,"[5] while often noting the limits and distortions of our senses. His attentiveness to human maxima might stem in part from personal exigency. Since infancy, Johnson was nearly blind in his left eye and severely impaired in his right, and he was also hard of hearing.[6] He was also uniquely aware of the limited range of his own vision: "Should I wish to become a botanist," he remarked during a garden tour, "I must first turn myself into a reptile" (*Life*, 1: 377, n2). More generally, Johnson remained skeptical of an individual's ability to perceive and retain reliable information, to locate meaningful patterns, and to document these phenomena in accurate and illuminating ways.

---

[4] Ian Donaldson, "Samuel Johnson and the Art of Observation," *ELH*, 53:4 (1986): 779–99.
[5] Donaldson, "Samuel Johnson," 782.
[6] See Lawrence C. McHenry and Ronald MacKeith, "Samuel Johnson's Childhood Illnesses and the King's Evil," *Medical History*, 10:4 (1966): 386–99.

Consequently, his own travelogues are, in the words of Deidre Lynch, "powerful demonstrations of the epistemological quandaries besetting such projects."[7] Indeed, *Rasselas* and *A Journey to the Western Islands of Scotland* pose trenchant questions about human experience and its role in the formation of knowledge.

One of Johnson's most popular works, both in the eighteenth century and today, *Rasselas* evinces the author's complex attitude toward travel and observation, while also exploring the nature of curiosity, wanderlust, and desire. His only work of prose fiction, *Rasselas* adopts the popular form of the "oriental tale," as we notice in its setting in Abyssinia (modern-day Ethiopia), or "the torrid zone"; its descriptions of luxury and despotism; its episodic structure; and its fairy-tale qualities. *Rasselas* is also a philosophical fable that structures its meditations via intimate conversations; in this way, it shares striking parallels with Voltaire's *Candide* (1759) and its related critique of mid-century optimism. In its philosophical searching, *Rasselas* elaborates themes that appear across Johnson's *oeuvre* and clearly aligns with *The Vanity of Human Wishes* (1749), a poem that grapples with the supreme egoism and emptiness of human desire. Finally, *Rasselas* engages travel and travel writing in important ways. While it employs the motif of travel to metaphorize the search after earthly contentment (which always exists a little beyond the horizon), and structures its plot as an adventure story, it is also an anti-travelogue of sorts in that it describes a quest that leads only to disappointment and ambiguity rather than enlightenment. In its formal permutations, then, *Rasselas* is a travelogue; a satire; a philosophical novel; an oriental tale or fable; and, more generally, an unsettling inquiry into the boundedness of human aspiration and the attainment of happiness, truth, and knowledge.

The plot of *Rasselas* is simple: the fourth son of the King of Abyssinia, Rasselas lives luxuriously but idly in the Happy Valley, knowing only "the soft vicissitudes of pleasure and repose" (*Rasselas*, 11). Although every desire is met, every physical need gratified, Rasselas grows restless in the beautiful, tranquil valley and yearns to see the world beyond its walls. He eventually escapes with his sister Nekayah, her servant Pekuah, and his poet–philosopher friend and tutor Imlac, and the group ventures out to locate people who are happy and might therefore inform their "choice of life." They travel first to Cairo, which appears to abound in joy and vivacity; soon, however, they learn that everyone is miserable. This basic pattern – promising illusions that reveal only

---

[7] Deidre Lynch, "Beating the Track of the Alphabet: Samuel Johnson, Tourism, and the ABCs of Modern Authority," *ELH*, 57:2 (1990): 357–405.

disillusionment, frustration, or despair – structures all their subsequent encounters, from pastoral existence to solitude to court life. They meet hermits and philosophers, astronomers and scholars, those living "according to nature" and urban dwellers; they discuss marriage, antiquity, and learning – but all ideals inevitably disappoint (suggesting that "ideals" are constructs that *cannot* exist in real life).[8] Finally, in "The Conclusion, in which nothing is Concluded," the group catalogues their remaining desires: Pekuah, "weary of expectation and disgust," wishes to join a convent and become prioress; the Princess hopes "to found," and to preside over, "a college of learned women"; the prince desires "a little kingdom," but "was always adding to the number of his subjects"; by contrast, Imlac and the astronomer are content "to be driven along the stream of life without directing their course to any particular port" (*Rasselas*, 175–76). However, they now recognize the futility of these desires and return to Abyssinia. This quick relinquishment of their newly formed aspirations – they are now self-conscious, even ironic – as well as the text's overt cue that "nothing is Concluded" creates an interpretive impasse that estranges and perplexes readers accustomed to more typically triumphant tales of travel and adventure.

Rasselas therefore foregrounds and urges us to question the relationship between epistemology and form. Specifically, the cyclical structure of *Rasselas* provides a counterpoint to the main conceits of the travel genre – usually, to reveal, to accumulate, or to transform – as the group returns to their original location and abandons their quest to discover a fulfilling "choice of life." It also undermines the fable, which usually facilitates the smooth interpretation of maxims. Here these lessons are difficult to discern. For instance, despite the group's failure to locate models of contentment, we are not necessarily to assume that they should have remained in the Happy Valley, ignorant of the world and of the comparative value of their positions. Perhaps, then, happiness is not an achievable state in itself, but rather a *process* or *search* that can expand our perspectival range and therefore our self-awareness. Yet even if the group has acquired the ability to "form a tacit comparison of [their] own state with that of others" (*Idler* 97, 298), establishing a "wider basis of analogy" (*Journey*, 40) and vanquishing idleness, we remain uncertain how to evaluate the main characters, especially in light of their final inventory of desires (wherein three of four hope to dominate a given hierarchy). And, although readers sometimes equate Johnson and the poet–philosopher Imlac, Imlac's serenity borders on stasis, which Johnson does not endorse.

---

[8] In his *Dictionary*, Johnson defines "ideal": "Mental; intellectual; not perceived by the senses."

We must therefore adopt a critical attitude toward all the protagonists, assimilating them into the array of lives we assess, as well as the genres that *Rasselas* engages. Fables were praised during the eighteenth century for their subtle didacticism, where a clear "Moral" exists, but, as Addison argues in *The Spectator* 512 (October 17, 1712), "we are made to believe we advise our selves," or "consider the Precepts ... as our own Conclusions."[9] In *Rasselas*, however, we find a fable that refuses to disclose its lesson, frustrating our inductive impulses. The text also shatters the certainty, confidence, and observational gains that usually underpin the travel genre, as Johnson forces readers to feel the frustration of *not* knowing and to recognize, in their very absence, the formal conceits and deceptions that we rely on but often fail to discern or examine.

Johnson's critical posture in regard to travel writing, and, more broadly, the human capacity to attain knowledge, emerges in its most sophisticated form in his *Journey to the Western Islands of Scotland*. Perhaps unsurprisingly, Johnson and Boswell's eighty-three-day circuit of the Highlands and Hebrides of Scotland, which started and ended in Edinburgh ("a city too well known to admit description" [*Journey*, 4]), produced a tremendous amount of writing. Johnson kept a notebook that he sometimes shared with Boswell,[10] while he also wrote a series of descriptive letters to friends. Boswell also kept a diary, which Johnson often read, and later published his own account, *The Journal of a Tour to the Hebrides* (1785). Finally, we have Johnson's *Journey* (1775), which appeared two years after their travels. *Journey*, therefore, is only one of several versions of the men's experiences in Scotland. The Hebrides venture must also be situated within its larger discursive context. Setting out later in life, or, in his words, "trembling on the brink of his own climacterick" (*Journey*, 84) (his sixty-seventh birthday), Johnson viewed this adventure as a long-awaited opportunity to contribute to the great questions of his age. He wrote in the midst of feverish enthusiasm surrounding Cook's voyages (and in fact "decided to tour the Hebrides ... in the very year that Cook was heading for the New Hebrides after crossing the Antarctic circle"), to which there are various references in both Johnson's and Boswell's Scotland accounts.[11] Although certainly less exotic than Polynesia or Australia, the remoter parts of Scotland would have been foreign indeed to Johnson's metropolitan

[9] [Joseph Addison and Richard Steele], *The Spectator*, 8 vols. (London: J. Tonson, 1733), 7: 145.
[10] See John B. Radner, *Johnson and Boswell: A Biography of Friendship* (New Haven, CT: Yale University Press, 2012), pp. 5, 120, 133–34.
[11] Thomas M. Curley, *Samuel Johnson and the Age of Travel* (Athens, GA: University of Georgia Press, 1976), p. 185.

readers, and he was eager to confirm firsthand what he had read, heard, and deduced about the history and culture of the region. Traveling and writing in the wake of authors like Daniel Defoe, Thomas Pennant, and Martin Martin, Johnson hoped to encounter in Scotland the "classic ground" (*Journey*, 25) that would eventually, he realized, give way to "the mono-chromatic land-scape – the international style, as it were – of a modern money economy,"[12] especially after the failed Jacobite rebellion of 1745. He was especially interested in Scotland's ancient sites, its folk and vernacular traditions, and, specifically, the oral language and histories that troubled the lexicographer's notions of stability and "gradual refinement" (*Journey*, 44).

Journey demonstrates Johnson's deep familiarity with the travel genre in the way that it subtly critiques and reformulates its conventions, and, like *Rasselas*, it tends to undercut our facility in reaching stable conclusions. But *A Journey* is more intently focused on exploring the role of the senses in our thinking lives, as well as the intellectual, moral, and generic consequences of their inevitable failures.[13] Initiating a pattern of seeing and not seeing that continues across *A Journey*, Johnson launches his narrative not with specific dates or places, and not with proclamations of veracity or exacti-tude, but with the complex genealogy of desire: "I had desired to visit the Hebrides, or Western Islands of Scotland, so long, that I scarcely remem-ber how the wish was originally excited" (*Journey*, 3). This pivot inward, toward the vagaries of memory, cognition, and desire, accomplishes much in one swoop: it signals Johnson's play with convention, to be sure, but also preemptively acknowledges the contingency of his perspective, which will emerge as a major theme in the text that follows. This fuzzy recollection launches a narrative that will work through not only what Johnson sees and reflects but also *how* he sees and reflects. Johnson soon returns to this interior landscape when he narrates how *A Journey* – the text we read – was conceived: "I sat down on a bank, such as a writer of romance might have delighted to feign. . . . Before me, and on either side, were high hills, which by hindering the eye from ranging, forced the mind to find entertainment for itself" (*Journey*, 40). The enclosure of this scene both metaphorizes and prompts a Lockean turn inward to contemplate one's own mind and ideas, thus anchoring his documentary account in reflection and imagination rather than perception. Lingering here and elsewhere on the interplay

---

[12] Lynch, "Beating the Track of the Alphabet," p. 379.
[13] See Anne M. Thell, *Minds in Motion: Imagining Empiricism in Eighteenth-Century British Travel Literature* (Lewisburg, PA: Bucknell University Press, 2017), pp. 189–226.

between mind and world – on the *effects* of sensory accrual or deprivation – Johnson stares down the *bête noire* of travel writing: that it pretends to document what it creates (like "a writer of romance"). While most travelers proclaim their disinterestedness and exactitude, Johnson carefully positions the human narrator who elaborates the gradual, imperfect, and idiosyncratic formation of new ideas. He also dramatizes the imaginative processes that transform *life* into *autobiography* and *travel* into *travel narrative*, as he makes apparent how he filters experience into synthetic narrative structures.

Such moments aggregate into a larger pattern, as Johnson weaves together perception and reflection, particular and general, in ways that reach far beyond a typical travel journal. Indeed, while *A Journey* describes what Johnson saw in Scotland – and, just as often, what he *failed* to see in a landscape he finds "barren," "naked," and "sterile" (*Journey*, 18, 139, 39) – it also articulates via form the gradual process of sensory apprehension. *A Journey* opens with a memory that he cannot precisely trace (his original desire to see Scotland) and follows with a scene that describes the numbing effects of habituation: Johnson's "curiosity was attracted by Inch Keith, a small island," which the local inhabitants had never explored, "though, lying within their view, it had all their lives solicited their notice" (3). Here, novelty enhances his perception, thus demonstrating how vision changes along with the perspective and context of the viewer. While on the Isle of Skye, Johnson devotes nearly six pages to assessing the possibility of extrasensory knowledge, the Highland concept of "second sight," a "receptive faculty" that supersedes ordinary perception by allowing certain individuals to see future or distant events (107). Finally, Johnson concludes *A Journey* by describing the students at Braidwood's Academy for the Deaf and Dumb in Edinburgh, where he marvels at students "who not only speak, write, and understand what is written," but also read lips so well "that it is an expression scarcely figurative to say, they hear with the eye" (*Journey*, 163). He is most impressed by the intellection that occurs despite sensory deprivation: the pupils *see* language and therefore reconfigure their senses to produce meaning. Such a feat celebrates the resilience of the mind in the face of loss, a reassuring concept, we might assume, to an aging empiricist with failing senses. Johnson's final paragraph cements his persistent focus on the limits of perception. "Such are the things which this journey has given me an opportunity of seeing," he remarks, "and such are the reflections which that sight has raised," although, as he muses, they "are the thoughts of one who has seen but little" (164). If Johnson explores the nature of perspective and its effect on vision across his writing life, he weaves these concerns into the fabric of *A Journey* as he narrates the provisional apprehension of perceptual data and explores the conditions that enhance or hinder one's access to knowledge.

Across *A Journey*, we find a variety of specific scenes that challenge our senses and purposefully illuminate the shifting nature of perspective. For example, early on at Slanes Castle, Johnson echoes Addison and Burke by describing sublime pleasure when "the eye wanders over the sea" and surveys "terrifick grandeur" from a venue of perfect safety, which allows him to test the power of his senses against the overwhelming natural scene (19). Similarly, entering the Buller of Buchan, a geological phenomenon "which no man can see with indifference," Johnson carefully details the strange optics of the cavity: his group is "inclosed" by walls "rising steep on every side," which trigger "the idea of insurmountable confinement." There is no light, only "a dismal gloom," with the "distant sky" above and the "profundity of water" below (20). Johnson explains that the Buller is terrible precisely because it restricts and channels sight; the gaze is forced far above or below, which inspires claustrophobic dread. Yet he pulls back from the scene with a characteristic maxim – "terror without danger is only one of the sports of fancy, a voluntary agitation of the mind that is permitted no longer than it pleases" (*Journey*, 20) – and therefore suggests that he has intentionally manipulated the effects of vision. Later, at the Fall of Fiers (modern-day Falls of Foyers), Johnson describes a magnificent chasm "of such dreadful depth, that we were naturally inclined to turn aside our eyes" (34). A moment later, he admits they visited at an "unseasonable time," when the site is "divested of its dignity and terror" (34). Yet Johnson continues to imagine the fall's potential impact, as the group "exercise[d] [their] thoughts, by endeavoring to conceive the effect of a thousand streams poured from the mountains ... discharging all their violence of waters by a sudden fall through the horrid chasm" (34). This recurring play with perception accentuates the active role of the imagination, which inflects and even choreographs phenomenology. It also illustrates what Johnson sees as one of the most valuable aspects of travel: that it estranges perspective; that is, travel makes our perception itself visible.

Instead of exhibiting a straightforward empirical zeal or a stolid faith in firsthand experience, Johnson tests, modulates, and thinks over and above his senses, a tactic that consolidates into a surprising moral of *A Journey to the Western Islands*: "Whatever withdraws us from the power of our senses ... advances us in the dignity of thinking beings" (148). Although he does not deny the importance of sight, he does question its accuracy and its sufficiency. Moreover, as Johnson deconstructs observation and

induction, and illuminates the perspectival complexities of producing
stable knowledge, he recognizes that what we see is necessarily conditioned
by idiosyncratic points of view; he therefore acknowledges difference and
what Mary Poovey calls an "emergent cultural relativism."[14] In this way,
A Journey interrogates even Johnson's own empiricist commitments, as he
investigates how our minds shape what we see and what we think we know.
On one hand, of course, his pragmatic metaphysics are rooted in the senses,
especially sight. But he also shows how the mind can maneuver over and
around the senses (receiving but also devising experience and knowledge),
while investigating its own operations in a way the senses cannot.
Surprisingly, then, we find tinges of Romantic thinking in *A Journey* as
Johnson treats imagination not as dangerously deluding, as we often find in
his moral writing, but as a nonsensory faculty that informs sense and
reason. Critical and self-aware even of Johnson's own long-held beliefs,
Journey operates at the intersection of epistemology and aesthetics and
offers a powerful response to a genre and a larger empiricist tradition that
apotheosize sense perception.

   The interest in epistemology that plays out across *Journey* might help to
illuminate the text's political dimensions. Many readers have noted the
imperial hue of *Journey*, which features a "southern stranger" assuming
cultural superiority and documenting a supposedly primitive society with
an eye "to cultivate the Hebrides" (*Journey*, 4, 164). Yet while Johnson
makes certain assumptions in *Journey*, especially in regard to the more
advanced culture of England, he lacks a clear colonial agenda. On the
contrary, he tends to express nostalgia and regret about the disappearance
of traditional Scottish life, as well as a desire to preserve history, which can
result in "odd tonal consequences."[15] Perhaps, then, as Ian Duncan has
suggested, the real imperialism of *Journey* appears in Johnson's strange
refusal to mention the Scottish Enlightenment thinkers – some of whom
he had met – who were precisely at this time theorizing many of the same
concepts that he explores in his travelogue.[16] The text dramatizes how we
think and know without ever acknowledging parallels with Scottish
authors like David Hume, Adam Smith, Lord Kames, and Hugh Blair,
although Johnson does, at other times, refer to their work positively. He

---

[14] Mary Poovey, *A History of the Modern Fact: Problems of Knowledge in the Sciences of Wealth and
   Society* (Chicago, IL: University of Chicago Press, 1998), p. 261; also pp. xxii, 257–64.
[15] Lynch, "Beating the Track of the Alphabet," p. 379.
[16] Ian Duncan, "The Pathos of Abstraction: Adam Smith, Ossian, and Samuel Johnson," in
   Leith Davis, Ian Duncan, and Janet Sorensen (eds.), *Scotland and the Borders of Romanticism*
   (Cambridge: Cambridge University Press, 2015), pp. 38–56.

therefore evacuates from Scotland "a flourishing cultural present," which is perhaps a means of enacting "revenge upon" a new-fangled "philosophical tradition that Johnson views as undertaking a kind of metaphysical desert-ification of knowledge and belief."[17] But Johnson's reticence might also stem from a concerted effort to pose his ideas as the product of travel and direct experience rather than books. Certainly, he must be aware that many of his concerns – the relationship between thinking subject and external world, the role of imagination in perception, the fictions we narrate to comprehend our lives – have deep resonance with Hume and other Scottish writers, although he leaves his readers to work through these connections as they reflect upon his travelogue.

At the end of his writing life, Johnson explores the limits of our senses and the resilience of the mind, as well as the epistemology of travel writing. In *Journey* and across his writing, he shows how travel stimulates thinking through difficult questions about human experience and is, therefore, a mode of self-examination that is always open-ended. He also vividly demonstrates the experimental nature of genre – for him, a way of seeing that can illuminate truths or fail to do so (creating "a picture of nothing" [*Life*, 2: 433]) – and ends his career questioning, probing, and critiquing, while refusing certainty and oversimplification (even in the case of an empiricism that he generally endorses). His refutation of Berkeleyan idealism – the boot kicking the rock with which I began this chapter – is therefore just as open to critical reevaluation as a probable avenue of human experience but not the only one we might explore or assess. Undercutting the authority of any single perspective by opening compara-tive frameworks that expand and proliferate, Johnson's travel discourse shows us how to wonder about the world, while also opening for inspection that "thinking thing" who seeks, always, to know.[18]

---

[17] Duncan, "The Pathos of Abstraction," p. 39.
[18] John Locke, *An Essay Concerning Human Understanding* ed. Peter H. Nidditch (Oxford: Oxford University Press, 1975 [1689]), p. 347.

CHAPTER 15

Johnson and Disability

Paul Kelleher

This chapter addresses the conjunction of Samuel Johnson and disability in several ways – with reference to biography, interpersonal relations, and literary style – and points readers toward other paths that might be taken in their own study of Johnson's relationship to disability.[1] As disability increasingly becomes a familiar topic in a number of spheres, from politics to Hollywood, and as ever more people gain at least a passing knowledge of, if not direct experience with, resources such as learning accommodations and workplace accessibility protocols, it is understandable if a twenty-first-century individual were to assume that determining what disability meant in Johnson's life and in his culture would be a fairly straightforward task. Consider this example of how such an assumption is made and encouraged. In the online catalogue of its holdings, the National Portrait Gallery begins its overview of Sir Joshua Reynolds's 1756 portrait of Johnson in the following manner:

> Massively ungainly and plagued with nervous tics, Dr. Johnson was a victim of melancholia and could not bear solitude. He had an immense circle of friends and was one of the greatest conversationalists of all time. This portrait of him as a man of letters was painted by his friend Reynolds shortly after the publication of his *Dictionary of the English Language* of 1755, a prodigious labour which remains a monument to his scholarship as well as to his forthright personality.[2]

Elsewhere on the gallery's website, in a short biographical entry for Johnson, we again find the sentence regarding his tics, melancholia, and dread of solitude, but now an additional sentence introduces a diagnostic turn: "James Boswell's *Life*, along with other biographies[,] documented

---

[1] I am grateful to Helen Deutsch, Martine W. Brownley, and Greg Clingham, who have supported my work on Johnson and modeled for me the Johnsonian art of using the mind well.
[2] See https://bit.ly/3JvhPAA.

his behaviour and mannerisms in such detail that they have informed the posthumous diagnosis of Tourette syndrome."[3]

What do we see in Reynolds's 1756 portrait of Johnson (see Chapter 16)? A dignified Johnson, sitting at a writing table. His right hand holds a quill; his left hand rests on a stack of paper, while the fingers of that hand curl inward. His head leans to the right; he looks alertly to his left, a posture accentuated by the deeper shadows given to the right side of his face. The asymmetrical line of his body is reinforced by how he diagonally sits in his chair. What are we meant to understand as we move between the portrait and its description? The textual cues supplied by the National Portrait Gallery suggest, quite simply, that the first thing the internet-surfing public needs to know about Samuel Johnson, celebrated man of letters and legendary conversationalist, is that he was "plagued" by and a "victim" of his disabilities. Further, there is the implication that Johnson's life's work, whether on the page or in conversation, can be understood variously as a flight from, a compensation for, or an overcoming of his disabled mind and body. True, the word "disability" is not used explicitly, but the condensed biographical narrative offered here is meant to bring Johnson closer to us, and we, in turn, are drawn to Johnson, because we already know and ostensibly take pleasure in the countless ways our culture has told this story: after much courageous struggle, a brilliant man finally triumphs over the obstacles posed by his disability.

The National Portrait Gallery's well-meaning curatorial staff has not gotten the facts wrong (despite the platitudinous use to which they are put). Johnson was a large man, and he did prefer to spend his time in company, engaged in animated conversation. Tics and melancholy did, indeed, feature in his life. We see that Reynolds subtly depicts some aspects of Johnson's unusual embodiment by, for instance, tilting his subject's head to one side and curling his fingers. These postures and gestures, captured on canvas, would have been immediately recognizable to Johnson's friends and acquaintances, given how often his "peculiarities," as they were characteristically called, are mentioned in the writings of James Boswell, Hester Thrale Piozzi, Frances Reynolds, and Fanny Burney, among many others. It is worth recalling that in his *Dictionary*, Johnson defined "peculiarity" as "Particularity; something found only in one." The negative connotation we now associate with "peculiarity" is largely absent; in its place, we find an emphasis placed on individuality and singularity. As we consider the various conjunctions of Johnson and

[3] https://bit.ly/3NVvmoN.

disability, the challenge will be to preserve the distance between eighteenth-century peculiarity and twenty-first-century disability, while at the same time remaining open and attentive to their surprising overlaps.

Biographical Disability

Was Samuel Johnson disabled?[4] From one perspective, this question can be answered with an unqualified *yes*. Whether we turn to the biographies written and the anecdotes collected by his contemporaries or consult the literary, academic, and medical assessments rendered by generations of his admirers and more than a few of his detractors, the Johnson who appears before our eyes would seem to be unmistakably and multiply disabled.[5] Indeed, Johnson's disabilities – among others, a childhood bout with scrofula (the "king's evil"); a nearly or totally blind left eye and a myopic right eye; partial deafness; uncontrollable tics, gestures, and vocalizations; obsessive rituals; and a lifelong susceptibility to depression ("melancholy") and hypochondria – get nearly the first and last word in James Boswell's monumental and monumentalizing *The Life of Samuel Johnson, LL.D.* (1791).

Early in this work, after noting how Johnson's father, Michael, suffered from "that disease, the nature of which eludes the most minute enquiry, though the effects are well known to be a weariness of life, an unconcern about those things which agitate the greater part of mankind, and a general sensation of gloomy wretchedness," Boswell reports Johnson's clear-eyed recognition of his troubled paternal inheritance and his unsparing self-diagnosis: "From him then his son inherited . . . 'a vile melancholy,' which in his too strong expression of any disturbance of mind, 'made him mad all his life, at least not sober'" (*Life*, 1: 35). The threat of madness casts a long, never-dispelled shadow across the hundreds of pages to follow, simultaneously immiserating Johnson the biographical subject and structuring Boswell's biographical enterprise. Always in the background are Johnson's

---

[4] In the disability community as well as in disability studies, there is an ongoing debate regarding terms related to "disability." In what is known as person-first language, one says or writes "person with a disability," whereas in what is known as identity-first language, one says or writes "a disabled person." Context – syntactical, historical, or conceptual, among others – often complicates a simple distinction between person-first and identity-first language. In this chapter, I use (for the most part) identity-first language, but depending on the context, I may use "disabled" or "disability." Moreover, I engage with disability studies scholars who themselves use "disabled" as a descriptor.

[5] The longstanding medical interest in Johnson's mind and body (including the infamous autopsy performed on his corpse) is examined in John Wiltshire, *Samuel Johnson in the Medical World: The Doctor and the Patient* (Cambridge: Cambridge University Press, 1991).

desperate, perhaps self-defeating fear that he will lose his reason and the implied but never confirmed connection between his "vile melancholy" and the numerous behavioral "peculiarities" documented in the *Life*. Moreover, the idiom of madness – "gloomy," "morbid," "dismal," and "melancholy" – provides Boswell some of his favored, oft-repeated words to capture the telling particularities of Johnson's character.

As he draws to a close, Boswell returns one last time to the subject of Johnson's singular mind and body, which at this point are well-trodden ground in the *Life*:

> His figure was large and well formed, and his countenance of the cast of an ancient statue; yet his appearance was rendered strange and somewhat uncouth, by convulsive cramps, by the scars of that distemper [the "king's evil"] which it was once imagined the royal touch could cure, and by a slovenly mode of dress. He had the use only of one eye . . . . So morbid was his temperament, that he never knew the natural joy of a free and vigorous use of his limbs: when he walked, it was like the struggling gait of one in fetters . . . . He was afflicted with a bodily disease, which made him often restless and fretful; and with a constitutional melancholy, the clouds of which darkened the brightness of his fancy, and gave a gloomy cast to his whole course of thinking. (*Life*, 4: 425, 427)

Years earlier, when Johnson and Boswell discuss the subject of "constitutional melancholy," Johnson asserts that it is "madness" to combat "distressing thoughts" by attempting to "*think them down.*" Instead, one must cultivate other "retreats" for the mind (for instance, by regaining composure through reading). "To have the management of the mind is a great art," Johnson declares, "and it may be obtained in a considerable degree by experience and habitual exercise" (*Life*, 2: 440). It is fitting, then, as a way to artfully complete the arc of Johnson's thought and to round off the form of Boswell's text, that Johnson's disabilities, in the end, are transcended by no longer needing to be mentioned: "his superiority over other learned men consisted chiefly in what may be called the art of thinking, the art of using his mind" (*Life*, 4: 427–28). And yet, can Boswell's reader truly forget – or, to invoke Johnson, *think down* – the dangerous proximity, hinted at throughout the *Life*, between using a mind and losing it?

From another perspective, the question of Johnson's disability is much less easily answered, precisely because the question assumes that we already know how disability – as a word, a concept, a lived experience, an identity – was understood in Johnson's lifetime and in the culture he inhabited. More perplexingly, the question also assumes that "disability" even existed in the eighteenth century. But how could disability not have existed in the age of

Johnson? As literary critics and historians working in the academic field of disability studies (many of whom study Johnson) have argued, some intellectual caution is needed when we go looking for "disability" before the nineteenth century. Diverse in their approaches and conclusions, these scholars nevertheless share some theoretical assumptions. First, they draw a distinction between an impairment (be it sensory, psychological, or bodily) and a disability. Concisely put, an "impairment is a physical fact, but a disability is a social construction."[6] An impairment, in other words, only becomes and is experienced as a disability in a specific – historical, cultural, infrastructural, and ideological – context. A classic example used in disability studies: while wheelchair users may have impaired mobility, they only become "disabled" in a built environment that lacks ramps, elevators, and curb cuts, and in a social world that sets them apart as a minoritized (even pathologized) population, as "other" than "normal." Second, these scholars are guided by the idea that the interplay of historical continuities and differences means that we can never assume that "disability" is an unchanging, transhistorical thing waiting to be unearthed and exhibited. The Enlightenment era certainly informs the principles of autonomy, moral dignity, and justice that animate later forms of disability embodiment and activism, but the differences between Johnson's time and our own are equally important. In order to capture historical difference faithfully, disability studies scholars attend to the specific textures of thought and language that shape eighteenth-century understandings of "extraordinary" bodies and minds.[7]

With regard to Johnson specifically, several compelling arguments have been made. Lennard Davis suggests that Johnson inhabits a transitional moment, one that predates the ideological regime of the "normal" and the "pathological" in the nineteenth century but one that has not yet fully detached from an early modern worldview in which "monstrosity" and "deformity" were deciphered as either signs of divine punishment (afflicted in body or mind by a deity who wishes to make visible and known a family's sins) or casualties of a mother's moral negligence (misshapen in the womb by the mysterious agency of a maternal imagination gone astray). In practice, according to Davis, this means that Johnson's contemporaries see him as "a brilliant man who had some oddities rather than

---

[6] Lennard Davis, "Dr. Johnson, Amelia, and the Discourse of Disability in the Eighteenth Century," in Helen Deutsch and Felicity Nussbaum (eds.), "Defects": Engendering the Modern Body (Ann Arbor: University of Michigan Press, 2000), pp. 54–71, 56.
[7] See, for example, Rosemarie Garland-Thomson, Extraordinary Bodies: Figuring Physical Disability in American Culture and Literature (New York: Columbia University Press, 1997).

a seriously disabled person."[8] "Caught between two paradigms," Johnson's body bears "the mark" but not the "sign" of disability. He is, in short, "neither normal nor abnormal."[9] Taking a more strictly historicist approach, David M. Turner calls into question the idea that the eighteenth century marked a transition between early modern and modern conceptions of disability. It has a more complicated story to tell, and Turner begins to piece together this story by shifting the focus from large-scale ideologies to more fine-grained, context-bound examples of how ordinary life and everyday language were experienced "before" medicalized understandings of disability took hold in the late eighteenth century. Turner, a professional historian, credits literary critics with making "inroads" into Enlightenment-era conceptions of humanity, but he also gently (and not quite fairly) faults these critics for paying attention to "a limited number of canonical texts or 'celebrity' disabled figures such as Alexander Pope or Samuel Johnson" instead of "attempting a broader analysis of cultural representations."[10] Finally, Helen Deutsch acutely explores how Johnson, in both life and death, exemplifies a constellation of elusive, often confounding binaries that lie at the very heart of our culture, including body and mind, originality and monstrosity, and not least, common reader and singular author. "Samuel Johnson," she observes, "in his embodied, diseased, and paradoxically representative particularity can thus be seen to occupy a charged and liminal position in a variety of cultural narratives."[11] Deutsch refrains from explicitly claiming Johnson as a "disabled" author or cultural icon, instead allowing the (often obsessive) desire to know Johnson, inside and out, to reveal itself as a culture's even deeper urge to encounter and master the uncanny, the deformed, and the excessive.

Staring at Johnson

Samuel Johnson provoked strong reactions. One of the most notorious of such reactions can be found in Thomas Babington Macaulay's review of John Wilson Croker's edition (1831) of Boswell's *Life*. Macaulay conjures a striking (indeed, patronizing and insulting) image of Johnson, one that had a lasting impact on Johnson's literary fortunes. Perhaps more than anyone else, Macaulay is responsible for shifting how Johnson was read – or more

---

[8] Davis, "Dr. Johnson," p. 55.   [9] Davis, "Dr. Johnson," p. 69.
[10] David M. Turner, *Disability in Eighteenth-Century England: Imagining Physical Impairment* (New York and London: Routledge, 2012), p. 3
[11] Helen Deutsch, *Loving Dr. Johnson* (Chicago, IL: University of Chicago Press, 2005), p. 25.

precisely, *not* read – in the nineteenth century. Johnson the personality, in Macaulay's hands, eclipses Johnson the author:[12]

> Everything about him, his coat, his wig, his figure, his face, his scrofula, his St. Vitus's dance, his rolling walk, his blinking eye, the outward signs which too clearly marked his approbation of his dinner, his insatiable appetite for fish-sauce and veal-pie with plums, his inextinguishable thirst for tea, his trick of touching the posts as he walked, his mysterious practice of treasuring up scraps of orange-peel, his morning slumbers, his midnight disputations, his contortions, his mutterings, his gruntings, his puffings, his vigorous, acute, and ready eloquence, his sarcastic wit, his vehemence, his insolence, his fits of tempestuous rage . . . all are as familiar to us as the objects by which we have been surrounded from childhood.[13]

Macaulay and Johnson were not contemporaries. And yet, given the emotional intensity with which Macaulay constructs this caricature, its immediacy heightened by the rapid-fire listing of objects, oddities, appetites, and passions, Macaulay makes it, so to speak, *personal*. The curious power of this caricature owes, in large part, to the fact that every biographical detail recorded here can be traced to an earlier account, sympathetically, even lovingly, written by one of Johnson's friends and companions. But it is not quite right to say that Macaulay's caricature of Johnson is cruel because brutally true. The cruelty lies in the way that Johnson's peculiarities are put on rhetorical display: one by one, they are collected, fixed, and magnified; but in order to accomplish this feat, Macaulay must utterly excise Johnson from the dense fabric of his life.

Looking at some of the accounts from which Macaulay cherry-picks his version of Johnson, we are reminded that mental and bodily impairments only come to signify, to take on interpersonal meaning and relevance, within a social context. For the most part, these encounters are not pleasing or comforting to contemplate; nevertheless, they are instructive, revealing to us the social norms and imaginative limits that determined how Johnson's "peculiarities" – and by extension, the peculiarities of unnamed and unknown others – were experienced in the eighteenth century. We glimpse, more specifically, moments when strangers, surprised by Johnson's unusual embodiment, are compelled to stop, stare, and wonder.[14] In a biographical

---

[12] See Bertrand H. Bronson, "The Double Tradition of Dr. Johnson," *ELH*, 18:2 (1951): 90–106.

[13] Thomas Babington, Lord Macaulay, "Samuel Johnson," in Hugh Trevor-Roper (ed.), *Critical and Historical Essays* (New York: McGraw-Hill, 1965), pp. 92–93.

[14] See Rosemarie Garland-Thomson, *Staring: How We Look* (New York and Oxford: Oxford University Press, 2009), for how staring can lead to transformative understandings of disability and bodily difference.

sketch published shortly after Johnson's death, Thomas Tyers notes Johnson's athletic prowess and bodily vigor, which are juxtaposed with, but not negated by, the fact that "he was to the last a convulsionary."[15] "He has often stept aside," Tyers recalls, "to let nature do what she would with him. His gestures, which were a degree of St. Vitus's dance, in the street, attracted the notice of many; the stare of the vulgar, but the compassion of the better sort."[16] Tyers finds himself in a complex public scene of looks exchanged and averted. When a convulsion comes on, Johnson steps aside, remaining in public but seeking a space of less exposure. Johnson is a surprising sight, and Tyers wants to suggest that social class dictates whether or not the curious gazes fixed on Johnson are tempered by a measure of politeness and charitable feeling. We get a vivid sense of how class and comportment were understood to function in the public spaces of eighteenth-century London; just as importantly, we learn something about what kinds of bodies and bodily movements, in a metropolis crisscrossed by strangers of all sorts, rise to the level of something to be stared at. Or, conversely, to be looked away from: as Tyers delicately adds, "This writer has often looked another way, as the companions of Peter the Great were used to do, while he was under the short paroxysm."[17] Strangers stare. Companions, already knowing what they would see if they indulged the impulse to stare, avert their eyes, and through this friendly, tactful gesture, give the "convulsionary" the gift of privacy.

Frances Reynolds, sister of Sir Joshua Reynolds and an artist in her own right, records another scene in which strangers gravitate toward the surprising figure Johnson cuts in public. She and Johnson are enjoying a Sunday morning in Twickenham Meadows, when Johnson's gestures grow so extraordinary "that men, women, and children gathered around him, laughing." "At last we sat down on some logs of wood by the river side," she continues, "and they nearly dispersed; when he pulled out of his pocket Grotius['s] *De Veritate Religionis*, over which he seesawed at such a violent rate as to excite the curiosity of some people at a distance to come and see what was the matter with him" (*JM*, 2: 297). The spectacle of laughing strangers, young and old, surrounding Johnson makes for difficult reading, and likely triggers a painful shudder of recognition in a disabled person today. At the same time, the light, unperturbed tone of Reynolds's recollection makes us wonder: is this laughter self-evidently and unequivocally mocking or malicious, and how was this laughter received?

[15] O M Brack, Jr. and Robert E. Kelley (eds.), *The Early Biographies of Samuel Johnson* (Iowa City: University of Iowa Press, 1974), p. 63.
[16] Brack and Kelley, *The Early Biographies of Samuel Johnson*, p. 63.
[17] Brack and Kelley, *The Early Biographies of Samuel Johnson*, p. 63.

Further, how are we to interpret the later moment, when Johnson's seesawing motions excite these strangers' "curiosity" to know "what was the matter with him"? Can curiosity be akin to care? These questions also prompt us to consider the role Reynolds plays here. Unlike Tyers, she makes no mention of turning her eyes away from her friend's convulsive motions – quite the opposite, given her carefully rendered portrait of Johnson's body. His "antics" involve both his feet and hands. Johnson's hands assume a shape that Reynolds likens to a "jockey" "holding the reins of a horse . . . on full speed." "But to describe the strange positions of his feet," she admits, "is a difficult task; sometimes he would make the back part of his heels to touch, sometimes his toes, as if he was aiming at making the form of a triangle, at least the two sides of one" (*JM*, 2: 297). Johnson's "antic" body excites Reynolds's imagination and impresses itself into her memory; although she cannot recall with certainty "whether these were his gestures on this particular occasion in Twickenham meadows . . . it is so long since," these extraordinary shapes expand and enrich her sense of what a body can do and become.

It is no surprise that Boswell's tenacious biographical efforts led him to capture several memorable "staring" episodes that complement those of Tyers and Reynolds and deepen our sense of how Johnson's body reworked, even momentarily, the forms of sociability in his midst. Early in the *Life*, Boswell notes that Johnson's "convulsive starts and odd gesticulations . . . tended to excite at once surprise and ridicule" (*Life*, 1: 95). The surprise and curiosity that motivate staring, I suggested a moment ago, might open a path toward a relationship of care or, at least, a genuine concern to understand another. The other possibility, of course, is ridicule, which forcefully closes down any chance for reciprocity and comprehension. But Johnson's future wife, Elizabeth ("Tetty") Porter, has a surprise of her own in store. As Boswell reports the anecdote, "Mrs. Porter was so much engaged by his conversation that she overlooked all these external disadvantages, and said to her daughter, 'this is the most sensible man that I ever saw in my life'" (*Life*, 1: 95). The familiar narratives of overlooking an impairment and overcoming an impairment go hand in hand – too easily, perhaps, since two clichés do not necessarily add up to one truth. Boswell means us to understand that, by overlooking his "external disadvantages," Mrs. Porter takes pleasure in her growing attachment to Johnson's sensible mind and engaging conversation. However, if we stress the visual dimension of her colloquial turn of phrase, "the most sensible man that I ever *saw* in my life," Johnson's beloved Tetty suggests something else: knowing and loving an extraordinary body, welcoming the arrival of something new, unforeseen, and transformative, entails a refusal of the mind–body divide and an embrace of the other's irreplaceable peculiarities.

Eighteenth-century painter and engraver William Hogarth had a famously discerning eye for the beautiful and the deformed, and it is fitting that he features in one of Boswell's most striking anecdotes about the disorienting effects of Johnson's mind and body. During a visit to Samuel Richardson, Hogarth's attention is caught by "a person standing at a window in the room, shaking his head, and rolling himself about in a strange ridiculous manner" (*Life*, 1: 146). Unacquainted with Johnson, Hogarth immediately concludes that the unusual stranger must be "an ideot [*sic*]," an unfortunate placed under the charitable care of Richardson, "a very good man" (*Life*, 1: 146, 147). Hogarth and Richardson are discussing the king's having allowed the execution of a rebellious partisan of the house of Stuart. A "warm partisan of George the Second," Hogarth's defense of the king forces Johnson to emerge from his reverie at the window. To Hogarth's "great surprise . . . this figure stalked forwards . . . and all at once took up the argument, and burst into an invective against George the Second" (*Life*, 1: 147). "In short," Boswell continues, Johnson "displayed such a power of eloquence, that Hogarth looked at him with astonishment, and actually imagined that this ideot [*sic*] had been at the moment inspired" (1: 147). As Hogarth looks at Johnson, what does he himself look like? Astonishment, a deeply visceral feeling of wonder and confusion, characteristically expresses itself from head to toe: staring eyes, mouth agape, limbs arrested. Johnson's surprising embodiment thus momentarily transforms the astonished Hogarth into something to be looked at in wonder. In other words, an extraordinary body is doubly surprising: first, it is a novel sight that attracts our curious eyes and awakens our questioning minds; second, in a more disorienting fashion, it triggers an involuntary response in our bodies that, however fleetingly and faintly, renews our sense of how truly strange it is to inhabit *any* body.

Imitating Johnson

Johnson's peculiarities drew stares (and sometimes, alas, provoked ridicule); they also famously inspired imitation and mimicry. While staring and imitating are different responses to an extraordinary mind and body, they share an important element: Brought face to face with a surprising shape or gesture, individuals often undergo an experience of bodily involuntarity and compulsion. They catch themselves, and fight the urge to continue, staring. They feel, and perhaps indulge, a visceral impulse to imitate a mannerism or speech pattern. To be sure, these represent instances of staring and imitating that carry a negative valence. But there are other, more positive, possibilities, such as the stares fixed on the beautiful or sublime or the intimacies that lead one friend to unconsciously adopt another friend's tone of voice or turn of phrase. Singular in the flesh and on the page, Johnson moved others to imitate – for a host of reasons, conscious and unconscious – both his bodily and literary style.

David Garrick, Johnson's former pupil and one of the eighteenth century's greatest actors, was famous for a number of his roles (Richard III, perhaps most spectacularly), but he played no role longer than that of Samuel Johnson. In his youth, while still under Johnson's tutelage, Garrick would join his fellow pupils in rendering Johnson's "oddities of manner" and "uncouth gesticulations" into a "subject of merriment" (*Life*, 1: 98). Boswell further reports that the "young rogues used to listen at the door of his bed-chamber, and peep through the key-hole, that they might turn into ridicule his tumultuous and *aukward* [*sic*] fondness for Mrs. Johnson" (*Life*, 1: 98). One can only begin to imagine the shapes and gestures these young men performed. In later years, Garrick took to entertaining fashionable drawing rooms with his imitations of Johnson. We find him indulging in a "ludicrous exaggeration," declaiming lines of Ovid (which invoke looking skyward) while continually looking downward, interrupting himself with "pauses and half-whistlings," and closing the lines of poetry by "absolutely touching the ground with a kind of contorted gesticulation" (*Life*, 2: 326). Elsewhere, we see Garrick mocking simultaneously the "provincial" Lichfield accent that Johnson "never got entirely free of" and the involuntary bodily motions that, by this point, Garrick knew intimately. As Boswell describes the scene, "Garrick sometimes used to take him off, squeezing a lemon into a punch-bowl, with uncouth gesticulations, looking round the company, and calling out, 'Who's for *poonsh?*' [i.e., punch]" (*Life*, 2: 464).

Boswell carefully records Garrick's nearly lifelong compulsion to imitate Johnson, but he passes over in silence his own desire to inhabit and perform Johnson's extraordinary body. Hannah More, however, freely informs us that Boswell was eager to join in the fun. As More recalls, she was made the "umpire in a trial of skill between Garrick and Boswell, which could most nearly imitate Dr. Johnson's manner." She decides to split her decision: "I remember I gave it for Boswell in familiar conversation, and for Garrick in reciting poetry" (*Life*, 2: 326, n2). If More's anecdote whets our appetite to know more about the urge Boswell felt to imitate Johnson, Fanny Burney reveals the profound depths of Boswell's investment in Johnsonian embodiment. Here she documents her first impressions of the young and ambitious James Boswell:

> He had an odd mock solemnity of tone and manner, that he had acquired imperceptibly from constantly thinking of and imitating Dr. Johnson, whose own solemnity, nevertheless, far from mock, was the result of pensive rumination. There was, also, something slouching in the gait and dress of Mr. Boswell, that wore an air, ridiculously enough, of purporting to personify the same model. His clothes were always too large for him; his hair, or wig, was constantly in a state of negligence; and he never for a moment sat still or upright upon a chair. Every look and movement displayed either intentional or involuntary imitation. Yet certainly it was not meant as caricature; for his heart, almost even to idolatry, was in his reverence of Dr. Johnson.[18]

Burney gives us a remarkable view into the intimate bond forged at the heart of this legendary friendship. Johnson's singular presence exerts an uncanny power over Boswell, whose practice of "constantly thinking of and imitating Dr. Johnson" brings him "imperceptibly" close to meta-morphosing into the man himself. Wearing "clothes . . . always too large for him," it is as if Boswell unconsciously awaits the moment when he will grow into Johnson's robust frame. Further, Johnson's signature gesticula-tions and rolling gait appear to have been internalized and reinterpreted as the restless motion that prevents Boswell, even for a moment, from sitting "still or upright upon a chair." Burney precisely captures how being in relation to Johnson means giving oneself over to a confusion between "intentional" and "involuntary" styles of moving, thinking, speaking, and, not least, writing.[19]

As we have seen, the pleasures and perils of imitation emerge, again and again, in the vicinity of Johnson's bodily peculiarities. But in the vast archive of Johnsoniana, when "imitation" and "peculiarity" are found on the same page, they are just as likely to refer to Johnson's prose style – its sumptuous arrangement of philosophical, often Latinate, words into striking parallelisms, antitheses, and triads, all of which move steadily toward the flourish of a resounding period. From his time to ours, these elements of Johnson's style have been passionately celebrated and imitated – and just as passionately criti-cized and rejected. Macaulay, unsurprisingly, has little good to say on

---

[18] [Fanny Burney], *Memoirs of Doctor Burney, Arranged from His Own Manuscripts, from Family Papers, and from Personal Recollections by His Daughter, Madame d'Arblay*, 3 vols. (London: Edward Moxon, 1832), 2: 191.

[19] [Burney], *Memoirs of Doctor Burney*, 2: 191.

this score: "The characteristic faults of his style are so familiar to all
our readers, and have been so often burlesqued, that it is almost
superfluous to point them out. . . . all these peculiarities have been
imitated by his admirers, and parodied by his assailants, till the public
has become sick of the subject."[20] Almost always lurking in the
background of such criticisms is an implied connection between
Johnson's two forms of peculiarity, as if his body and his prose were
mirror images of one another. Horace Walpole, with characteristic
acidity, explicitly makes the case. "A marked manner," he writes,
"when it runs thro[ugh] all the compositions of any master, is
a defect in itself, and indicates a deviation from Nature." Indeed,
for Walpole, Johnson's prose suggests that he is not fully and properly
human: "It is the clumsy gambol of a lettered elephant."[21] But more is
at stake, given that it is the nature of peculiarities to propagate
themselves, one intentional or involuntary imitation at a time.
Walpole thus feels that it is his duty "to caution young authors against
partiality" to Johnson's "style and manner," both of which he deems
"uncommonly vicious" and "unworthy of imitation by any man who
aims at excellence in writing his own language."[22] In contrast to
Walpole's ungenerous (not to say, phobic) critique, recall Boswell's
exuberant desire to have his mind *strongly impregnated with the
Johnsonian aether*" (*Life*, 1: 421; original emphasis) and his fervent
hope that, by preserving Johnson in the wildly successful *Life*, he
has "Johnsonised the land" (*Life*, 1: 13). Walpole and Boswell could
not be more diametrically opposed. But, setting their differences aside,
it is illuminating to see that Johnson inspires a strong, passionate
response precisely when the boundaries – moral, intellectual, and
literary – between men are felt to be either degradingly or pleasurably
collapsed.

By way of closing, we can briefly return to the question posed
earlier: was Samuel Johnson disabled? One way to proceed is to
decline to answer this question with a simple *yes* or a *no*. Better yet,
after immersing ourselves in the richness, strangeness, and, at times,
uncanny familiarity of the eighteenth century, we can begin to for-
mulate better questions. For example: Is "peculiarity" a conceptual

---

[20] Macaulay, "Samuel Johnson," pp. 113, 114.
[21] Horace Walpole, "General Criticism of Dr. Johnson's Writings," in James T. Boulton (ed.), *Samuel Johnson: The Critical Heritage* (London and New York: Routledge, 1971), pp. 324, 325.
[22] Walpole, "General Criticism," p. 324.

forerunner of "disability"? How would claiming Johnson as "disabled" shift our understanding of eighteenth-century culture and the forms of authorship that flourished in that century? How would this, in turn, revise the shape of British literary history? Of course, the fundamental question will be: How, as we read his works and study his life, do we do justice to the peculiar, singular, and, in the end, wholly inimitable Samuel Johnson?

CHAPTER 16

Representing Johnson in Life and After

Heather McPherson

Representing Samuel Johnson, whose towering intellect and larger-than-life persona dominated his era, posed a challenge for portrait painters and caricaturists alike. Even for Joshua Reynolds, a close friend and gifted portraitist, portraying Johnson's exceptional mind and unwieldly body was daunting. Beyond the traditional iconographic attributes of writers such as pen-and-paper and books, there were few artistic models for representing intellectual prowess or literary genius. Reynolds's portraits for the Thrales's library at Streatham, which have been compared to intimate biography, are the most ambitious attempt at linking creative genius with eccentricity and physical defects.[1] Reynolds's multiple portraits of Johnson, which track his public persona and inner life at different moments in time, arguably constitute a serial portraiture.[2] Over three decades, Johnson sat to many different artists, including James Barry, Joseph Nollekens, John Opie, Frances Reynolds, Thomas Trotter, and Johan Zoffany.[3] The portraits, some of which exist in multiple versions, were engraved and widely disseminated, attesting to their commodification and exchange value. Although Johnson himself did not commission any portraits, he took an interest in them and prized their talismanic significance as tokens of friendship to be collected and exchanged. The erroneous belief that he cared little about his image is contradicted by his willingness to pose for portraits and his awareness of their power in shaping his public image and posthumous reputation. His tolerance for being caricatured, likewise, speaks to his understanding that caricatures were a mark of celebrity that kept the subject in the public eye.

[1] Nadia Tscherny, "Reynolds's Streatham Portraits and the Art of Intimate Biography," *Burlington Magazine*, 128 (1986): 4–11.
[2] Whitney Davis, "Serial Portraiture and the Death of Man in Late Eighteenth-Century Portraiture," in Dana Arnold and David Peters Corbett (eds.), *A Companion to Art 1600 to the Present* (Chichester: Wiley Blackwell, 2013), pp. 502–31.
[3] See Lawrence Fitzroy Powell, "The Portraits of Johnson," *Life*, 4: 447–64.

If portraitists struggled to represent Johnson's elevated mind and ponderous physique, caricaturists were stymied by his notorious ugliness. That may explain why most caricatures of Johnson are fairly anodyne or merely nominal likenesses, based primarily on his writings.[4] Johnson's physical idiosyncrasies exceeded the distortions caricaturists typically deployed to deface their subjects and render them ridiculous, making him virtually impervious to personal satires. The exception is James Gillray, whose *Apollo and the Muses, Inflicting Penance on Dr. Pomposo, round Parnassus* (1783), pictures Johnson as an obese, bare-chested penitent being scourged by Apollo and the Muses. As we shall see, in Johnson's portraits, his physical imperfections, rather than stigmatizing him, were integral components of his identity and became emblematic of his exceptional mind.

Johnson's public image, which coalesced over several decades, continued to mutate and proliferate long after his death. Throughout the nineteenth century, depictions of Johnson multiplied, from prints and illustrations, to posthumous statues and monuments, to sentimental genre paintings in which he was domesticated and recast as a cozy Victorian, or an elegant 'gallant', as in William Powell Frith's imagined encounter of *Dr. Johnson and Mrs. Siddons* (1884). Expanding the idea of serial portraiture, this chapter examines pairs or clusters of related images across various artists and media, focusing on the formative function of Johnson's portraits in and after life and their central role in mythologizing him as a literary colossus. I am particularly interested in tracing how visual representations of Johnson morphed over time, were appropriated and reproduced, and interacted dialogically, creating a kaleidoscopic, multifaceted, evolving and complex portrait of Johnson. As his close ties with artists, his support of the Society of Arts and the Royal Academy, his personal collection of prints, and his collaboration in the creation of numerous portraits amply demonstrate, Johnson was not the ignorant philistine disinterested in his image that he at times professed to be.

"Dictionary Johnson": Type and Countertype

Reynolds's earliest portrait of Johnson (1756–7), which largely adheres to iconographic conventions, portrays him as a writer and a thinker (Figure 16.1). Its countertype – Gillray's subversive caricature, *Old Wisdom Blinking at the Stars* (1782) – alludes to and deconstructs that tradition and

---

[4] Morris R. Brownell, *Samuel Johnson's Attitude to the Arts* (Oxford: Clarendon Press, 1989), pp. 91–104.

Figure 16.1. Joshua Reynolds, *Samuel Johnson*, 1756–7. Oil on canvas. National
Portrait Gallery, London. © National Portrait Gallery, London.

derides literary celebrity (Figure 16.2). Reynolds painted Johnson's portrait
soon after they met (c. 1755), presumably as a speculative venture.[5] Still
building his reputation as a celebrity portraitist, Reynolds depicted Johnson
shortly after the publication of his *Dictionary* (1755), which propelled him
into literary fame. Awkwardly sprawled at a small desk, his head tilted to the
right, Johnson holds a quill pen in his limp right hand, recalling depictions
of the Apostles. His claw-like left hand anchors a pile of papers; a pen and an
ink bottle and two volumes are visible at far right. Pictured as a writer with
the tools of his trade, the off-kilter, oblique pose and unfocused gaze,
connoting inspiration, and disjointed body destabilize the image,

---

[5] David Mannings, *Sir Joshua Reynolds: A Complete Catalogue of His Paintings*, 2 vols. (New Haven,
CT: Yale University Press, 2000), 1: 280, number 1011.

Figure 16.2. James Gillray, *Old Wisdom Blinking at the Stars*, 1782. Hand-colored etching. Beinecke Rare Book and Manuscript Library, Yale University.

foregrounding the inner workings of Johnson's mind and eliding his genius with his physical anomalies. His massive body, which fills the pictorial space, reinforces his aura of authority. Although the portrait remained in Reynolds's studio and was not exhibited or engraved during Johnson's lifetime, it would subsequently play a crucial role in shaping his posthumous image and reputation.

In *Old Wisdom Blinking*, Gillray portrays Johnson in classical profile
view but cunningly metamorphoses him into a monstrous hybrid – an
owl's body with an ass's ears, perched atop his famous *Dictionary* and the
Lives of the Poets, with the *Beauties of Johnson* lying open on the floor.
Although Gillray reprises the venerable physiognomic tradition of representing human character through animal traits, the owl's traditional association with wisdom is subverted by the ass's ears. Behind, books are
haphazardly stacked on shelves and the irradiated busts of Pope, Milton,
and two unidentified poets are displayed on pedestals, as authors' busts
commonly were in libraries. In this brilliant dialogic caricature, Gillray
strikes deeper, pointedly alluding to Johnson's extreme myopia and blindness in one eye, which is wittily parlayed into his critical blindness to the
genius of certain poets including Pope and Milton.[6] Johnson's harsh
silhouette also recalls Thomas Trotter's etched profile portrait, drawn
from life, which was rejected as the frontispiece for *The Beauties of
Johnson* (first published by George Kearsley in 1782) due to its ugliness,
but whose half-length seated portrait was published in 1786. Cleverly
melding diverse visual sources and iconographic traditions to denigrate
Johnson and mock literary fame, Gillray adopted the popular oval format
used for miniatures and Wedgwood medallions of illustrious moderns.

After Johnson's death, Reynolds's portrait was modified and resurfaced
as "Dictionary Johnson" in James Heath's 1791 engraving. In 1789,
Reynolds had given the previously unknown portrait to Boswell, who
wished to have it engraved as the frontispiece for his *Life of Johnson*. In
a curious reversal, which is corroborated by documentary evidence and the
four successive states of the engraving, the 1757 portrait was repainted by or
under Reynolds's supervision to duplicate the changes he had asked Heath
to make after seeing the first state of his engraving (c. 1790).[7] Recent
technical analysis has revealed that a number of changes were made to
the original portrait, including modifications to the waistcoat, the substi-
tution of a large square writing table, and the addition of the quill and ink
bottle and Johnson's iconic *Dictionary*. In a bizarre Wildean twist,
Johnson's wig was refreshed and his face was artificially aged to better
conform with more recent images, resulting in a composite retrospective
portrait.[8] When the painting was cleaned and restored in 1976, the post-
1757 alterations were removed, including the square writing table and quill

---

[6] James Gillray, *Old Wisdom Blinking at the Stars*, 1782, British Museum (BM) 6103.
[7] On the four states of Heath's engraving, see National Portrait Gallery (NPG) 1597.
[8] Richard Wendorf, *The Elements of Life: Biography and Portrait-Painting in Stuart and Georgian England* (Oxford: Clarendon Press, 1990), pp. 256–58.

and ink bottle, and the books were painted over.[9] The portrait had faded, due to Reynold's experimental technique and unstable pigments, and the overpainting made it difficult to distinguish the various paint layers. After the portrait was attacked with a hammer in 2007, it underwent yet further conservation. At that time the decision was made to "restore" the additions to the 1757 portrait that Reynolds had approved, including the *Dictionary*, quill, and ink bottle, but not the invasive writing table.[10]

Gillray's caricature, which uncannily anticipated the addition of the *Dictionary*, cruelly plays off Johnson's harshly etched features against the idealized, irradiated effigies of Pope and Milton, giving him an exaggeratedly hooked nose and accentuating his heavy eyebrows and thick lips. Although Trotter's ponderous profile of Johnson was considered unflattering, it was not universally reviled. Fanny Burney, a close friend in Johnson's later years, considered it "as like him as it can look."[11] Trotter's powerful profile of Johnson, drawn from life, is not grotesque and does not stigmatize him as "blinking Sam," as Gillray's caricature would. Trotter's etching was the model for John Flaxman's Jasperware medallion of 1784, which softens Johnson's profile and imbues it with classical gravitas, enshrining him as an illustrious "modern."

Reckoning with Likeness in Life and Death

One of the central premises of portraiture is likeness – the accurate transcription of an individual's physiognomy – and preserving that image for posterity. Before photography, the most indexical impressions of the human face were death masks, which were often taken of prominent individuals and could be used in sculpting effigies.[12] Because portraits were generally commissioned, they were governed by social conventions and decorum and inflected by fashion. Not surprisingly, individual sitters tended toward the formulaic and were often "improved" by correcting physical flaws. Johnson's appearance and physical idiosyncrasies were documented by friends and contemporaries who knew him. He was roughly six feet tall and powerfully built, had light blue or gray eyes, was extremely myopic and virtually blind

---

[9] Bettina Jessell, "A Study of the Paint Layers of a Portrait of Dr. Johnson by Sir Joshua Reynolds P.R. A.," *The Conservator*, 5:1 (1981): 36–40.

[10] NPG 1597.

[11] Quoted in Joyce Hemlow, "Dr. Johnson and the Young Burneys," in Frederick W. Hilles (ed.), *New Light on Dr. Johnson* (New Haven, CT: Yale University Press, 1959), p. 330.

[12] See Marcia Pointon, "Casts, Imprints, and the Deathliness of Things: Artifacts on the Edge," *Art Bulletin*, 96 (2014): 170–95.

in his left eye, and subject to strange tics and uncontrollable gestures. Although Johnson's nearsightedness and massive torso figure prominently in his portraits, artists' strategies for representing his mental prowess and transcribing his physical anomalies varied considerably. James Barry's vivid sketch of Johnson's head taken from life (c. 1778–80), which remained in his studio, is the most striking painted likeness. Barry knew and admired Johnson. Although no sittings are recorded, it was made as a preparatory study for *The Distribution of Premiums in the Society of Arts*, the fifth mural in Barry's cycle on *The Progress of Human Culture*, painted for the Great Room at the Adelphi.[13] In his 1783 account of the murals, Barry explained that Johnson was pointing out the example of Mrs. Montagu's philanthropy. Unfortunately, in the completed mural, Johnson's detached head is relegated to the back row and awkwardly squeezed behind the luminous full-length portraits of the young Duchesses of Rutland and Devonshire, effacing the vivacity of Barry's sketch.[14]

The most authentic effigy of Johnson is the painted plaster bust by William Cumberland Cruikshank and James Hoskins, which incorporates his death mask (Figure 16.3). Despite its verisimilitude, the bust is less straightforward than it appears.[15] Neither strictly original nor fabricated, it is a direct imprint of the dead subject's face that was used to produce multiple copies distributed to Johnson's friends. The "original" death mask, which was built up to form the head, was cast in three parts, the face and the two ears. The head was then attached to an unrelated torso in Hoskins's studio, and the plaster was painted to resemble marble. Immediately after Johnson's death, Reynolds ordered Hoskins to make a plaster cast of his face. Although directly molded from Johnson's features, the eyes are closed and the face is immobilized, making it appear deathlike. Johnson's head is not tilted to the right, as it was in life due to a neurological injury, and his features have been smoothed out, though the crease of his habitual frown and scrofula scars are discernible. Although Dr. Cruikshank, Johnson's attending physician, claimed it was a remarkable likeness, it has a reductive quality and a sort of blandness.[16] His absent gaze distances Johnson and makes his visage appear inscrutable. While it is reminiscent of a Roman portrait bust, the naturalistic detail – the scarred facial topography and imprints of individual hairs – make it disconcertingly life-like. The bust

---

[13] William Pressly, *The Life and Art of James Barry* (New Haven, CT: Yale University Press, 1981), pp. 105–09.
[14] NPG 1185.   [15] NPG 4685.
[16] Matthew H. Kaufman and Robert McNeil, "Death Masks and Life Masks at Edinburgh University," *British Medical Journal*, 298 (1989): 506–07.

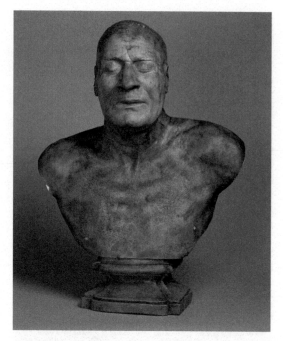

Figure 16.3. William Cumberland Cruikshank and James Hoskins, *Bust Incorporating Death Mask of Samuel Johnson*, 1784. Plaster cast. National Portrait Gallery, London. © National Portrait Gallery, London.

has been compared to Reynolds's profile portrait of Johnson as a classical orator (1769–70), his eyes shuttered, likewise distancing him from the spectator. Despite its hybridity and liminality, the posthumous bust/death mask is the most accurate material record we have of Johnson's face.

Joseph Nollekens's bust of Johnson, the only sculptural portrait modeled from life, provides an intriguing comparison (Figure 16.4). Exhibited at the Royal Academy in 1777, it exists in six versions: four plaster casts, a terracotta, and a lead cast, made after the original clay version (now lost).[17] Although Nollekens did not execute a marble version, there is an extended marble copy by Edward Hodges Baily (1828).[18] Nollekens's fame rests primarily on his portrait busts *à l'antique*, with cropped hair and classical drapery, which were much in demand. Nollekens and Johnson became acquainted around 1772 through the magistrate Saunders Welch, who was Nollekens's father-in-law

[17] See John Thomas Smith, *Nollekens and His Times*, 2 vols. (London: John Lane, 1917), 1: 46–48.
[18] NPG 996. A version of the bust is installed above Johnson's grave at Westminster Abbey.

Figure 16.4. Joseph Nollekens, *Samuel Johnson*, 1777. Plaster. Yale Center for British
Art, Paul Mellon Fund.

and an old friend of Johnson's. Johnson probably began sitting for his bust in
late 1776. Nollekens gave Johnson a cast of the bust, which he sent to his
stepdaughter, Lucy Porter. In 1778 Johnson wrote her: "My Bust was made for
the Exhibition, and shown for the honour of the artist," and bragged about
Nollekens's unrivaled reputation (*Letters*, 3: 108–09). Although Francis
Chantrey considered it Nollekens's finest bust, Johnson's female coterie –
Mrs. Thrale, Frances Reynolds, and Mrs. Garrick – disliked his wigless
appearance and condemned it. Johnson thought it a good likeness except
for the flowing locks, modeled on the hair of an Irish beggar, but objected to
appearing without his wig, insisting that "sitters should be shown as they are
seen in company."[19] Though Nollekens portrayed Johnson as an ancient poet

[19] Herman W. Liebert, *Johnson's Head: The Story of the Bust of Dr. Samuel Johnson* (New Haven, CT:
Yale University Press, 1960), np.

and draped him in a toga, his features are highly individualized and animated. It is a powerful but subtle likeness that evokes Johnson's inner psyche – his forthrightness, fortitude, and fierce mental concentration – to an extraordinary degree.

Like many sculptors, Nollekens made death masks, which he occasionally used in sculpting portraits. Having restored and probably counterfeited ancient sculpture in Rome in the 1760s, he was thoroughly versed in classical antiquity. Although the bust of Johnson appears complete when viewed from the front, the torso, as in many Roman busts, is hollow cast so, like a death mask, it displays the physical marks of its production inside. Only the head is fully in the round, making the sculpture a body fragment, a sort of synecdoche of the subject that, by focusing on Johnson's massive head, underscores his mind and the thinking process.

The portrait of *Bennet Langton Contemplating the Bust of Johnson* (c. 1785), attributed to Zoffany, thematizes Nollekens's bust, transforming it into an object of melancholic contemplation by channeling Rembrandt's famous depiction of *Aristotle Contemplating the Bust of Homer* (1654) (Figure 16.5).[20] Langton, a classical scholar and longtime friend, may have commissioned the portrait shortly after Johnson's death, as a sort of *memento mori* to memorialize their friendship. What makes the picture compelling is the intense exchange of gazes between Langton and the bust of his deceased friend. The massive larger-than-life bust dwarfs the pen, ink bottle, and paper, traditional writers' attributes, on the table below. In this moving double portrait, Johnson is resurrected and commemorated in the social sphere of friendship and intimate conversation.

The bust of Johnson was engraved by William Thomas Fry in 1815, and posthumous marble versions were produced, testifying to Nollekens's success at creating a timeless iconic image of Johnson as an ancient but touchingly human sage. Boswell described Johnson's countenance as cast in the mold of an ancient statue, but somewhat disfigured (*Life*, 5: 18–19). After Johnson's death, statues and public memorials commemorating him proliferated.

---

[20] Johnson sat for Zoffany in late 1782 just before Zoffany departed for India, so he could not have painted it c. 1785. Based on the pose, Kai Kin Yung suggests it could be a self-portrait, since Langton could paint. Kai Kin Yung, *Samuel Johnson, 1709–84* (London: The Arts Council of Great Britain, 1986), p. 93.

Figure 16.5. Unknown artist, attributed to Johan Zoffany, *Bennet Langton Contemplating the Bust of Johnson*, c. 1785. Oil on canvas. Samuel Johnson Birthplace Museum, Lichfield.

Reading Johnson: The Conundrum of *Blinking Sam*

Blinking Sam, whose date and early history are uncertain, is arguably Reynolds's least-loved portrait of Johnson (Figure 16.6). Depicted half-length in close-up, three-quarter view, Johnson voraciously devours a book, held up to his face, highlighting his extreme myopia. Further complicating the plot, *Blinking Sam* inspired other artists and survives in multiple versions: an oil sketch attributed to Gilbert Stuart, a free copy by Frances Reynolds, and another attributed to Theophila Palmer

Figure 16.6.   Joshua Reynolds, *Samuel Johnson "Blinking Sam,"* 1775. Oil on canvas.
The Huntington Library, Art Museum, and Botanical Gardens. Gift of Frances and
Loren Rothschild.

(Figure 16.7).[21] The "original" version belonged to Edmond Malone,
a friend of both Johnson and Reynolds, but it is unclear when or how it
entered his collection. James Northcote, Reynolds's assistant and biographer, dated it 1775, and linked it with Mrs. Piozzi's "Blinking Sam"
anecdote.[22] Based on a notation on the mount of John Hall's 1787
engraving in the British Museum, which states the head was painted
from memory after Johnson's death, David Mannings has dated it c. 1786.[23]
Further muddying the waters, *Blinking Sam* is easily confused with the
half-length portrait Reynolds painted for the Streatham library. What light

---

[21]   See Loren Rothschild, "Blinking Sam: The True History of Sir Joshua Reynolds's Portrait of Samuel
Johnson," *AJ*, 15 (2004): 141–50.
[22]   James Northcote, *Memoirs of Sir Joshua Reynolds* (London: H. Colburn, 1813), p. 218.
[23]   Mannings, *Sir Joshua Reynolds*, 1: 282, number 1016.

Figure 16.7. Attributed to Gilbert Stuart, *Dr. Samuel Johnson, L.L.D.*, 1783? Oil on canvas. *2003JM-15, Houghton Library, Harvard University.

(if any) can be shed on *Blinking Sam*'s murky origins, contested date, and the nexus of copies it engendered? How does the portrait encapsulate Johnson's public and private personas, and what explains its pariah status? To represent Johnson, renowned for his ability to instantly grasp a book's essence, absorbed in the act of reading, seems obvious, even axiomatic. Reading was thematized in Barry's pendant portraits of Giuseppe Baretti and Dr. Christopher Nugent reading, exhibited at the Royal Academy in 1773, and in Reynolds's more decorous *Portrait of Baretti* for Streatham, exhibited the following year. Barry's vivid depiction of Baretti, holding up a magnifying lens to his eye, has the same casual intimacy and laser-like focus on the act of reading as *Blinking Sam*.

According to Mrs. Piozzi's witty anecdote in *Anecdotes of the Late Samuel Johnson*, Johnson strenuously objected to the portrait, telling her, "he would not be known by posterity for his *defects* only." When she pointed to Reynolds's *Self-Portrait as a Deaf Man* (c. 1775) hanging nearby, he testily replied, "He may paint himself as deaf if he chuses; but I will not be '*blinking Sam*'" (*JM*, 1: 313). Johnson's sharp rebuke indicates his touchiness about how his defective vision was portrayed, as well as his awareness of the power of portraits in shaping and projecting his image. But there are problems with Mrs. Piozzi's account. The portrait depicts Johnson reading a book, rather than "looking into the slit of his pen," as Mrs. Piozzi described it in her *Anecdotes*, while Northcote recounted a different scenario in which Johnson reproved Reynolds "for painting him in that manner and attitude," finding it unfriendly "to hand down the imperfections of any man to posterity." Reynolds viewed it as "characterizing the person represented and adding to the value of the portrait."[24] Mrs. Piozzi's description seems closer to the unfinished sketch in the Hyde Collection, which is closely modeled on *Blinking Sam* but depicts a bound book and what looks like a penknife. It bears a nineteenth-century inscription stating it was painted from life during Johnson's 1783 visit to the home of William Bowles, for whom it was made and who thought it an excellent likeness.[25] Although not conclusive, Stuart was in London, 1775–87 and knew Reynolds, whose portrait he painted in 1784. The preponderance of evidence does not support Mannings's posthumous 1786 dating, nor his proposal that the moniker "Blinking Sam" be applied to the Streatham portrait instead.[26] The dimensions and compressed format of *Blinking Sam* accord with the other "Streatham Worthies," raising the intriguing possibility that it could have originally been intended for the library.[27] As previously noted, it resembles the *Portrait of Baretti* (1773), reading a small book held up to his nose, which Baretti disliked, but remained on display. Reynolds's candid portrayal of Johnson's myopia would have formed a pendant to his *Self-Portrait as a Deaf Man*, cupping his hand to his ear. In *Blinking Sam*, Reynolds, who saw Johnson regularly, observed him in a private, unguarded moment, and captures his authenticity in an attitude that registers their intimacy.[28] Johnson's visual disability is subsumed into his passion for knowledge and enhances his intellectual aura.

---

[24] Northcote, *Memoirs of Sir Joshua Reynolds*, p. 218.
[25] Hyde Collection, Harvard University, 2003 JM-15.
[26] Mannings, *Sir Joshua Reynolds*, 1: 281–82, number 1014.
[27] Robert Folkenflik, "*Blinking Sam,* 'Surly Sam', and 'Johnson's Grimly Ghost'," in Howard Weinbrot (ed.), *Samuel Johnson: New Contexts for a New Century* (San Marino: Huntington Library, (2014), pp. 265–94, 278. Yung, *Samuel Johnson*, p. 112, suggests it may have been conceived as a private joke.
[28] See Wendorf, *Elements of Life*, p. 254.

The book's print appears slightly blurred, and the cover is folded over and held slightly off-center, bringing it closer to his good eye.[29] The 1756–7 portrait, which *Blinking Sam* resembles, remained in Reynolds's studio. Although Johnson objected in principle to women painting portraits, in 1783 he sat repeatedly for Reynolds's youngest sister, Frances, for a portrait, possibly begun in 1780, that he ironically dubbed "Johnson's grimly Ghost" (*Letters*, 4: 188). Frances, who managed Reynolds's household from 1752 until the late 1770s, painted miniatures and portraits, two of which were exhibited at the Royal Academy, and made copies after Reynolds. Though her portraits are becoming better known, her painting career, which Reynolds discouraged, is poorly documented.[30] Her portrait of Johnson is a free copy, darker and slightly extended, with variants, including the waistcoat, which resembles the Streatham portrait. Johnson's features are heavier and the effect is less vivid, bringing to mind Northcote's cruel quip that her portraits were exact imitations of Reynolds's defects.[31] What remains unclear is why Johnson would have posed repeatedly for a copy after a portrait that he disliked.

There is yet another related portrait of Johnson reading, attributed to Northcote, known today through a crude 1813 etching by Ignace Joseph de Claussin.[32] It depicts Johnson in a hideous wig, turned almost frontally, awkwardly grasping a bound book. Although Boswell mentions a portrait by Northcote, there is no evidence Johnson sat for him. Northcote, who lived in Reynolds's house from 1771 to 1776, could have seen *Blinking Sam* in the studio when it was painted. Indeed, Reynolds's depiction of Johnson reading was a powerfully expressive and characteristic likeness that struck a chord among contemporaries despite the subject's aversion to it. It is an unfiltered image painted by a close friend, which may explain Johnson's aversion to it and sense of betrayal. In baptizing it "blinking Sam," he unwittingly ensured its lasting fame. It continued to resonate as Hall's ornate oval engraving, published in 1787 for the first edition of Johnson's *Works*, and later impressions of *Blinking Sam* demonstrate. Particularly fascinating is the devolution of the image of Johnson reading, appropriated by multiple artists during his lifetime. The genesis of *Blinking Sam* can

[29] Herman W. Liebert, "Portraits of the Author: Lifetime Likenesses of Samuel Johnson," in *English Portraits of the Seventeenth and Eighteenth Centuries; Papers Read at a Clark Library Seminar, April 14, 1973* (Los Angeles: William Andrews Clark Memorial Library, University of California, 1974), pp. 47-88, 56.
[30] See Richard Wendorf, *Sir Joshua Reynolds: The Painter in Society* (Cambridge, MA: Harvard University Press, 1996), pp. 68–81.
[31] Cited in Wendorf, *Sir Joshua Reynolds*, p. 77.
[32] Powell, "The Portraits of Johnson," *Life*, 4: 457–58; BM 18680808.1707.

probably be traced back to Reynolds's *Girl Reading* (c. 1771), a popular theme in French painting, exhibited at the Royal Academy in 1771. It portrays Theophila Palmer, Reynolds's niece, close-up, in left profile, absorbed in reading Richardson's *Clarissa*, and was engraved in 1775.[33] In *Blinking Sam*, Reynolds reprised the reader theme, transforming Johnson's myopia into an emblem of his insatiable mind.

Johnson in Old Age

Although Johnson's lifetime portraits stretch across decades, the majority depict him in old age. These valedictory images portray him as a benevolent sage, whose formidable intellect is cloaked in serenity. John Opie's magisterial portraits (1783–4), which Greg Clingham has recently discussed, are noteworthy examples.[34] A more obscure late effigy (c. 1784) continues to perplex scholars (Figure 16.8). Though embraced as a moving portrayal of Johnson in old age, its authorship is an open question. Hailed by L. F. Powell as "the finest of all portraits of Johnson" and long considered the finale in Reynolds's series, the attribution has been rejected by others, who ascribe it to an unknown artist (*Life*, 4: 452). Various names have been put forward – none of them convincing. The portrait is a cautionary example of the reliability and limitations of historical documentation and pictorial evidence in determining authorship. Though not mentioned by Boswell or other early sources, the likeness is undeniable and the provenance is well established. Painted for Dr. John Taylor of Ashbourne, one of Johnson's oldest friends, the portrait passed down to his heir. That Reynolds would have painted a final portrait of Johnson for Taylor is plausible, though no payments are recorded. Besides the paucity of evidence, Yung's rationale for deattributing the portrait is based on stylistic factors such as paint application and the modeling of the head, which brings us back to the picture itself.

Johnson is depicted frontally, at half-length, against a red curtain, his head tilted to the right, as in Reynolds's first portrait. The light blue eyes, nose, and mouth are clearly Johnson's, though the features appear strained and the face longer, indicating aging and illness. The body is a dark undifferentiated mass, focusing the viewer's attention on the illuminated face. What stands out and differentiates it from Reynolds's earlier portraits

---

[33] Mannings, *Sir Joshua Reynolds*, 1: 362–63, number 1389.
[34] Greg Clingham, "John Opie's Portraits of Dr. Johnson," *Harvard Library Bulletin*, 28:2 (2017): 57–80.

Figure 16.8. Unknown artist, *Samuel Johnson*, c. 1784. Oil on canvas. Quaker and
Special Collections, Haverford College, Haverford, PA.

is the directness and poignancy of the gaze. Max Beerbohm, who knew it
only through reproduction, recognized its uniqueness, as his scribbled
annotations attest: "It's far more convincing and *telling* than any of the
others. ... This is intimately the dear man himself – not the legendary
monster."[35] I suspect its vulnerability and unstinting depiction of old age
may have mitigated against its wider critical acceptance. That Reynolds
was capable of painting such an image is demonstrated by his final *Self-
Portrait* (c. 1788), in which he depicted himself wearing spectacles, alluding
to his near blindness. Edmond Malone recognized that picture, of which
he owned a copy, as representing Reynolds "exactly as he appeared in his
latter days."[36] Although the authorship of this portrait, now at Haverford

---

[35] Max Beerbohm, annotations from Newton's *A Magnificent Farce*, Hyde Collection.
[36] Mannings, *Sir Joshua Reynolds*, 1: 51, number 21.

College, remains uncertain, and critical opinion diverges, its authenticity as a movingly human image of Johnson at the end of his life is indisputable.

Reinventing Johnson: Imaginary and Fictive Portraits

Besides their commemorative function and instrumental role as tools for registering identity, portraits are often perceived as historical documents, though it may be more accurate to view them as historical fiction. This concluding section considers imaginary or ingeniously fabricated images that complicate and enrich the indexical function of portraiture by weaving fictions about the sitter. Fancy pictures of children or infants, which enhanced the subject imaginatively or allegorically, were a popular sub-genre in the late eighteenth century. Beginning in the 1770s, Reynolds delighted in composing such pictures because they freed him from the drudgery of portrait painting, giving him latitude to invent and experiment with new ideas, as in the *Infant Hercules* and the *Infant Johnson* (c. 1780) (Figure 16.9).[37] The latter depicts a pudgy naked infant seated in a forest setting, looking down pensively, his hands clasped in his lap. According to Mrs. Jameson, Reynolds "intended it to represent Dr. Johnson when a year old. One can imagine him something like that at that age."[38] The picture, which was not exhibited or engraved, remained in Reynolds's studio. Although the identity of the infant has been questioned and cannot be wholly proven,[39] the downcast gaze, serious expression, and introspective air differentiate him from Reynolds's more conventional cherubic infants. The challenge of representing Johnson's literary genius in embryonic form would doubtless have appealed to Reynolds's creative imagination. The solidly built *Infant Johnson*, with his large squarish head and inward focus, suggests the act of thinking. Also, Carey McIntosh associates the infant's pose with melancholy, which Johnson suffered from and was traditionally associated with genius. As with the *Infant Hercules*, the interest lay in inventing a sort of *Jüngen Legend*, in tracing the figure's greatness back to infancy and exploiting the tension between the infant and the mature literary colossus.[40] Johnson's interest in Reynolds's infants is demonstrated

---

[37] Mannings, *Sir Joshua Reynolds*, 1: 541, number 2097.
[38] Mrs. Jameson, *Companion to the Most Celebrated Private Galleries of Art in London* (London: Saunders & Otley, 1844), p. 329.
[39] See Edward Hudson, "Joshua Reynolds and the Infant Johnson: New Light on an Old Riddle," *JNL*, 73:1 (2022): 19–21.
[40] Carey McIntosh, "Reynolds's Portrait of the Infant Johnson," in William Henry Bond (ed.), *Eighteenth-Century Studies in Honor of Donald F. Hyde* (New York: Grolier Club, 1970), pp. 279–96.

Figure 16.9. Joshua Reynolds, *The Infant Johnson,* c. 1780. Oil on canvas. *2003JM-4, Houghton Library, Harvard University.

by his felicitous renaming of *The Infant Academy* (1782) in the 1783 engraving after it, as noted in *The World,* January 9, 1787. The fact that Reynolds, whose fancy pictures were highly marketable, kept the painting is a further indication of the personal significance it held for him.

Long after his death, Johnson's image continued to circulate and mutate across media, sometimes giving rise to peculiar hybrid composites. One such example is the plaster modello by Joseph Boehm (1881?) after Reynolds's profile portrait (1769–70) (Figure 16.10).[41] The half-length figure, translated from two into three dimensions, is depicted frontally rather than in profile, and is abruptly cut off at the waist. Johnson's eyes are closed and his features are smoothed out and regularized, making it

[41] NPG 621.

Figure 16.10. Joseph Edgar Boehm, *Samuel Johnson*, 1881. Plaster modello. National Portrait Gallery, London. © National Portrait Gallery, London.

resemble a death mask. His eccentric gesticulations have been tamed and recast as a self-referential gesture rather than uncontrollable nervous tics. Only the head appears worked up; the body is rapidly modeled and roughly textured. What intrigues me is Boehm's bold attempt at "translation" across media to sculpt an invented bust of Johnson in the guise of an ancient orator. It stands in sharp contrast to Nollekens's lively bust, modeled from life. Another imaginary bust of Johnson appears in James Sayers's satirical print *The Biographers* (1786).[42] It is an inventive reworking

[42] BM 7052.

of the iconic Streatham portrait, notably the oddly tilted head and grimace
of concentration, with a bit of Opie thrown in. Recalling the poets' busts in
Old Wisdom, the bust of Johnson gazes down balefully at his biographers,
who have been busy fabricating his biography. Johnson is wearing his
habitual waistcoat with buttons, but his body is reduced to a truncated
bust, the arms abruptly hacked off below the shoulders.

Epilogue

Kehinde Wiley's inkjet print *After Sir Joshua Reynolds Portrait of Samuel
Johnson* (2009), from his Black Light series, appropriates and deconstructs
Reynolds's classical profile portrait, recasting it in contemporary hip hop
style with cinematic lighting and aggressively bright colors and patterns.
Wiley's typical modus operandi is critical intervention – to interrogate and
subvert famous old master portraits by replacing white protagonists with
young male African Americans. The models pose in their own clothes in
the studio under special lighting and assume attitudes from well-known
paintings, undermining hierarchies of race and power. The traditional
literary attributes – the books, quill pen and ink, and scroll – and the
classical references – the toga and stern profile view – have been replaced
with a swirling red foliage pattern. Only Johnson's odd hand gesticulations, aptly characterized as the mind preying upon itself, remain as
a signifier of power and eloquence. The model is rotated a quarter turn
to face the viewer, and the gesture is cool and assertive. The sitter's artfully
tilted pale green baseball cap replaces Johnson's cropped hair, and his
baseball jacket replaces the antiquated toga, as emblems of contemporary
identity. Wiley's transformation of Reynolds's portrait of Johnson as an
antique philosopher reminds us of the powerful role portraiture continues
to play in registering identity and shaping images past and present.
Johnson, who once observed that "Fame is a shuttlecock. . . . To keep it
up, it must be struck at both ends" (*Boswell's Scotland*, 390), would
doubtless be amused that his image has not fallen into oblivion and still
matters enough to be mimicked in the twenty-first century.

CHAPTER 17

Johnson among the Scholars

Robert DeMaria, Jr.

As a young man, Johnson sought to join an ideal European community of scholars and poets, comprising late Renaissance humanists such as Angelo Poliziano, whose poetry he wished to edit, and Joseph Scaliger, to whom he addressed a self-deprecating autobiographical poem (*Life*, 1: 89–90).[1] Johnson identified with the scholars following Erasmus, whom he revered (*Diaries*, 194), who studied the classics and wrote their own Latin and Greek poetry. Johnson never gave up this aspirational identity, but necessity forced him to write and edit in the vernacular – if not to become a Grubstreet hack, at least to do "booksellers' jobbs," as one critic called his *Dictionary*.[2] Despite his fall from humanistic grace, Johnson engendered a community of scholars who have adopted his animating spirit and become learned in a humanistic way by studying Johnson and publishing books about his life and works. It would please Johnson to know this, for even in his lifetime he was pleased to be the "benefactor" of authors who excerpted his works – collectors both of "Beauties" and "Deformities" (*Letters*, 4: 28).

To be learned in Johnson – or Johnsonian – is a category of intellectual achievement that was recognized early on in Johnson's afterlife. Boswell praised Edmund Malone, the first editor of Boswell's *Life*, as "an acute and knowing critic" and "*Johnsonianissimus*."[3] G. B. Hill borrowed the praise of Malone for the dedication of his edition (1887) of Boswell's *Life of Johnson* to Benjamin Jowett, the classicist and Master of Balliol College, Oxford. Countless Johnsonians since have used the term in inscriptions and introductions. As the dedication indicates, however, being very Johnsonian is not the same as being "an acute and knowing critic." The distinction is important: it separates knowing a great deal about a subject from being

---

[1] The poem is "Know Thyself" (*Poems*, p. 271).
[2] Thomas Edwards, cited by James Sledd and Gwin Kolb, *Dr. Johnson's Dictionary: Essays in the Biography of a Book* (Chicago, IL: University of Chicago Press, 1955), p. 135.
[3] To Richard Temple, 28 November 1789, *Letters of James Boswell*, 2 vols., ed. Chauncey Brewster Tinker (Oxford: Clarendon Press, 1924), 2: 381.

scholarly in a general way. Being Johnsonianissimus requires a thorough knowledge of Johnson's works, but it also means being especially learned in Boswell's *Life of Johnson* and Hill's notes. It often goes beyond that, to include the many works that have added to our knowledge of the Great Cham. The most impressive of these remains Allen Lyell Reade's *Johnsonian Gleanings*, 11 vols. (1909–52). No one amassed more knowledge of Johnson than Reade, but even mastering all the knowledge in Reade is not enough to make a scholar on the model of the great humanists that Johnson admired. What is lacking in many devoted Johnsonians is an acutely critical approach to Johnson's works. There were admirers of Johnson in his lifetime and there have been many since who deserve the accolade "Johnsonian," or even "Johnsonianissimus," whose knowledge of Johnson and his works, even if comprehensive, is not critical.

A dictionary of Johnsonians would include well-known figures such as Boswell, Hester Thrale Piozzi, and Frances Burney, who were members of Johnson's circle; somewhat less-well-known people such as Samuel Parr, the so-called "Whig Dr. Johnson"; and some obscure scholars, such as Rev. John Brickdale Blakeway (1765–1826), who contributed fifty-six notes to the Johnson–Malone edition of Shakespeare (1821) and wrote numerous learned articles for the *Gentleman's Magazine* as "Sciolus," many of them revealing a detailed knowledge of Johnson's works. A history of Johnsonians would cover Hill, who eventually became an honorary fellow of Pembroke College; pass through Leslie Stephen, the creator of the *Dictionary of National Biography*; and go on into the great Johnsonians of the twentieth century: J. D. Fleeman, Allen Hazen, Donald Greene, James Clifford, John H. Middendorf, Mary Hyde Eccles, Walter Jackson Bate, Bertrand Bronson, Gwin Kolb, and Howard Weinbrot.[4] At some point, however, one would observe a rift in these Johnsonians between the purists and those who were scholars first and Johnsonians second. There were of course many hybrid cases, but those more committed to scholarship than to Johnson probably have to be called academics.

Despite Johnson's well-known disdain for academies and his protestation in the preface to the *Dictionary* that he did not write his book "under the shelter of academick bowers," "academic" was not a dirty word for him. The last work attributed to Johnson by J. D. Fleeman in his great *Bibliography of the Works of Samuel Johnson*[5] is "The Duty of an

[4] I omit the names of living Johnsonians.
[5] John David Fleeman, *A Bibliography of the Works of Samuel Johnson: Treating His Published Works from the Beginnings to 1984*, 2 vols. (Oxford: Clarendon Press, 2000).

Academick." Johnson elevates the purpose of the academic to a very high station: "Our colleges may be considered as the citadel of truth, where he is to stand on his guard as a sentinel, to watch and discover the approach of falsehood, and from which he is to march out into the field of controversy, and bid defiance to the teachers of corruption" (*Demand*, 612). Johnson associated closely with academics at Oxford, such as Robert Chambers and Thomas Warton, and at Cambridge, such as the scholar James Farmer. He also delighted to be included in academic institutions, as is clear, for example, in his letter of thanks to Vice-Chancellor George Huddesford, the official responsible for granting his Oxford MA in 1755 (*Letters*, 1: 99). He was happy too in having his *Dictionary* praised by the Accademia della Crusca in Florence (*Life*, 1: 443).

There was clearly an ambivalence in Johnson's attitude to academic pursuits. He could play Augustine in his famous treatise *Against the Academics* in, for example, asking the scholar in the *Vanity of Human Wishes* to "pause a while from letters, to be wise" (*Poems*, 99, 158). On the other hand, he could praise academics, consort with them, and even behave like them in, for example, the philologically oriented notes to his edition of Shakespeare or those to his editions of Roger Ascham's *English Works* and Thomas Browne's *Christian Morals*. This ambivalence about the academy plays itself out in the long history of Johnson scholars, but for present purposes it is necessary to focus on a shorter span of time and a more limited area of work on Johnson. The history of the Yale Edition of the Works of Samuel Johnson in twenty-three volumes (1958–2018) provides a convenient focus for tracing the conversation between the academics and the Johnsonians.[6] The work was largely begun by Johnsonians and largely completed by academics. Many of the men and women involved in the project were a bit of both: no pure Johnsonian could do the scholarly work, and no pure academic is likely to have undertaken such a daunting project. It required some romantic feeling for Johnson, which isn't a feature of the purely academic mind. The distinction comes down to a concern for Johnson's texts versus a concern for the person who created them: a hard-headed materialism versus a romantic love of a lost personality and a bygone age – in short, it's biography vs bibliography.

---

[6] I have told parts of this story in three articles: "A History of the Collected Works of Samuel Johnson: The First Two Hundred Years," in Howard Weinbrot (ed.), *Samuel Johnson: New Contexts for a New Century* (San Marino, CA: Huntington Library, 2014), pp. 343–66; "Careful and Careless: Epic Tales in the Editing of Dr Johnson," *Times Literary Supplement*, March 6, 2015, pp. 14–15; and "The Yale Edition of the Works of Samuel Johnson, 1958–2018," *The Book Collector*, 69:3 (2020): 487–96.

In the beginning, on the romantic side, was Mary Hyde (later, Hyde Eccles), and among the academics Allen Hazen. A third party present from the start, though not formally involved in the project, was J. D. Fleeman. Hyde and Hazen were both close to Fleeman, argued with him, and in many ways defined their relationship to the great project in relation to him. Mary Hyde operated in concert with her husband Donald, but I emphasize Mary because she had more influence on the Edition, both because of her superior scholarship and her longevity. Donald died in 1966 while Mary lived until 2003, continued to build the greatest private collection of Johnsoniana in the world, and bequeathed her treasures to Harvard University.

Mary Hyde organized the first meeting of the Johnsonians of America in 1946 as a bit of fun on Johnson's birthday. She knew of British Johnsonian societies in London (founded 1928) and Lichfield (founded 1910), as well as the Johnson Club derived from the original Club (founded in 1764), although it had already devolved by then into a more high-toned society, denizened by a select few of the great and powerful. By 1946, the Hydes were important collectors of Johnsonian books and manuscripts: They invited friends – other collectors, such as Herman W. Liebert (who qualified as a "founder member") – and some university librarians and professors to Four Oaks Farm, their house in Somerville, New Jersey. By 1951 there were forty-eight active members and nine honorary members (all British), who presumably would be unable to attend the annual dinner (though at least R. W. Chapman and L. F. Powell did attend a dinner each). The Yale Edition of Johnson's works was conceived by members of this group, and one can imagine that it was a romantic impulse that stimulated them. Other collectors, such as Frederick B. Adams, Ralph H. Isham, Halsted B. Vander Poel, and Arthur A. Houghton, Jr. were among the group. There were also future biographers of Johnson – Joseph Wood Krutch, James Clifford, and Walter Jackson Bate. I would say these men, for all their scholarship and academic credentials, were nevertheless coadjutants in pressing the romantic claims for an edition: biography is inherently romantic in an essential sense. At the beginning there were also more textually or philologically oriented scholars present, such as William Todd, Allen Hazen, and William Wimsatt. Allen Hazen was asked to write up the first proposal for the Edition in 1951 and he became its first general editor. With a Yale BA (1927) and PhD (1935), Hazen was a Yale library cataloguer (1942–5), and later director of the library at the University of Chicago (1947–8). When he arrived at Columbia University in 1948 it was as Professor of English in the school of Library Service. As a bibliographer,

Hazen was squarely in the camp of the academics. His correspondents and friends included other bibliographers, such as Graham Pollard, Dard Hunter, and David Fleeman. His most distinctive work is the catalogue of the library of Horace Walpole (1969). In 1935, he prepared the catalogue of the exhibition of first editions of the works of Samuel Johnson at Yale and he edited *Johnson's Prefaces and Dedications* (1937), a collection of many of Johnson's fugitive works. Given Hazen's background, it is not surprising that his inaugural proposal for the Yale Edition emphasized the production of a "sound text" (a phrase that purposely avoids adherence to any specific theory of the copy-text) and played down commentary and criticism. He reflected the interests of "purer" Johnsonians in proposing an edition that would be unencumbered by academic apparatus, focused on Johnson's major works, and finished quickly. He proposed in 1951:

> The edition is planned . . . in 12 volumes; the Letters and Debates probably to be omitted. . . . the apparatus is to be minimal. The text printed is to be sound, as the first requisite, with enough apparatus to enable users to follow the textual problems. Non-technical bibliographical notes should identify clearly the textual problems involved. Explanatory annotation is to be helpful and adequate, but never discursive or all-inclusive. . . . the edition ought to be ready to print within about two years.[7]

"Two years" is perhaps the most romantic phrase in the proposal, and since the Edition took sixty years to complete, the most ironic. The proposal could be described as an attempt to marry the ideas behind the Library of America, a virtually unannotated series of books (begun at that time by Hazen's Columbia University colleague Jacques Barzun), with the instincts of a bibliographer. A sign that Hazen was compromising his own scholarly inclinations is that many of the works he edited in *Prefaces and Dedications* would have no place in the Yale Edition as originally planned. In this work, Hazen also produces texts that follow more conservative editorial principles than those he recommended for the Yale Johnson (e.g., he retains more of the original typography of the works included).

Hazen, with his impeccable bibliographical credentials, was the first general editor of the Edition, but the first chairman of the Editorial Committee, one of two committees in the group that Mary Hyde founded, was Herman (Fritz) Liebert. Liebert was about six years younger than Hazen, having graduated from Yale in 1933. He was a newspaper reporter for a time, and during World War II he worked for the Office of Strategic

---

[7] Houghton Library, Harvard University, MS Hyde 98 (827).

Services, the predecessor to the CIA. After the war, he worked on the drafting committee for Truman's Committee on Foreign Aid, which included the development of the Marshall Plan. After that, he conducted private research before returning to Yale as an assistant librarian and becoming, in 1963, the first librarian of the Beinecke Rare Book and Manuscript Library. He was never a member of any academic department. He was a librarian of the enlightened amateur sort; he did not have a masters in Library Science, though there had been Schools of Library Science since 1887. Like Hazen, Liebert was a bibliographer, but his interest in describing books was included in his passion for collecting them. His gifts to Yale, following those of his teacher Frederick Pottle (also a curator of rare books at Yale), vastly increased the Johnsonian holdings of the Beinecke. Liebert co-authored a long essay on Johnson's Club,[8] but his publications are largely introductions to catalogues and exhibitions, and he often used these occasions to write more broadly about the history of books and the eighteenth-century British book trade. He prepared many keepsakes for the Johnsonians' dinners, including the rare and fascinating "Who Dropped the Copy for Rambler 109?" (1966). Liebert bridged the gap between the Johnsonians who started the Edition and academics like Hazen who would, in the end, complete it. He understood both worlds, and his position as chairman of the committee united them. As the organizer of the Editorial Committee, he asked Mary Hyde to join, before asking others. He was also at the center of fund-raising for the Edition, and he supplied funds himself.[9] After Liebert's death, the position of chairman of the Editorial Committee was eliminated and the general editor from then on served in that role. That is one way in which some of the romance of Johnson gave way to the academic interest in the evolution of the Edition.

The *tertium aliquid* in that evolution, though he was not actually involved in it for many years, was J. D. Fleeman. He was a student of L. F. Powell (1881–1975), who was a member of the Editorial Committee. Powell, who never took a degree, worked in several Oxford libraries and as a member of the team assembling the *Oxford English Dictionary*. In 1923, R. W. Chapman asked him to revise Hill's edition of Boswell's *Life*, which led to further Johnsonian editing – particularly, Boswell's *Journal of*

---

[8] Lewis Perry Curtis and Herman W. Liebert, *Esto Perpetua: The Club of Dr. Johnson and His Friends, 1764–1784* (Hamden, CT: Archon Books, 1963).

[9] Although the edition had a grant from the Aaron E. Norman Fund of New York, most of the money came from "four private individuals" (presumably the Hydes, Liebert, and Houghton); it was later augmented by other individuals and the National Endowment for the Humanities.

a Tour to the Hebrides, which became volume 5 in the Hill–Powell edition of the *Life* (1950), and Johnson's contributions to the *Adventurer* in the Yale Edition. As Fleeman writes in Powell's *Oxford Dictionary of National Biography* entry, "It was one of his few boasts that he had never taken an academic examination in his life." Nevertheless, after his retirement as librarian of the Taylorian Institute, Powell supervised dissertations at Oxford until his death in 1975, when he was at work on a further edition of the Hill–Powell Boswell. Crucially, he inspired and supervised Fleeman's dissertation on the history of editions of Johnson's complete works. Fleeman's presentation copy of his dissertation to Powell registers the depth of his gratitude to Powell, whom he calls, in Shakespearean fashion, "the onlie begetter of these ensuing pages." Fleeman's dissertation is devoted to dismantling the reputation of the so-called Oxford Edition of Johnson's Works (1825), against which Powell evidently had a grudge, saying of it, "Its only value is that it is an object lesson in the delusive fascination which printed copy-text has exerted over generations of printers and editors."[10] He looked forward to the Yale Edition, writing hopefully in 1963 in the Preface to his dissertation, "The progress of the new Yale edition of Johnson's Works has and is continuing to make it of less moment to depose the 1825 edition from the eminence which it had unworthily enjoyed."[11]

Fleeman was not immune to the romance of Johnson and was exceedingly generous with anyone who studied him devotedly, encouraging me and other young scholars. At his prompting, I attended Johnson's birthday celebration in Lichfield in 1980. He showed me books and artifacts, asked me about my Johnsonian connections, and particularly wanted to know if I had met James Clifford. I had shaken his hand, but that was all. "You touched the hem of the garment," Fleeman replied, suggesting we were all apostles of Clifford's attempts to further Johnson's reputation.[12] For all his love of Johnson, however, Fleeman was an academic first and a Johnsonian second. His primary concern as a professional was for the text of Johnson and then, in his *Bibliography*, for the universe of Johnson's writings in print. In maintaining this material emphasis, he was following his mentor, L. F. Powell. Fleeman's predilections as a bibliographer and textual scholar led both to his high hopes and to his

---

[10] L. F. Powell, *"A Critical Study of the Transmission of the Texts of the Works of Dr. Samuel Johnson,"* University of Oxford, doctoral dissertation, 1965, p. 407.
[11] Powell, *"A Critical Study,"* p.iii.
[12] Clifford founded the *Johnsonian News Letter* in 1940. He was known for his generosity in communicating his knowledge to other researchers.

disappointment in the Yale Edition. He argued vociferously with Hazen, perhaps because he believed that at heart Hazen was like himself, a bibliographer first and a Johnsonian second. Their correspondence, preserved in the Fleeman Papers at the University of St. Andrews, attests to the strength of Fleeman's views as well as the depth of his friendship with Hazen. Fleeman may have felt betrayed, as though Hazen had given in to the Johnsonians, including popular writers on the Yale Editorial Committee such as Walter Jackson Bate (who had no interest in textual scholarship) and collectors such as the Hydes. Fleeman had in fact fallen out with the Hydes earlier for other reasons, but Fleeman's argument with both the Hydes and Hazen show the tensions between Johnsonians and academics at the start of the Yale Edition.

Fleeman's argument with Hazen boiled over after the publication of the Yale *Rambler* in 1969. The Edition, as proposed by Hazen in 1951, reflects his academic, bibliographical bent, and must have given Fleeman hope for the Yale Edition. When the volumes began appearing, however, hope turned to fear and anger. The first volume, *Dairies, Prayers, and Annals* (1958), was disappointing and attracted criticism. Using a strong light, Fleeman was able to read many obliterated or illegible words in the manuscripts that form the basis of this volume, and he published his critical findings in "Some Notes on Johnson's Prayers and Meditations."[13] Fredson T. Bowers, a fierce academic uninfluenced by Johnsonian romance, condemned the textual scholarship on other grounds. He concluded that "the editors' transcriptions and their notes on the formation of the completed text are insufficiently trustworthy for scholarly use ... [and] we have no definitive editions of the texts that appear here."[14] This volume is anomalous, being edited largely from manuscripts (rather than printed texts) at Pembroke College or in the Hyde Collection and also because its contents are so personal. R. W. Chapman in fact urged the Hydes not to publish it as part of the Edition. In September 1956 he wrote, "What would SJ have said if he had been told that Aegri Ephemeri [daily pains] should be put beside [the] Rambler? ... Do please think again."[15] Mary was determined, however, and reminded Chapman that she was supporting the publication financially. More romantic Johnsonians were also determined and pleased. The

---

[13] J. D. Fleeman, "Some Notes on Johnson's Prayers and Meditations," *Review of English Studies*, NS, 19:74 (1968): 172–79.

[14] Fredson Bowers, "Book Review: Samuel Johnson: Diaries, Prayers, and Annals," *Journal of English and Germanic Philology*, 58 (1959): 132–37, 137.

[15] Hyde MS 98, p. 613.

volume provided a great deal of grist for the mill of Walter Jackson Bate, whose biographical work on Johnson, including his inspiring teaching, was becoming popular at this time, winning the friendship and confidence of the Hydes.

Bate was the most influential of the romantic Johnsonians and, despite his high standing in the academy, the antithesis of academics like Fleeman and, at least in theory, Hazen. He was not as popular in Britain as he was in America. His psychological approach to Johnson baffled Chapman, who wrote to Mary Hyde in October 1955:

> Bate has just sent me his book [*The Achievement of Samuel Johnson*], but I have read only 20 pages so far .... I think most of us find that the fashionable kind of literary criticism especially in America but also in the TLS & elsewhere, leaves us cold. I feel myself that I just don't know what they mean. There is, I think, a cleavage between the critical journality and the majority of the academics, who tend to stick to detail.[16]

"Critical journality" is one way of characterizing an aspect of the spirit that animated the formation of the Yale Edition, despite the fact that its general editor was a scholar who in his own work, such as the catalogue of the library of Horace Walpole, stuck to details with a vengeance.

Chapman's criticism of Bate suggests that there was a split between the British and the American approaches to the Edition, which comes up in Bate's correspondence with Mary Hyde. He calls the British members of the editorial committee mere "ornaments," and he complains about L. F. Powell, with whom he was uneasily yoked in collaboration on volume 2 of the Edition, comprising the *Idler* and the *Adventurer*. In a letter to the Hydes in March 1964, Bate resisted a suggestion that he meet up with L. F. in England:

> I'll not see Powell or even let him know I'm coming, or I'd pick up a book & crown him; he took a year to change my notes to the Adventurer by simply making them wordier ... he then took another 3 years to write his 3-page textual note. He now wants me to make some changes in the form of my Idler notes.

Bate was equally frustrated with his coeditor of the *Rambler* (vols. 3–5), Albrecht Strauss. In March 1964 he wrote to the Hydes:

> I'd hoped, in February, to wrap up the Rambler .... But A. Strauss wrote his text won't be ready till August! – so it goes, year after year. They all pretend to

---

[16] Hyde MS 98, p. 613.

be so busy! Keast had 8 years in which to add a few notes to G. B. Hill's *Lives of the Poets* – a full year sabbatical. I wonder what they do with their time . . . . My enthusiasm is almost zero now. . . . let's just drop the nonsense & start up a Harvard Edition of Johnson – which we'll finish with dispatch.[17]

Like Powell, Strauss was an academic first: his correspondence with Hazen and Middendorf, Hazen's Columbia University colleague who gradually took over the general editorship of the Edition, shows how carefully he worked through the text.[18] Liebert loaned him the necessary editions of the *Rambler*, and he corresponded in letters and on the phone with Hazen and Middendorf about numerous specific editorial choices.

No amount of academic effort, however, for Fleeman could make up for the fact that Yale had chosen the wrong copy-text for the edition of the *Rambler* (the 4th), which (as with the *Idler*) had been heavily revised by Johnson, and that they had decided to modernize capitalization and italicization. Fleeman's review was highly critical. He found this practice amounts

> to nothing more than the reprint of a selected "best text." Such texts are modernized and use the chosen version simply as a basis for literary or historical annotation. Inevitably such editions exhibit a low standard of textual scrupulosity.[19]

Fleeman goes on to decry what is lost when spelling variants are not recorded before discussing the way modernizing capitals obscures one of Johnson's most salient stylistic habits – personification. He points out the superiority of the original textual layout and argues against the Yale editors' assertion that Johnson did not really care very much about spelling or capitalization and submitted instead to "House style," which Fleeman calls an invention of modern editors, "a kind of magic handkerchief into which editorial problems may be persuaded to disappear." He concludes his evaluation of the Yale *Rambler* grimly, saying, "We are as far from a definitive and critical text of Johnson today as we have ever been."[20]

This review evoked from Hazen what he described to Albrecht Strauss as "a sharp letter," which he began on a note of disingenuous paternal concern:

> Dear David, I am disappointed for you that you chose to take such a jaundiced view of the Yale Rambler in your review; I think you will not

---

[17] W. J. Bate to Donald and Mary Hyde, March 17, 1964, Houghton MS Hyde 98 (514).
[18] Strauss's correspondence relevant to the Edition was donated to the present General Editor by his wife, Nancy Strauss.
[19] J. D. Fleeman, "REVIEWS," *Review of English Studies*, 22:87 (1971): 348–52, 351.
[20] Fleeman, "REVIEWS," 352.

give people the impression that you are a balanced and scholarly reviewer with sound judgment and clear facts to support your complaints.[21]

Hazen goes on to pull professional rank as well: "I have known and praised Greg's Rationale ever since I heard it as originally read for him by Fred Bowers at the English Institute," but, he says, Yale chose the 4th edition of the *Rambler* for practical reasons and saw no point in going back to the Folio for accidentals.

For all the heat of Hazen's letter, he acknowledges in a marginal comment "all the help you & Isabel furnished on the textual collations," and he concedes the low level of scholarly commentary in the edition (blaming Bate, whom he was "unable to budge"). Finally, Hazen concludes, "Christmas greetings and all good wishes to you and Isabel." Fleeman responded to this sharply worded letter with a four-page, single-spaced, typewritten defense of his views. The tone, however, is genial:

> It looks as though we must agree to differ on some general attitudes towards textual criticism, though I hope I am not being stubborn without good reason. I don't think I have any creed about it: I certainly didn't want to imply that I consider Greg's "Rationale" to be Holy Writ – very far from it in fact: I object to those who do so consider it; but because such an argument cannot be taken as a rule, it behooves every editor to make very clear just what principles he has evolved for the particular work he has done. It was assumed that the adoption of the 1756 text was the right thing to do: I complained because I was not given a full argument in favour of that procedure ... I felt also the concession that the folios were inescapably nearer to SJ's MS practice showed that the editors were almost sinning against the light.[22]

The evangelism Fleeman felt about Johnsonian studies is as apparent here as in his remark to me about touching the hem of Clifford's garment. After going into greater detail concerning his views, Fleeman closes,

> Isabel joins me in our most affectionate greetings to you both, and in belated but sincere good wishes for the new year; I hear good things of your talk and only wish I could have heard it. I have been asked to preside at Lichfield this September ('72) and am very flattered by the invitation: but what can I say to them? I wish I could wander into New York to steal ideas from you.[23]

---

[21] Strauss's letters were supplied to me by his widow, Nancy Strauss. Hazen shared his letter to Fleeman with Strauss but it also is archived in the J. D. Fleeman Collection at the University of St. Andrews, MS 38384/5/7.

[22] Fleeman Collection, University of St. Andrews, MS 38384/5/23f.

[23] Fleeman Collection, University of St. Andrews, MS 38384/5/23f.

David Fleeman was certainly not pleased with volumes 1–6 of the Yale Edition, and he was never reconciled to the Edition's policy on capitalization, but as time wore on, he was happier with the way the Edition evolved. Arthur Sherbo was an editor more to his liking – more bibliographically oriented – and his edition of Johnson's Shakespeare (vols. 7–8, 1968) garnered better reviews from academics. Mary Lascelles's *Journey to the Western Islands* (vol. 9, 1971) was nearly exempt from Fleeman's criticism: she was a student of L. F. Powell. However, Fleeman prepared his own, more rigorously annotated edition of the *Journey* (Oxford, 1985). Donald Greene's *Political Writings* (vol. 10, 1977) went its own way, with much richer annotation than Yale prescribed. Immediately following its publication, Greene, who was also working on a bibliography of Johnson's works, resigned from the Edition. Jean Hagstrum and James Gray's *Sermons* (1978) and Joel Gold's *Voyage to Abyssinia* (1985) were also better bibliographically in Fleeman's view, but the turning point for him was Gwin Kolb's edition of *Rasselas* (1990). Rigorously edited, with full explanation of the editorial policy, and richly annotated, this volume not only won Fleeman's approval, it convinced him to accept an offer to serve on Yale's editorial committee.

With Fleeman as a bellwether, one can discern that by 1990 the transformation of the Yale Edition from a work born of Johnsonian enthusiasm to a work prepared and administered by academics was complete. Better than anyone else's, Kolb's work registered the new approach and new tone. In volume 18 (2005), *Johnson on the English Language*, Kolb, who was in charge of the text, departed entirely from the Yale protocols, even retaining Johnson's italics and capitalization, as well as all kinds of unusual characters in his "Grammar" and "History of the English Language." Kolb's practice was not quite followed in later volumes, but *Johnson on the English Language* established a precedent that gave later editors free rein to indulge their academic, bibliographical commitments, to the extent that they saw fit.

Are the changes that occurred in the history of the Yale Edition characteristic of the changes that have occurred in the community of people who study Johnson? What sort of scholars is Johnson now among? The membership of Mary Hyde's Johnsonians has become gradually more academic, but only in the sense that a high percentage of its members have university appointments. Many of the younger members are neither bibliographically oriented nor romantic Johnsonians. (For many, Johnson is not a primary interest.) There are still enthusiastic Johnsonians in the world. The Johnson clubs in London, Lichfield, Melbourne, Tokyo, and Los

Angeles have healthy numbers, so something of the romance of Johnson persists. What seems lacking, however, is the sort of pure academic (a textual scholar) who is also a romantic Johnsonian: a Malone, a Fleeman, or a Kolb. Are there true academics now who aspire to be Johnsonianissimus/Johnsonianissima? One problem is that books do not hold as crucially important a place in the lives of scholars today as they did for Johnsonians of old, from Fleeman to Kolb. We inhabit a different media ecology, and we should expect different norms of scholarship. It is difficult for me, however, to imagine a Johnsonian scholar who is not bookish – who doesn't share some of Johnson's lifelong immersion in books, as a reader, a writer, and a collector of them, in some fashion.

Every age will have its own Johnson, and Donald Greene's angry young man is as dated now as Boswell's infant Hercules of Toryism. This is inevitable because criticism is always changing, and Johnson will take on new forms in the next generation. Textual scholarship, however, takes a steadier course. Its job, from the humanists of the Renaissance down to editors of Johnson, has been to improve the accuracy of texts and complete our understanding of who wrote what and when. For further work in this kind of scholarship, the groundwork has certainly been laid by the older generation of Johnson scholars. The Yale Edition, Fleeman's *Bibliography*, Lonsdale's *Lives*, Redford's *Letters*, and all the other products of the twentieth century's scholarly Johnsonians provide the materials for future scholars to renew Johnson's place in the shelter of academic bowers. None of these great works is definitive, and there is much still to do: we need an edition of Johnson's *Dictionary*; new versions of Yale 1–6, with adequate annotation; a revision of Fleeman's *Bibliography*. Some of these projects are underway. Others we may hope for, if there are those with the fortitude and the love to complete them.

Further Reading

Scholarship on the life and writings of Samuel Johnson is prodigious. Comprehensiveness is neither possible nor necessary. This section falls into three categories – primary texts and repositories, biographies, and criticism. It aims to inform the reader new to Johnson while also offering the seasoned scholar a reminder. Some of the information here duplicates that in the *Cambridge Companion to Samuel Johnson* (1997), but much new work has appeared since then, notably, J. D. Fleeman's monumental *Bibliography of the Works of Samuel Johnson: Treating his Published Works from the Beginning to 1984*, 2 vols. (Oxford: Clarendon Press, 2000). Criticism – not included in Fleeman – is well served by James L. Clifford and Donald J. Greene's *Samuel Johnson: A Survey and Bibliography of Critical Studies* (Minneapolis: University of Minnesota Press, 1970), Donald Greene and John A. Vance's *A Bibliography of Johnsonian Studies, 1970–1985* (Victoria, BC: English Literary Studies, 1987), and (post-1986) the works cited in Jack Lynch's "A Bibliography of Johnsonian Studies, 1986–" (http://jack lynch.net/Johnson/sjbib.html).

The Age of Johnson: A Scholarly Annual, started by Paul J. Korshin, now edited by Jack Lynch and J. T. Scanlan, and in its twenty-fourth volume (2021), is the only journal devoted to the life and works of Johnson and to his broader historical moment. Johnsoniana – including scholarly articles and reviews – are informatively and entertainingly published by the *New Rambler*, the journal of the Johnson Society of London (founded in 1928), edited by Catherine Dille, and by *The Johnsonian News Letter* (founded in 1940), edited by Robert DeMaria, Jr. These publications are indicative of Johnson's appeal to nonacademics, replicated in the popularity of Johnson societies and clubs – in Britain (Lichfield and London), Australia, Japan, and the USA (the Johnsonians, a Johnson Society of the West, and a Johnson Society of the Central Region).

Primary Works, Repositories, and Selections

The most important repository of early editions of Johnson's works, manuscripts, and Johnsoniana is the Hyde Collection, Houghton Library, Harvard, although other libraries also have significant holdings (e.g., Beinecke Library, Bodleian Library, John Rylands Library, and British Library). After sixty years, under the general editorship of Allen T. Hazen (1951–66), John H. Middendorf (1966–2007), and Robert DeMaria, Jr. (2007–), the *Yale Edition of the Works of Samuel Johnson* has been completed in twenty-three volumes (1959–2019). It includes all of Johnson's canonical works except his *Dictionary* and letters. All twenty-three volumes are in print and free online at www.yalejohnson.com/front/end.

Yale is the standard scholarly edition of Johnson's works, but earlier editions continue to be of scholarly and historical import, primarily G. B. Hill's *The Lives of the English Poets*, 3 vols. (Oxford: Clarendon Press, 1905) and R. W. Chapman's *Letters*, 3 vols. (Oxford: Clarendon Press, 1952). Apart from Yale, some works exist in excellent scholarly editions, most obviously Roger Lonsdale (ed.), *The Lives of the Most Eminent English Poets; With Critical Observations Upon Their Works*, 4 vols. (Oxford: Clarendon Press, 2006), David Nichol Smith and Edward L. McAdam (eds.), *The Poems of Samuel Johnson* (Oxford: Clarendon Press, 1941), *The Complete Poems* (New Haven: Yale University Press, 1971) and *A Journey to the Western Islands of Scotland* (Oxford: Clarendon Press, 1985), both edited by J. D. Fleeman, and Geoffrey Tillotson and Brian Jenkins' *The History of Rasselas Prince of Abissinia* (London: Oxford University Press, 1971). Johnson's Latin and Greeks poems have been edited and translated with a commentary by Barry Baldwin (London: Duckworth, 1995), and his Latin poems have been edited and translated by Niall Rudd (Lewisburg, PA: Bucknell University Press, 2005).

Some works are available in paperback, most usefully Niall Rudd's parallel text edition of *The Vanity of Human Wishes* and *London* with Juvenal's third and tenth satires (Bristol Classical Press, 1981), and, from the same press, Philip J. Smallwood's edition of Johnson's *Preface* to Shakespeare (1985). Similarly, Peter Levi's Penguin edition of Johnson and Boswell's separate journeys in Scotland (1984), several editions of *Rasselas* – by John P. Hardy (Oxford University Press, 1968 and 1988), Jessica Richard (Broadview, 2008), and Thomas Keymer (Oxford University Press, 2009) – and Nicholas Seager and Lance Wilcox (eds.), *The Life of Mr Richard Savage* (Broadview, 2016), all provide useful contextual and interpretive resources.

Johnson's letters, not in Yale, are available, in addition to Chapman, in the five-volume Hyde edition, edited by Bruce Redford (Princeton University Press and Oxford University Press, 1992–4). The prefatory material to the *Dictionary of the English Language* is in Yale. Apropos the *Dictionary* itself, Jack Lynch has produced a useful selection (New York: Levenger Press, 2002), facsimile reprints (1967, 1968, 1979, and 1980) of the first (1755) folio edition, which is out of print but available secondhand. A searchable CD-ROM of the first (1755) and revised fourth (1773) editions (Cambridge University Press, 1996), edited by Anne McDermott, is now unfortunately obsolete (due to software incompatibility), but an online scholarly edition of these editions is underway at the University of Central Florida (https://projects.cah.ucf.edu/sjd/#about). In the meantime, the first edition, by Brandi Besalke (2010), is searchable online at https://johnsonsdictionaryonline.com/. Supplementary to all these, Brian Grimes is compiling an extensive website of the authorial, historical, and biographical sources on which Johnson and his associates drew in writing the *Dictionary*: www.sjdictionarysources.org/. Among other relevant works not included in Yale is Sir Robert Chambers' *A Course of Lectures on the English Law 1767–1773*, ed. Thomas M. Curley, 2 vols. (Madison: University of Wisconsin Press, 1986), to which Johnson contributed.

Paperback selections of Johnson's works include Donald Greene's Oxford Authors, *Samuel Johnson* (Oxford; New York: Oxford University Press, 1984), reprinted as *Samuel Johnson: The Major Works* (2000), while Oxford has issued a further selection, *Samuel Johnson Selected Writings* (2020), by David Womersley. In culmination of the Yale edition, Yale University Press has also published Robert DeMaria, Jr., Stephen Fix, and Howard D. Weinbrot (eds.), *Samuel Johnson Selected Works*, (2021).

Finally, high-quality scanned versions of all Johnson's texts are available in multiple editions on ECCO (Eighteenth-Century Collections Online) and EBBO (Eighteenth-Century Books Online).

Biographies

Johnson is the subject of numerous contemporary and later biographies, especially James Boswell's *The Life of Samuel Johnson, LL.D.* (1791, 2nd ed. 1793) and *Journal of a Tour to the Hebrides with Samuel Johnson, LL.D.* (1785), the standard editions of which, together, are by G. B. Hill, revised by Lawrence Fitzroy Powell, 6 vols. (Oxford: Clarendon Press, 1934–64). Boswell's *Life* is now available in the Research Edition of the Yale Editions of the Private Papers of James Boswell (2012–20), 4 vols., based on the original manuscripts, an indispensable supplement to Hill–Powell, while the one-volume paperback edition, edited by R. W. Chapman (Oxford University Press, 1980), offers accessibility.

The other major contemporary biographies of Johnson are Sir John Hawkins' *The Life of Samuel Johnson, LL.D.* (1787), ed. O M Brack, Jr. (Athens, GA: University of Georgia Press, 2009), Arthur Murphy's *Essay on the Life and Genius of Samuel Johnson, LL.D.*, published as the first volume of Murphy's twelve-volume edition of Johnson's *Works* (1792), and Hester Lynch [Thrale] Piozzi's *Anecdotes of the Late Samuel Johnson* (1786), *Letters to and from the Late Samuel Johnson, LL.D.* (1788), and Katherine Balderston (ed.),*Thraliana: The Diary of Mrs. Hester Lynch Thrale (Later Mrs. Piozzi), 1776–1809*, 2 vols. (Oxford: Clarendon Press, 1942). Murphy and Thrale-Piozzi's *Anecdotes* are included, along with other contemporary Johnsonian memoirs and anecdotes, in G. B. Hill (ed.), *Johnsonian Miscellanies*, 2 vols. (Oxford: Clarendon Press, 1897). It, in turn, is supplemented by O M Brack, Jr. and Robert E. Kelley (eds.), *The Early Biographies of Samuel Johnson* (Iowa City: University of Iowa Press, 1974), lesser-known lives of Johnson mostly omitted from *Johnsonian Miscellanies*. The most comprehensive compendium of biographical information about Johnson is Allen Lyell Reade's *Johnsonian Gleanings*, 11 vols. (1909–52).

Boswell, Hawkins, Piozzi, and Murphy have generated their own substantial scholarship, much of which sheds light on Johnson's life, but this falls outside the parameters of this section.

Modern Biographies of Johnson Include:

Bate, Walter Jackson. *Samuel Johnson* (London: Chatto & Windus, 1978).
Clifford, James L. *Dictionary Johnson: The Middle Years of Samuel Johnson.* London: Heinemann, 1979).
Young Sam Johnson (New York: McGraw Hill, 1955).
DeMaria, Jr., Robert. *The Life of Samuel Johnson* (Oxford: Blackwell, 1993).
Hudson, Nicholas. *A Political Biography of Samuel Johnson* (London: Routledge, 2013).
Radner, John B. *Johnson and Boswell: A Biography of Friendship* (New Haven, CT: Yale University Press, 2012).

Selected Criticism

Alkon, Paul K. *Samuel Johnson and Moral Discipline* (Evanston, IL: Northwestern University Press, 1967).
Alkon, Paul and Robert Folkenflik. *Samuel Johnson: Pictures and Words.* Papers Presented at a Clark Library Seminar, October 23, 1982 (Los Angeles, CA: William Andrews Clark Memorial Library, 1984).
Basker, James G. "Dancing Dogs, Women Preachers and the Myth of Johnson's Misogyny," *AJ*, 3 (1990): 63–90.
"Radical Affinities: Mary Wollstonecraft and Samuel Johnson," in Alvaro Ribiero, SJ, and James G. Basker (eds.), *Tradition in Transition: Women Writers, Marginal Texts, and the Eighteenth-Century Canon* (Oxford: Clarendon Press, 1996), pp. 41–55.
"Samuel Johnson and the African-American Reader," *The New Rambler* (1994–5): 47–57.
Bate, W. J. *The Achievement of Samuel Johnson* (Chicago, IL: University of Chicago Press, 1955).
Battersby, James L. "Life, Art, and the *Lives of the Poets*," in David Wheeler (ed.), *Domestick Privacies: Samuel Johnson and the Art of Biography* (Lexington: University of Kentucky Press, 1987), pp. 26–56.
Berglund, Lisa. "Dr. Johnson's Apology for the Married Life of Hester Thrale: Hester Lynch Piozzi's *Letters to and from the Late Samuel Johnson, LL.D.*," in Tanya M. Caldwell (ed.), *Writing Lives in the Eighteenth Century* (Lewisburg, PA: Bucknell University Press, 2020), pp. 19–44.
Boulton, James T. (ed.). *Johnson: The Critical Heritage* (London: Routledge & Kegan Paul, 1971).
Bronson, Bertrand H. *Johnson Agonistes and Other Essays* (Berkeley: University of California Press, 1946).

Brownell, Morris R. *Samuel Johnson's Attitude to the Arts* (Oxford: Clarendon Press, 1989).

Chapin, Chester. *The Religious Thought of Samuel Johnson* (Ann Arbor: University of Michigan Press, 1968).

Clingham, Greg (ed.). *The Cambridge Companion to Samuel Johnson* (Cambridge: Cambridge University Press, 1997).

Johnson, Writing and Memory (Cambridge: Cambridge University Press, 2002).

"Johnson and China: Culture, Commerce, and the Dream of the Orient in Mid- Eighteenth-Century England," *1650–1850: Ideas, Issues, & Aesthetics in the Early Modern Era*, 24 (2019): 178–242.

Clingham, Greg and Philip Smallwood (eds.). *Samuel Johnson after 300 Years* (Cambridge: Cambridge University Press, 2009).

Damrosch, Leo. *Fictions of Reality in the Age of Hume and Johnson* (Madison: University of Wisconsin Press, 1989).

"Johnson's *Rasselas*: Limits of Wisdom, Limits of Art," in Douglas Lane Patey and Timothy Keegan (eds.), *Augustan Studies: Essays in Honor of Irvin Ehrenpreis* (Newark: University of Delaware Press, 1985), pp. 205–14.

Samuel Johnson and the Tragic Sense (Princeton, NJ: Princeton University Press, 1972).

The Uses of Johnson's Criticism (Charlottesville, VA: University of Virginia Press, 1976).

Davis, Philip. *In Mind of Johnson: A Study of Johnson the Rambler* (Athens, GA: University of Georgia Press, 1989).

DeMaria, Robert, Jr. *Johnson's "Dictionary" and the Language of Learning* (Chapel Hill, NC: University of North Carolina Press, 1986).

Samuel Johnson and the Life of Reading (Baltimore, MD: Johns Hopkins University Press, 1997).

Deutsch, Helen. *Loving Dr. Johnson* (Chicago, IL: University of Chicago Press, 2005).

Eliot, T. S. "Johnson as Critic and Poet," in *On Poets and Poetry* (London: Faber and Faber, 1971), pp. 162–92.

"The Metaphysical Poets," in *Selected Essays* (London: Faber and Faber, 1972), pp. 281–90.

Engel, James (ed.). *Johnson and His Age* (Cambridge, MA: Harvard University Press, 1984).

Fix, Stephen. "Distant Genius: Johnson and the Art of Milton's *Life*," *Modern Philology*, 81 (1984): 244–64.

"Johnson and the Duty of Reading *Paradise Lost*," *ELH*, 52 (1985): 649–71.

Folkenflik, Robert. *Samuel Johnson, Biographer* (Ithaca, NY: Cornell University Press, 1978).

Fussell, Paul. *Samuel Johnson and the Life of Writing* (London: Chatto & Windus, 1972).

Greene, Donald J. *The Politics of Samuel Johnson* (New Haven, CT: Yale University Press, 1960).

Grundy, Isobel (ed.). *Samuel Johnson: New Critical Essays* (London: Vision, and Barnes & Noble, 1984).

Samuel Johnson and the Scale of Greatness (Leicester: Leicester University Press, 1984).

Hagstrum, Jean. *Samuel Johnson's Literary Criticism* (Minneapolis: University of Minnesota Press, 1952 [2nd ed., Chicago, IL: University of Chicago Press, 1967]).

Hinnant, Charles H. *Samuel Johnson: An Analysis* (New York: St. Martin's Press, 1988).

Horrocks, Thomas A. and John Overholt. *A Monument More Durable Than Brass: The Donald & Mary Hyde Collection of Dr. Samuel Johnson. An Exhibition.* (Cambridge, MA: Houghton Library, Harvard University, 2009).

Horrocks, Thomas A. and Howard D. Weinbrot (eds.). *Johnson after Three Centuries: New Light on Texts and Contexts*, Special Issue of the *Harvard Library Bulletin*, 20:3–4 (2011).

Hudson, Nicholas. *Samuel Johnson and Eighteenth-Century Thought* (Oxford: Clarendon Press, 1988).

Samuel Johnson and the Making of Modern England (Cambridge: Cambridge University Press, 2003).

Johnston, Freya. *Samuel Johnson and the Art of Sinking, 1709–1791* (Oxford: Oxford University Press, 2005).

"Samuel Johnson's Classicism," in David Hopkins and Charles Martindale (eds.), *The Oxford History of Classical Reception in English Literature, Vol 3: 1660–1790* (Oxford: Oxford University Press, 2012), pp. 615–46.

Johnston, Freya and Lynda Mugglestone (eds.). *Samuel Johnson: The Arc of the Pendulum* (Oxford: Oxford University Press, 2012).

Jones, Emrys. "The Artistic Form of Rasselas, *Review of English Studies*, n.s. 18 (1967): 387–401.

Keast, William R. "The Theoretical Foundations of Johnson's Criticism," in R. S. Crane (ed.), *Critics and Criticism* (Chicago, IL: University of Chicago Press, 1957), pp. 169–87.

Kemmerer, Kathleen. *"A Neutral Being between the Sexes": Samuel Johnson's Sexual Politics* (Lewisburg, PA: Bucknell University Press, 1998).

Kermode, Frank. "The Survival of the Classic," in *Renaissance Essays* (London: Collins, 1971), pp. 164–80.

Korshin, Paul J. (ed.). *Johnson after Two Hundred Years* (Philadelphia: University of Pennsylvanian Press, 1986).

Leavis, F. R. "Johnson and Augustanism," in *The Common Pursuit* (Harmondsworth: Penguin, 1969), pp. 97–115.

"Johnson as Critic," in *"Anna Karenina" and Other Essays* (London: Chatto & Windus, 1973), pp. 197–218.

Lee, Anthony W. (ed.). *Community and Solitude: New Essays on Johnson's Circle* (Lewisburg, PA: Bucknell University Press, 2019).

Dead Masters: Mentoring and Intertextuality in Samuel Johnson (Bethlehem, PA: Lehigh University Press, 2011).

New Essays on Samuel Johnson: Revaluation (Newark, DE: University of Delaware Press, 2018).

(ed.), *Samuel Johnson among the Modernists* (Clemson, SC: Clemson University Press, 2019).

Lipking, Lawrence. *Samuel Johnson: The Life of an Author* (Cambridge, MA: Harvard University Press, 1988).

Lynch, Jack. *The Age of Elizabeth in the Age of Johnson* (Cambridge: Cambridge University Press, 2003).

(ed.), *The Oxford Handbook of Samuel Johnson* (Oxford: Oxford University Press, 2022).

(ed.), *Samuel Johnson in Context* (Cambridge: Cambridge University Press, 2012).

Lynch, Jack and Anne McDermott (eds.). *Anniversary Essays on Johnson's "Dictionary"* (Cambridge: Cambridge University Press, 2005).

Lynn, Steven. *Samuel Johnson after Deconstruction: Rhetoric and "The Rambler"* (Carbondale, IL: Southern Illinois University Press, 1992).

Morris, John. "Samuel Johnson and the Author's Work," *Hudson Review*, 26 (1973): 441–61.

Mugglestone, Lynda. *Samuel Johnson and the Journey into Words* (Oxford: Oxford University Press, 2015).

Ogawa, Kimiyo and Mika Suzuki (eds.). *Johnson in Japan* (Lewisburg, PA: Bucknell University Press, 2021).

Parke, Catherine N. *Samuel Johnson and Biographical Thinking* (Columbia, MO: University of Missouri Press, 1991).

Parker, Fred. *Johnson's Shakespeare* (Oxford: Clarendon Press, 1989).

Scepticism and Literature: An Essay on Pope, Hume, Sterne, and Johnson (Oxford: Oxford University Press, 2003).

Potkay, Adam. *The Passion for Happiness: Samuel Johnson and David Hume* (Ithaca, NY: Cornell University Press, 2000).

Reddick, Allen. *The Making of Johnson's Dictionary 1746–1773* (Cambridge: Cambridge University Press, 1990; revised 1996).

Ricks, Christopher. "Literary Principles as against Theory," in *Essays in Appreciation* (Oxford: Oxford University Press, 1996), pp. 311–32.

Rogers, Pat. *The Samuel Johnson Encyclopedia* (Westport, CT: Greenwood Press, 1996).

Scherwatzsky, Steven. "Samuel Johnson and Eighteenth-Century Politics," *Eighteenth-Century Literature*, 15 (1991): 113–24.

Schwartz, Richard B. *Samuel Johnson and the New Science* (Madison, WI: University of Wisconsin Press, 1971).

Samuel Johnson and the Problem of Evil (Madison, WI: University of Wisconsin Press, 1975).

Smallwood, Philip. *Critical Occasions: Dryden, Pope, Johnson, and the History of Criticism* (New York: AMS Press, 2011).

(ed.), *Johnson Re-Visioned: Looking Before and After* (Lewisburg, PA: Bucknell University Press, 2001).

Johnson's Critical Presence: Image, History, Judgment (Aldershot: Ashgate, 2004).

Vance, John A. *Samuel Johnson and the Sense of History* (Athens, GA: University of Georgia Press, 1985).

Weinbrot, Howard D. *Aspects of Samuel Johnson: Essays on His Arts, Mind, Afterlife, and Politics* (Newark, DE: University of Delaware Press, 2005).

Samuel Johnson: New Contexts for a New Century (San Marino, CA: Huntington Library, 2014).

Wiltshire, John. *Samuel Johnson in the Medical World* (Cambridge: Cambridge University Press, 1991).

Wimsatt, William K. *The Prose Style of Samuel Johnson* (New Haven, CT: Yale University Press, 1941).

Yung, Kai Kin (ed.). *Samuel Johnson 1709–84* (London: Arts Council of Great Britain and the Herbert Press, 1984).

Index

Cambridge Companions To ...

AUTHORS

John Updike edited by Stacey Olster
Mario Vargas Llosa edited by Efrain Kristal and John King
Virgil edited by Fiachra Mac Góráin and Charles Martindale (second edition)
Voltaire edited by Nicholas Cronk
David Foster Wallace edited by Ralph Clare
Edith Wharton edited by Millicent Bell
Walt Whitman edited by Ezra Greenspan
Oscar Wilde edited by Peter Raby
Tennessee Williams edited by Matthew C. Roudané
William Carlos Williams edited by Christopher MacGowan
August Wilson edited by Christopher Bigsby
Mary Wollstonecraft edited by Claudia L. Johnson
Virginia Woolf edited by Susan Sellers (second edition)
Wordsworth edited by Stephen Gill
Richard Wright edited by Glenda R. Carpio
W. B. Yeats edited by Marjorie Howes and John Kelly
Xenophon edited by Michael A. Flower
Zola edited by Brian Nelson
Topics
The Actress edited by Maggie B. Gale and John Stokes
The African American Novel edited by Maryemma Graham
The African American Slave Narrative edited by Audrey A. Fisch
African American Theatre by Harvey Young
Allegory edited by Rita Copeland and Peter Struck
American Crime Fiction edited by Catherine Ross Nickerson
American Gothic edited by Jeffrey Andrew Weinstock
American Horror edited by Stephen Shapiro and Mark Storey
American Literature and the Body by Travis M. Foster
American Literature and the Environment edited by Sarah Ensor and Susan
   Scott Parrish
American Literature of the 1930s edited by William Solomon
American Modernism edited by Walter Kalaidjian
American Poetry since 1945 edited by Jennifer Ashton
American Realism and Naturalism edited by Donald Pizer
American Travel Writing edited by Alfred Bendixen and Judith Hamera
American Women Playwrights edited by Brenda Murphy
Ancient Rhetoric edited by Erik Gunderson
Arthurian Legend edited by Elizabeth Archibald and Ad Putter
Australian Literature edited by Elizabeth Webby
The Beats edited by Stephen Belletto
Boxing edited by Gerald Early
British Black and Asian Literature (1945–2010) edited by Deirdre Osborne
British Fiction: 1980–2018 edited by Peter Boxall
British Fiction since 1945 edited by David James
British Literature of the 1930s edited by James Smith

Printed by Printforce, United Kingdom